MOMENT II:
OLD TESTAMENT DEVOTIONS FOR TODAY
(Genesis – 1 Kings)

DR. JERRY D. INGALLS

NORTHSIDE
AN AGF IMPRINT

New Castle, Indiana

All scripture references are from The New American Standard Bible: 1995 Update (La Habra, CA: The Lockman Foundation, 1995), unless otherwise noted.

Copyright © 2022 Jerry D. Ingalls

All rights reserved. No portion of this book may be reproduced, stored in a retrieval system, or transmitted in any form or by any means – electronic, mechanical, photocopy, recording, or any other – except for brief quotations in printed reviews, without the prior permission of the publisher.

Published by Northside Books & Media, an imprint of AGF Publishing LLC.

ISBN: 978-1-955709-10-1

DEDICATION

I dedicate this book to my beloved church family at the First Baptist Church of New Castle, Indiana. The Holy Spirit is using our life together to conform us into the image of Jesus Christ, and for that I am eternally grateful for God's call to be your pastor. May the Lord bless you and keep you; the Lord make His face to shine upon you and be gracious to you; the Lord lift up His countenance upon you and give you peace.

Soli Deo Gloria!

CONTENTS

Introduction	1
Genesis	5
Exodus	57
Leviticus	99
Numbers	127
Deuteronomy	165
Joshua	201
Judges	227
Ruth	249
1 Samuel	255
2 Samuel	287
1 Kings	313
Acknowledgments	337
About the Author	339

INTRODUCTION

We are on a journey together. This is a journey of reading the Bible, reflecting upon every chapter, and praying over how God's Word applies to our everyday lives. It's a journey where we are intentionally learning how to be more like Jesus by the end of each day. That's God's good pleasure for your life; it's why He chose you! Paul explained this in Romans 8:29, "For those whom He foreknew, He also predestined to become conformed to the image of His Son, so that He would be the firstborn among many brethren."

What intentional steps have you taken to experience this promise of God in your life?

I'm sharing this part of my spiritual formation journey with you because it has been so fruitful in my life, and in the life of my local church. As I invest significant time and energy to write a *Seize the Moment* devotion on every chapter of the Bible, it is my prayer for you, a fellow sojourner of faith, that you will be "transformed by the renewing of your mind" (Romans 12:2). Your Christlikeness is God's good pleasure for your life, which is a *promise* with a *praxis*. In other words, there is something you are invited to do to experience the good fruit of God's grace at work in your daily life. This is the yokefellow life of Christian discipleship, as Paul invites in Philippians 2:12-13:

> So then, my beloved, just as you have always obeyed, not as in my presence only, but now much more in my absence, work out your salvation with fear and trembling; for it is God who is at work in you, both to will and to work for His good pleasure.

The process of writing the *Seize the Moment* devotional series has increased my spiritual vitality – the quality of possessing a living faith. As a pastor in the trenches of demanding local church ministry, this devotional practice has provided the daily structure and weekly rhythm I need to abide in the Vine and take on the easy yoke of Jesus in a consistent, reliable way. My favorite time of the day has become my early morning Bible reading and devotion writing. It is at this time of the day that I envision myself getting back into the easy yoke of Jesus for a day of co-laboring in the harvest fields, side-by-side with Jesus. My ministry to my family, congregation, and community flows out of this daily starting point of grace, when I experience the peace of God and rest for my soul. Please join with me, and experience

God's proven way to bring about fruitfulness and effectiveness in your Christian life.

This book, the second installment of the *Seize the Moment* devotional series, is not a program; rather, it is a rhythm of life that intends to focus you, the reader, on sitting at the feet of Jesus to listen to His Word (Luke 10:38-42). This book is a daily invitation to find rest for your soul by taking on the easy yoke of Jesus, learning from Him how to become gentle and humble in heart (Matthew 11:28-30). This is the way of grace, learning how to rely upon the Holy Spirit to bear fruit upon your branch as you abide in the Vine (John 15:1-5).

The *Seize the Moment* devotional series is a daily invitation into an effective spiritual formation journey – a long slow obedience in the same direction, becoming more like Jesus Christ. My invitation is for you to soak your heart, soul, and mind in the Word of God. The method is simple and time-tested:

1. **Read God's Word daily.** I designed this devotional series to have you read the Bible in a systematic way, one chapter per day, over four years, with a day or two of grace built into each week. Regardless of whether you start with Genesis and read straight through the Old Testament, or with Matthew and read through the New Testament, the goal is the same – for you to receive maximum benefit from your Bible reading. If you have never read through the Bible, then I encourage you to start with the Gospel of Matthew and *Seize the Moment: New Testament Devotions for Today*, the first book of this devotional series. Whichever book you start with, I have a big request to make of you: please read your Bible as of first importance to your day.

2. **Meditate on what you read.** How many times have you read your Bible, then forgot what you read within a short amount of time? I want you to know God's Word. There are no short cuts to this goal, so you must prioritize time and energy for it. Give it the best time of your day, when your mind is clear, and your heart is open. This devotional series is intended to help you create a structure and rhythm to fulfill Joshua 1:8 in your life, "This book of the law shall not depart from your mouth, but you shall meditate on it day and night, so that you may be careful to do according to all that is written in it; for then you will make your way prosperous, and then you will have success." A warning: reading God's Word, or using a devotional book, cannot be a box you check before you get on with the important stuff of your day. It is intended to be that which informs and inspires your entire day to be lived with God, to seize

the moment for His glory, and your good. Therefore, pray first by asking the Holy Spirit to teach you, to open the eyes of your heart as you read; then, ask God to hide His Word in your heart so that you may live according to it. By reading the corresponding daily devotion with your daily Bible reading plan, you will find yourself pondering God's Word throughout the day. The Holy Spirit will bring it back to your mind when you need it the most, so that you can live according to it.

    3. **Prayerfully apply to your life.** How many times have you read a chapter of the Bible and felt there was no practical way it could apply to your life? If we must be honest with ourselves, we know every word of the Bible is God's Word, including some of the hard chapters of the Old Testament, but we just don't know how any of it applies to our lives today. Jesus taught that a wise person was the one who heard His words and put them into practice (Matthew 7:24-27). Every *Seize the Moment* devotion was written to help members of the local church be hope-bearers in their everyday lives. These devotions are purposefully brief, so that you can read each one in under two minutes, pray about the *Seize the Moment* application opportunity found at the end of each devotion, and then get going with your day to live on mission for God. The devotions are intended to be simple, but not simplistic, so that you can gain understanding. I encourage you start your day this way, first thing, so that your daily Bible reading, in partnership with these devotions, empowers you to join with Jesus in His ongoing mission work in the world today, right where you find yourself.

    The *Seize the Moment* devotional series takes you on a four-year spiritual formation journey through every chapter of the Bible. It started with a five-day per week, year-long daily discipline where you were invited to read the 260 chapters of the New Testament. Today, you are taking the next step of this life-transforming experience through the renewal of your mind (Romans 12:1-2). This book will guide you on a six-day per week, year-long daily discipline through the first third of the 929 chapters of the Old Testament – the 313 chapters of Genesis through the end of 1 Kings. It is essential, to gain the maximum impact from this book, to read God's Word each day, not just the devotional I have written to help you remember it and apply it to your daily life of living on mission for Jesus. The prophet wrote to us in Isaiah 55:10-11:

> For as the rain and the snow come down from heaven, and do not return there without watering the earth and making it bear and sprout, and furnishing seed to the sower and bread to the eater; so will My word

be which goes forth from My mouth; it will not return to Me empty, without accomplishing what I desire, and without succeeding in the matter for which I sent it.

May God accomplish in and through you that which He has purposed for your life. May each moment of your day be blessed with God's grace, and may His Word and Spirit lead you in every task you undertake, every conversation you embrace, and every circumstance you face.

Seize the moment!

GENESIS

GENESIS 1
THE UNFORCED RHYTHMS OF GRACE!

Did you know that Jesus invites you to live in His unforced rhythms of grace?

This has been God's intent from the very beginning, revealed in the ancient pattern of thought found in the creation account of Genesis 1, "And there was evening and there was morning, one day ... and there was evening and there was morning, a second day ... and there was evening and there was morning, the next day" for six days, but not on the seventh day, for that day was set apart as different; it was consecrated – made "holy."

Read Genesis 1 to see how deeply imbedded this refrain is into the entire creation account – it's all grace! Pastor Eugene Peterson explained the importance of this refrain:

> The Hebrew evening/morning sequence conditions us to the rhythms of grace. We go to sleep, and God begins his work. As we sleep, he develops his covenant. We wake and are called out to participate in God's creative action. We respond in faith, in work. But always grace is previous. Grace is primary. We wake into a world we did not make; into a salvation we did not earn. Evening: God begins, without our help, his creative day. Morning: God calls us to enjoy and share and develop the work he initiated. Creation and covenant are sheer grace and there to greet us every morning. George MacDonald once wrote that sleep is God's contrivance for giving us the help he cannot get into us when we are awake.[1]

Seize the moment and rest in the unforced rhythms of grace that God designed you for from the beginning. Get in the easy yoke of Jesus Christ today and find rest for your soul (Matthew 11:28-30).

---

[1] Eugene H. Peterson, "The Good-for-Nothing Sabbath," *Christianity Today* (Carol Stream, IL: Christianity Today, 1994), 34.

GENESIS 2
STOPPING IS HOLY WORK!

Do you find it hard to take a day off in your busy schedule? Do you find it challenging to disconnect from social media for a day? Do you find it hard to not buy or sell something whenever you want? Do you have trouble turning off your worry?

Sabbath means "to cease," and is rooted in God's creative intent, as recorded in Genesis 2:1-3:

> Thus the heavens and the earth were completed, and all their hosts. By the seventh day God completed His work which He had done, and He rested on the seventh day from all His work which He had done. Then God blessed the seventh day and sanctified it, because in it He rested from all His work which God had created and made.

God sanctified, made holy, the seventh day because it was the day that He rested to delight in His completed work. Interestingly, in the Genesis creation account, only the Sabbath day is called "holy." Jewish theologian Abraham Joshua Heschel commented,

> It is, indeed, a unique occasion at which the distinguished word *qadosh* is used for the first time: in the Book of Genesis at the end of the story of creation. … There is no reference in the record of creation to any object in space that would be endowed with the quality of holiness.[2]

Here is the key point: **Stopping is God's idea!** Boundaries on your work and worry are a good thing. When we cease striving, we will know that He is God (Psalm 46:10). Sabbath is a faithful practice of proclaiming the preeminence of Jesus Christ in our lives (Colossians 1:15-18).

Seize the moment and submit to God's creative intent for rest! Stopping is holy work!

---

2 Abraham Joshua Heschel, *The Sabbath: Its Meaning for Modern Man* (New York, NY: Farrar, Straus and Giroux, 1951), 9.

GENESIS 3
A WALK IN THE GARDEN!

Did you know that God desires a personal relationship with you? We see this from the very beginning. Genesis 3:8-9 describes a very tragic scene in a very relational way:

> They heard the sound of the LORD God walking in the garden in the cool of the day, and the man and his wife hid themselves from the presence of the LORD God among the trees of the garden. Then the LORD God called to the man, and said to him, "Where are you?"

God knew exactly where the first humans were, but he was inviting Adam and Eve into a conversation with Him. Why? Because it had become their habit to walk together in the garden. How do I know this? Because like a child who knows the familiar sound of her parent's footsteps, so Adam and Eve knew the sound of God's footsteps.

But, this time, they hid from God because they had committed the first sin – Adam and Eve had disobeyed God.

Do you know what sin does? Sin breaks relationships!

Brokenness is not God's desire for you and me. God's desire for us is to have a personal relationship with Him. That is why He sent His Son Jesus Christ – to deal with the sin issue, once for all, and restore us back into a right relationship with God (John 3:16-17).

"Where are you" in your relationship with God today?

Seize the moment and walk with God through a personal relationship with Jesus. Jesus came so that we can love God, and one another, as God intended from the very beginning.

Dr. Jerry D. Ingalls

GENESIS 4
THERE IS A WAY OF VICTORY!

Did you know that God has made a way for you to return to Him? No matter what you have done!

Genesis 4:5b-7 demonstrates God's unrelenting desire to have a healthy relationship with His people. In this passage we hear God speak to Adam and Eve's son, Cain, regarding his anger at how Abel's offering was accepted, while his offering was not:

> So, Cain became very angry, and his countenance fell. Then the LORD said to Cain, "Why are you angry? And why has your countenance fallen? If you do well, will not your countenance be lifted up? And if you do not do well, sin is crouching at the door; and its desire is for you, but you must master it."

Just because Cain's first attempt at offering a right sacrifice was rejected by God doesn't mean that Cain himself was cut off from God. Even though God made a way of victory for Cain, Cain allowed his anger and resentment to build up; he rejected God's way and killed Abel.

We must choose to walk in the way of victory. Paul encourages believers in 1 Corinthians 10:13 to trust that God has made a way:

> No temptation has overtaken you but such as is common to man; and God is faithful, who will not allow you to be tempted beyond what you are able, but with the temptation will provide the way of escape [victory] also, so that you will be able to endure it.

Seize the moment and walk in God's way of victory. Jesus Christ has made a way for you; He is the way (John 14:6)!

GENESIS 5
CREATED IN THE IMAGE OF GOD!

How do you view people? How do you view yourself?

Genesis gives us a strong foundation in understanding the reality of humanity. Genesis 5:1-2 begins with a genealogy of the descendants of Adam and Eve:

> This is the book of the generations of Adam. In the day when God created man, He made him in the likeness of God. He created them male and female, and He blessed them and named them Man in the day when they were created.

We are created in the image of God, and we are blessed by God. Our origins are holy, even if our history is marked by sin. The Bible does not run from either reality. We can't oversimplify our view of people and simply categorize them according to our views and biases.

We must see each other as God created us to be. It is important to see how the author of Genesis echoes the earlier language of Genesis 1:26-28:

> Then God said, "Let Us make man in Our image, according to Our likeness; and let them rule over the fish of the sea and over the birds of the sky and over the cattle and over all the earth, and over every creeping thing that creeps on the earth." God created man in His own image, in the image of God He created him; male and female He created them. God blessed them; and God said to them, "Be fruitful and multiply, and fill the earth, and subdue it; and rule over the fish of the sea and over the birds of the sky and over every living thing that moves on the earth."

Seize the moment and worship God; in doing so, you will reflect the glory of God to the world He created.

Dr. Jerry D. Ingalls

GENESIS 6
ONE PERSON DOES MAKE A DIFFERENCE!

The beautiful thing about reading through the Old Testament together is that we find the classic Sunday School lessons (Sorry no flannel graphs.). Today, we start one of the most famous Bible stories: The flood and Noah's ark, found in Genesis 6-10.

Can one person truly make a difference in today's world?

The story of the world-wide flood and Noah's ark is the story of the second rebellion of humanity against God's rightful rule. As usual, God's response to our sin is found in a person. This template of response was ultimately fulfilled thousands of years later in Jesus Christ.

Genesis 6:7-8 gives God's response to man's universal rebellion against Him:

> The LORD said, "I will blot out man whom I have created from the face of the land, from man to animals to creeping things and to birds of the sky; for I am sorry that I have made them." But Noah found favor in the eyes of the LORD.

All had rebelled, but one. How would this one person named Noah respond to God's covenant to choose him and use him to rescue all of humanity and all of God's living creatures? Genesis 6:22 explains Noah's response, "Thus Noah did; according to all that God had commanded him, so he did."

In the New Testament, written thousands of years later, Noah is remembered in Hebrews 11:7:

> By faith Noah, being warned by God about things not yet seen, in reverence prepared an ark for the salvation of his household, by which he condemned the world, and became an heir of the righteousness which is according to faith.

Seize the moment and live by faith; like Noah, you will make a difference in your generation. God is still using individuals to make a difference in the world today. Be one of them!

GENESIS 7
IN THE DAYS OF NOAH!

Do you ever wonder what it would have been like to experience the flood in the days of Noah?

Genesis 7:21-23 describes the horrifying judgment that was the world-wide flood:

> All flesh that moved on the earth perished, birds and cattle and beasts and every swarming thing that swarms upon the earth, and all mankind; of all that was on the dry land, all in whose nostrils was the breath of the spirit of life, died. Thus He blotted out every living thing that was upon the face of the land, from man to animals to creeping things and to birds of the sky, and they were blotted out from the earth; and only Noah was left, together with those that were with him in the ark.

I believe this was a real historic event – the judgment of God upon humanity's rebellion against His rightful rule. I hold this conviction because of Jesus' words. Jesus referenced Noah and the flood as a historical reality and used it to describe His second coming in Matthew 24:37-39:

> For the coming of the Son of Man will be just like the days of Noah. For as in those days before the flood they were eating and drinking, marrying and giving in marriage, until the day that Noah entered the ark, and they did not understand until the flood came and took them all away; so will the coming of the Son of Man be.

Jesus not only referenced it, He was there for it as the sovereign God. The reason Jesus came from Heaven to Earth was to create an ark by which all can be saved from God's righteous judgment of sin. He made the way!

Seize the moment and get in the ark of faith in Jesus Christ today! You don't have to face a world-wide flood to know that you need a savior … *do you?*

GENESIS 8
THE RIGHT RESPONSE OF GRATITUDE!

Does it matter how you respond to God's blessings in your life?

Let's think about that question from a simple perspective: How do you feel when you give someone a gift, or you do something nice for them, and they take it for granted and don't say thank you or show any gratitude in word or deed?

Genesis 8:20-22 captures the scene of Noah's first activity after leaving the ark. Noah could have been wrapped up with lots of concerns and thoughts about what had just happened because of the world-wide flood, or about what should happen next now that they had to start life and civilization all over again, but instead Noah did this:

> Then Noah built an altar to the LORD, and took of every clean animal and of every clean bird and offered burnt offerings on the altar. The LORD smelled the soothing aroma; and the LORD said to Himself, "I will never again curse the ground on account of man, for the intent of man's heart is evil from his youth; and I will never again destroy every living thing, as I have done. While the earth remains, seedtime and harvest, and cold and heat, and summer and winter, and day and night shall not cease."

God's blessings come in many forms, shapes, and sizes. We are invited to praise God for all His gracious gifts. Gratitude in word and/or deed goes a long way toward offering God a right response to His blessings in your life.

Seize the moment and say thank you to God! Remember that God often uses people to give you His many blessings. Be sure to say thanks to the people God uses to bless you along the way.

GENESIS 9
THE PROMISE OF COVENANT!

After the flood receded and Noah had worshipped God, God did something unexpected. He established an unconditional covenant with Noah. God not only started over with Noah, but God promised to persevere with Noah's descendants. That's us!

Genesis 9:9-13 emphasizes the promise of the unconditional covenant that God gave Noah and all living creatures:

"Now behold, I Myself do establish My covenant with you, and with your descendants after you; and with every living creature that is with you, the birds, the cattle, and every beast of the earth with you; of all that comes out of the ark, even every beast of the earth. I establish My covenant with you; and all flesh shall never again be cut off by the water of the flood, neither shall there again be a flood to destroy the earth." God said, "This is the sign of the covenant which I am making between Me and you and every living creature that is with you, for all successive generations; I set My bow in the cloud, and it shall be for a sign of a covenant between Me and the earth."

This unconditional covenant to not flood the earth again doesn't mean there isn't a judgment of sin (Hebrews 9:27). There must be, because God is righteous and just (Romans 2:1-16).

This is the importance of Jesus Christ! We all deserve the same fate as those who lived in the days of Noah; therefore, we each need a savior. Paul said in Romans 6:23, "For the wages of sin is death, but the free gift of God is eternal life in Christ Jesus our Lord." Praise God for the promise of covenant!

Seize the moment and receive the gracious gift of God by putting your faith in Jesus Christ for the forgiveness of sin and life everlasting.

Dr. Jerry D. Ingalls

GENESIS 10
GOD KNOWS YOUR NAME!

Do you believe that God knows you by name?

If you ever wonder if God cares about names, take notice of how many names are in the Bible. Genesis 10 and 11 are great examples of this, as these chapters list the good fruit of Noah's faith – name by name!

God kept His word to Noah and preserved humanity through Noah's three sons. Listen to the bookends of Genesis 10:1 and 32:

Now these are the records of the generations of Shem, Ham, and Japheth, the sons of Noah; and sons were born to them after the flood. … These are the families of the sons of Noah, according to their genealogies, by their nations; and out of these the nations were separated on the earth after the flood.

The timeline of all these generations, and their separations, and the events of the Tower of Babel in Genesis 11 can be unclear, but what is very clear is God's faithfulness to keep His promise to Noah. Did you see how many people are listed in these chapters? Praise God for His faithfulness to all generations; He brings the increase (Psalm 100)!

God not only preserved a small remnant through Noah, but he quickly multiplied them on the face of the earth, not as a nameless mass of people, but as individuals with names because each person represented the promise of God.

God loves you and knows your name. Jesus said in Luke 12:7, "Indeed, the very hairs of your head are all numbered. Do not fear; you are more valuable than many sparrows."

Seize the moment and remember that Jesus knows your name and finds great value in you. You are precious in His sight (Psalm 139:17). Find your worth in God today.

GENESIS 11
THE STAGE HAS BEEN SET!

Have you ever jumped into a movie late? The big picture has been set and the main characters have been introduced. You can still enjoy the movie, but you don't fully understand the story.

The same happens with the Bible. Genesis 11 is the end of the prologue and the setting of the stage for the choosing of Abram in Genesis 12. You most likely know him as the great patriarch, Father Abraham, the man who is considered the father of Judaism, Christianity, and Islam.

Understanding the story to which he was introduced is very important to understanding the whole. The Table of Nations is described in Genesis 10, but it is Genesis 11 that explains why the descendants of Noah went from being a unified family tree to scattered branches across the land. Listen to Genesis 11:8-9, which gives you a summary of the Tower of Babel story:

> So the LORD scattered them abroad from there over the face of the whole earth; and they stopped building the city. Therefore its name was called Babel, because there the LORD confused the language of the whole earth; and from there the LORD scattered them abroad over the face of the whole earth.

It was the pride and presumption of humanity that led to our disunity, but it would be in the humility of one man that would ultimately lead to our unification with God!

Pride and humility are both forces unto themselves – one divides and destroys; the other unites and builds. Abram believed God, whereas the rest wanted to be gods!

Seize the moment and believe God! The stage has been set, and you are invited to join the story that unites you to God and builds up God's people.

Dr. Jerry D. Ingalls

GENESIS 12
GOD USES REAL PEOPLE!

Do you think that the characters in the Bible were perfect people who walked in their faith without fear, or anxiety, or disbelief, or sin?

I want to quickly disabuse you of this notion. From the very beginning of the story, with the choosing of Abram in Genesis 12:1-3, we see that God used real people to carry out His purposes to bless the nations:

> Now the LORD said to Abram, "Go forth from your country, and from your relatives and from your father's house, to the land which I will show you; and I will make you a great nation, and I will bless you, and make your name great; and so you shall be a blessing; and I will bless those who bless you, and the one who curses you I will curse. And in you all the families of the earth will be blessed."

If you were in Abram's shoes, sounds like a no brainer, right? If God would so clearly talk with you and make this promise to you, then you would walk obediently – never wavering along the way. *Right?*

Abram certainly did waver along the way, and you don't have to wait long to see it. Genesis 12:13 records when he asked his wife to lie for him, "Please say that you are my sister so that it may go well with me because of you, and that I may live on account of you."

I am so glad that the Bible never exalts human nature, but rather tells the true story of how God calls real people to Himself, with all their imperfections, so that the families of world may be blessed through God's grace.

Seize the moment and answer God's call. Don't worry if you feel disqualified! God will use you if you let Him because God is still using real people to carry out His purposes to bless the nations!

GENESIS 13
BLESSED ARE THE PEACEMAKERS!

Are you a peacemaker?

It is only possible to be a peacemaker when you dwell in the security of God's promises. Genesis 13 is a wonderful example of being a peacemaker, as we watch God's chosen man graciously deal with a close family member.

Genesis 13:8-9 shows us how Abram dealt with his nephew Lot, who was getting too big for his britches:

So Abram said to Lot, "Please let there be no strife between you and me, nor between my herdsmen and your herdsmen, for we are brothers. Is not the whole land before you? Please separate from me; if to the left, then I will go to the right; or if to the right, then I will go to the left."

We know that Abram was a powerful man, but instead of using his power of position and wealth to get his way, he made a way for his nephew to prosper, and he cultivated peace through generosity and grace.

Are there situations in your life, today, where you can do the same thing?

Immediately afterwards, in Genesis 13:14-15, God gave Abram the assurance of His covenant faithfulness, "Now lift up your eyes and look from the place where you are, northward and southward and eastward and westward; for all the land which you see, I will give it to you and to your descendants forever."

God honored Abram for being a peacemaker and, in doing so, assured Abram of His promise. Just as Jesus assures His disciples in Matthew 5:9, "Blessed are the peacemakers, for they shall be called sons of God."

Seize the moment and be a peacemaker in your relationships, and in the situations of our world, starting with those closest to you.

GENESIS 14
PURE MOTIVES!

Do you ever struggle with selfish motives when having to make difficult decisions?

Abram demonstrated a resolve to defend his family in Genesis 14. In a rare moment, we see him put on the hat of a warrior-prince. Why? To rescue Lot, that nephew of his – the same one we saw Abram be so gracious and generous to in the previous chapter. Because Lot chose to live in Sodom, he got caught up in a regional conflict and was captured. Abram rescued Lot and, in the process, he won a large and lucrative victory.

Would Abram's motives remain pure when financial prosperity fell in his lap? At this defining moment of Abram's life, a new and important character was introduced in Genesis 14:18-20:

> And Melchizedek king of Salem brought out bread and wine; now he was a priest of God Most High. He blessed him and said, "Blessed be Abram of God Most High, Possessor of heaven and earth; and blessed be God Most High, Who has delivered your enemies into your hand." [Abram] gave him a tenth of all.

Abram willingly gave a tenth of all the plunder to Melchizedek, which means, "King of Righteousness." This was a defining moment for Abram. It demonstrated that he did not rescue Lot or defeat this invading army for personal gain.

The victory belonged to God, and Abram wanted to declare that with a sacrificial gift. Abram wanted God to get all the glory, not only from this military campaign, but in his life. He did not let anything steal his heart – neither success nor prosperity.

Seize the moment and make sure your motives are pure and that you do all things for the glory of God. In the same way that gold is refined by fire, so often the motives of a person's heart are refined by gold.

GENESIS 15
ABRAM'S FAITH!

The Genesis story of Abram highlights the primary work of God's grace, and the essential importance of faith – the act of believing God for His promises.

Do you have a hard time believing the promises of God in the face of your everyday situations?

Abram had good reasons to doubt God's promise to make his family into a great nation, and bless all the nations of the world through his family. Abram was an older man, and his wife was barren. To Abram, it seemed impossible that he would ever become a father. That is why his story is an essential part of the Bible, and a critical connection between the Old and New Testaments. This is highlighted in Genesis 15:1, 5-6:

> After these things the word of the LORD came to Abram in a vision, saying, "Do not fear, Abram, I am a shield to you; Your reward shall be very great." … And He took him outside and said, "Now look toward the heavens, and count the stars, if you are able to count them." And He said to him, "So shall your descendants be." Then [Abram] believed in the LORD; and He reckoned it to him as righteousness.

We are saved by faith, and not by works, so that no one can boast. The Apostle Paul proclaimed this to us in Ephesians 2:8-9. Paul emphasized the Abram story as the foundation for his gospel presentation in Romans 4. Paul said in verse 16, "For this reason it is by faith, in order that it may be in accordance with grace, so that the promise will be guaranteed to all the descendants, not only to those who are of the Law, but also to those who are of the faith of Abraham, who is the father of us all." It is only because of God's grace that we now sing songs of faith about Father Abraham.

Seize the moment and believe God in the face of your everyday situations. God keeps His promises on time, every time!

… Dr. Jerry D. Ingalls

GENESIS 16
PATIENCE WINS THE DAY!

Have you ever taken matters into your own hands, only to make the situation worse?

That is exactly what happened in Genesis 16, and humanity is still dealing with the effects of this ancient couple's impatience. The same is true in our lives – a momentary decision to take matters into our own hands can have an unexpected ripple effect.

The heart of the issue is trust! Abram and Sarai became impatient with God to keep His promise to provide a child for them, so Sarai invited her husband to be with Hagar the Egyptian, her handmaid, in hopes of her conceiving the child. They took matters into their own hands!

It worked, but at what cost? Their sin manifested in a broken community and marital strain. Their mistrust of God led to mistrust in one another. Genesis 16:5-6 records the immediate effects:

And Sarai said to Abram, "May the wrong done me be upon you. I gave my maid into your arms, but when she saw that she had conceived, I was despised in her sight. May the LORD judge between you and me." But Abram said to Sarai, "Behold, your maid is in your power; do to her what is good in your sight." So Sarai treated her harshly, and she fled from her presence.

Hollywood has nothing on this epic story! This is soap opera material, and it all comes down to this basic human issue: Trust! Patience is the good fruit of trusting God to do what He says He will do and to wait upon Him and learn that He is God, and we are not.

Seize the moment and wait on God! This will save you a lot of headaches now, and you never know how much future heartache you will save your family, church, and community.

GENESIS 17
THE POWER OF A NEW NAME!

Have you ever noticed how often people's names are changed in the Bible?

In the New Testament, Jesus changed the fisherman Simon's name to Peter when Jesus invited him to become His follower (John 1:42). When God gives someone a special task, He doesn't want anything to stand in his or her way, even a name.

There is power in a name. Sometimes keeping an old name can keep a person caught up in the old life, and sometimes receiving a new name can free a person to fulfill God's purposes for his or her life. This is what was happening in Genesis 17.

First, God changed Abram's name in Genesis 17:3-5:

Abram fell on his face, and God talked with him, saying, "As for Me, behold, My covenant is with you, and you will be the father of a multitude of nations. No longer shall your name be called Abram, but your name shall be Abraham; for I will make you the father of a multitude of nations."

Second, God changed Sarai's name in Genesis 17:15-16:

As for Sarai your wife, you shall not call her name Sarai, but Sarah shall be her name. I will bless her, and indeed I will give you a son by her. Then I will bless her, and she shall be a mother of nations; kings of peoples will come from her.

For us, when we enter a relationship with Jesus, we are given a new identity (2 Corinthians 5:17). Identifying as a Christian means that our new priority is to do God's will. Is there anything standing in the way of you fulfilling God's purposes for your life?

Seize the moment and walk in the new identity of Christian. Jesus has placed His name on your life. May your life and legacy exalt the name of Jesus, the name above all names and the only name by which anyone can be saved.

GENESIS 18
THE SON OF LAUGHTER!

Have you ever been so surprised by God's goodness and grace in your life that you laughed? Not the laughter of a scoffer, but the laughter of amazement – the laughter that says, "Wow! Go God!"

Listen to one of the matriarchs of our faith laugh in Genesis 18:10-14:

He said, "I will surely return to you at this time next year; and behold, Sarah your wife will have a son." And Sarah was listening at the tent door, which was behind him. Now Abraham and Sarah were old, advanced in age; Sarah was past childbearing. Sarah laughed to herself, saying, "After I have become old, shall I have pleasure, my lord being old also?" And the LORD said to Abraham, "Why did Sarah laugh, saying, 'Shall I indeed bear a child, when I am so old?' "Is anything too difficult for the LORD? At the appointed time I will return to you, at this time next year, and Sarah will have a son."

But Sarah wasn't the only one to laugh. Abraham fell on his face and laughed for the same reason in Genesis 17:17. It was in response to his laugh that God commanded them to name their son Isaac, which means, "he laughs" (Genesis 17:19).

I love that, when God heard them laugh at the audacity of His promise, He had them name their son Isaac, a name that would remind them of His awesomeness!

We all need reminders in our lives. I recently heard a mom say to me that, every time she looks at her baby, she thinks of Jesus.

What are some of God's reminders to you that He has placed in your life to demonstrate how much bigger He is than your problems or your solutions?

Never forget Jesus' words from Luke 18:27, "The things that are impossible with people are possible with God."

Seize the moment and believe God can and will do the impossible.

GENESIS 19
THE LORD'S COMPASSIONATE RESCUE!

The story of Sodom and Gomorrah in Genesis 19 is the classic judgment story. It is a hard story for modern people to comprehend, but as you read the story in Genesis 18:17 – 19:29, you will see that, even in the pouring out of His wrath, God is compassionate.

The story of God's rescue of Lot is told in Genesis 19:15-16:

When morning dawned, the angels urged Lot, saying, "Up, take your wife and your two daughters who are here, or you will be swept away in the punishment of the city." But he hesitated. So the men seized his hand and the hand of his wife and the hands of his two daughters, for the compassion of the LORD was upon him; and they brought him out, and put him outside the city.

God sent His messengers to rescue Abraham's nephew Lot and his family from the impending destruction. This was not the first time Lot had gotten himself into a bind because of his desire to live in Sodom. The Lord was compassionate both times, the first time through Abram's rescue of him and the second time through angelic intervention.

Yet, even so, Lot hesitated to accept God's rescue, just like so many people from Jesus' day through today have hesitated to accept God's compassionate rescue through Jesus Christ.

As Jesus prepared His disciples to live on mission, Jesus referenced this judgment story in Matthew 10:14-15:

Whoever does not receive you, nor heed your words, as you go out of that house or that city, shake the dust off your feet. Truly I say to you, it will be more tolerable for the land of Sodom and Gomorrah in the day of judgment than for that city. (cf. Matthew 11:20-24)

Jesus is God's compassionate rescue from the coming wrath.

Seize the moment and turn to God today. Put your faith in Jesus, "who rescues us from the wrath to come" (1 Thessalonians 1:10).

Dr. Jerry D. Ingalls

GENESIS 20
HONESTY IS THE BEST POLICY!

While most of us would agree that honesty is the best policy, I think it is safe to say that at some point in all our lives, we have been in situations where we felt it would easier, if not better, to give a half-truth or an outright lie, rather than be truthful.

Whether or not this moral dilemma has happened to you more than one time I don't know, but I do know that the great patriarch of our faith, Father Abraham, was in that situation repeatedly in his life.

According to Genesis 20:13, Abraham asked Sarah to consistently lie by giving a half-truth about their relationship, "When God caused me to wander from my father's house, that I said to her, 'This is the kindness which you will show to me: everywhere we go, say of me, "He is my brother."'"

Genesis 20 records the second time that Abraham's policy of deception caused a problem. Genesis 20:2-3 begins the story:

> Abraham said of Sarah his wife, "She is my sister." So Abimelech king of Gerar sent and took Sarah. But God came to Abimelech in a dream of the night, and said to him, "Behold, you are a dead man because of the woman whom you have taken, for she is married."

There is much in this story that is alien to us because it happened thousands of years ago in an ancient culture with different cultural values and social norms, but what can we learn from it and apply to our lives today?

Honesty is the best policy! Don't make situations more complicated than they need to be. Bring light to the darkness and walk in the truth, trusting God every step of the way.

Seize the moment and speak the truth in love; be gentle and walk in the light of God's love as you live in the way of Jesus through your daily life.

GENESIS 21
A CHILD OF PROMISE!

Did you know that every believer in Jesus Christ is a child of the promise of God?

Genesis 21:1-3 begins the story of what it means to be a child of promise:

Then the LORD took note of Sarah as He had said, and the LORD did for Sarah as He had promised. So Sarah conceived and bore a son to Abraham in his old age, at the appointed time of which God had spoken to him. Abraham called the name of his son who was born to him, whom Sarah bore to him, Isaac.

Paul used the ancient story of Abraham's son Isaac and his half-brother Ishmael to describe who Christians become because of the work of the Spirit through faith in Jesus Christ. In Galatians 4:28, Paul contrasts being a child of promise and being a child of the flesh, "And you brethren, like Isaac, are children of promise" (cf. Romans 9:8).

We become children of promise by the grace of God through faith in Jesus Christ. This is the work of the Holy Spirit, who grafts us into the family tree of God's people (Romans 8:15-17; 11:17-24; cf. Galatians 3:29; 1 John 3:1).

We are, like Isaac, the children of promise. Therefore, Jesus Christ came from Heaven to Earth, as John taught in John 1:12-13, "But as many as received Him, to them He gave the right to become children of God, even to those who believe in His name, who were born, not of blood nor of the will of the flesh nor of the will of man, but of God."

This is what it means to be born again, not of flesh, but of God, to be transformed from a child of the flesh to a child of the promise of God!

Seize the moment and put your faith in Jesus Christ. You are a child of God!

Dr. Jerry D. Ingalls

GENESIS 22
THE LIFE OF SACRIFICE!

Have you ever been in a situation where you had to let go of an important relationship and entrust it to God? What did it feel like to make that sacrifice?

Genesis 22:15-18 describes God's reward to Abraham for his faithfulness to let go of his most prized person, his son Isaac, the unique child of promise:

> Then the angel of the LORD called to Abraham a second time from heaven, and said, "By Myself I have sworn, declares the LORD, because you have done this thing and have not withheld your son, your only son, indeed I will greatly bless you, and I will greatly multiply your seed as the stars of the heavens and as the sand which is on the seashore; and your seed shall possess the gate of their enemies. In your seed all the nations of the earth shall be blessed, because you have obeyed My voice."

While this ancient story has much in it that is confusing and upsetting to our modern sensibilities, the emphasis of the story is on God's faithfulness to provide for His promise. It is here to remind His people to trust Him, no matter what is asked of us.

The life of sacrifice can feel confusing and upsetting when you begin it, but as you learn to trust God, you truly learn of His faithfulness. It is not until you are willing to follow Jesus and obey Him that you learn of the greater rewards of the life of sacrifice.

Jesus invites you in Mark 8:34-35, "If anyone wishes to come after Me, he must deny himself, and take up his cross and follow Me. For whoever wishes to save his life will lose it, but whoever loses his life for My sake and the gospel's will save it."

Seize the moment and trust God with whatever it is you are clutching. There are great blessings in a life of sacrifice.

GENESIS 23
DEEP ROOTS IN THE PROMISES OF GOD!

Do you have deep roots in the promises of God?

Abraham's wife Sarah passed away at the beginning of Genesis 23. In verse 2, it is recorded, "Sarah died in Kiriath-arba (that is, Hebron) in the land of Canaan; and Abraham went in to mourn for Sarah and to weep for her."

The rest of the chapter is about a real estate transaction for her burial site in the Promised Land (3-20). The story focuses more on the negotiations for the purchase of land than on the death and burial itself. Why?

Because there was no going back! Abraham was purchasing the family burial plot in the Promised Land of Canaan, rather than going back to where they came from. In the face of death, Abraham was literally planting their roots deeply into the promises of God by placing his wife into the Promised Land itself.

This was a loud statement of faith! This real estate transaction was a big deal. That is why the chapter is bookended by statements of geographical location. Genesis 23:19-20 ends the chapter:

After this, Abraham buried Sarah his wife in the cave of the field at Machpelah facing Mamre (that is, Hebron) in the land of Canaan. So the field and the cave that is in it, were deeded over to Abraham for a burial site by the sons of Heth.

Upon Sarah's death, Abraham declared to Isaac, and to all successive generations, that God's promise of this land had been secured – the land was God's land by His promise, and now God's people through Abraham and Sarah have a foothold in it through this legal transaction and the burial of the matriarch in the land itself.

Seize the moment and stake your claim in the promises of God! It may not be through a real estate transaction, but how does your lifestyle today plant gospel seeds? How do your plans declare your deep roots in the promises of God to future generations?

Dr. Jerry D. Ingalls

GENESIS 24
THE SERVANT'S PRAYER!

It is important to know who you are talking to when you are praying because prayer is neither a pep talk nor a pity party; it is a direct communication with God, who desires a relationship with you.

Genesis 24:12-14 records an ancient prayer of one of God's people – Abraham's servant who was sent to find a wife for Isaac:

He said, "O LORD, the God of my master Abraham, please grant me success today, and show lovingkindness to my master Abraham. Behold, I am standing by the spring, and the daughters of the men of the city are coming out to draw water; now may it be that the girl to whom I say, 'Please let down your jar so that I may drink,' and who answers, 'Drink, and I will water your camels also' – may she be the one whom You have appointed for Your servant Isaac; and by this I will know that You have shown lovingkindness to my master."

As we listen to the servant's prayer, and the conversation between Abraham and his servant prior to this prayer, we learn that they believed in both God's providence and God's direct involvement in their daily affairs. This is the same faith we hold today – God is sovereign over all, and God is personally involved with each of us.

In Matthew 6:9-13, Jesus taught His disciples to pray to God according to these same truths:

> Our Father, who art in Heaven
> Hallowed be thy Name
> Thy Kingdom Come, thy will be done
> On earth as it is in Heaven
> Give us this day our daily bread, and
> Forgive us our sins as we forgive those who sin against us
> Lead us not into temptation, but deliver us from evil
> For thine is the Kingdom, and the power, and the glory, forever.
> Amen

Seize the moment and pray in this way as you grow in God's sovereign grace. Prayer is powerful because of the One you are addressing in prayer!

GENESIS 25
COMFORT IN GRIEVING!

I officiate and participate in a lot of funerals. It is a part of my calling to provide pastoral care for the congregation and as an outreach ministry to the community. What a joy it is to give people hope in a time of such grief and sorrow.

There is a powerful sentence about Abraham's death in Genesis 25:8 that deeply struck me this morning, especially as I was preparing the message for a senior saint's funeral this afternoon, "Abraham breathed his last and died in a ripe old age, an old man and satisfied with life; and he was gathered to his people."

God blessed Abraham with a long fruitful life, and then he was gathered with the saints who had gone to be with God before him. What else could we ask of God?

Psalm 116:15 proclaims, "Precious in the sight of the LORD is the death of His godly ones."

Revelation 14:13 promises, "Blessed are the dead who die in the Lord from now on!"

One of the great gifts of our faith in Jesus Christ is the peace God's presence gives us in the face of life's trials and temptations, including the trials caused by death and dying. The Lord has not only given us a heavenly peace, but also a certain assurance that we will join with Jesus in His resurrection; the death of this body does not have the final word!

Jesus said in John 11:25-26, "I am the resurrection and the life; he who believes in Me will live even if he dies, and everyone who lives and believes in Me will never die. Do you believe this?"

Seize the moment and believe in Jesus Christ. Because He lives, you can face tomorrow. Because He lives, all fear is gone.

Dr. Jerry D. Ingalls

GENESIS 26
FAITH GIVES HOPE!

The situation became dire for God's people as a famine fell upon the Promised Land. The new and inexperienced family leader, Isaac, was feeling the heavy weight of responsibility ever since his father Abraham had died. He needed clear instructions on what to do so that his wife and twin boys wouldn't perish in the desperate days of famine.

Would God keep His promise to Isaac and his family?

The Lord both reassured and commanded Isaac in Genesis 26:3, "Sojourn in this land and I will be with you and bless you, for to you and to your descendants I will give all these lands, and I will establish the oath which I swore to your father Abraham."

From his time with God, Isaac trusted God and made a go at it. While the forecast looked desperate, his faith kept him hopeful. He had the courage to live out his faith and trust God during difficult circumstances. Isaac responded faithfully to God's great provision in Genesis 26:25:

> So he built an altar there and called upon the name of the LORD, and pitched his tent there; and there Isaac's servants dug a well. He worshipped the Lord by building an altar to worship God and remember God's power and provision to keep His promises.

When you are faced with a dire forecast and finding it difficult to trust the promises of God, remember how God has come through for you and your family time and time again in the past. He will do so, again and again, in the future.

Seize the moment and trust God's power and provision for you and your family.

GENESIS 27
BE A PERSON OF BLESSING!

Have you ever been prayed over by a parent, or by a parent-figure, in your life? Have you ever been in the position of authority over someone and prayed a blessing over them?

There is power in giving and receiving a blessing. Watch how Isaac blessed his son Jacob in Genesis 27:27-29:

> So he came close and kissed him; and when he smelled the smell of his garments, he blessed him and said, "See, the smell of my son is like the smell of a field which the LORD has blessed; now may God give you of the dew of heaven, and of the fatness of the earth, and an abundance of grain and new wine; may peoples serve you, and nations bow down to you; be master of your brothers, and may your mother's sons bow down to you. Cursed be those who curse you, and blessed be those who bless you."

While this is a sordid story, there is something of great value that we can learn from it – the importance of giving a blessing. A blessing, simply stated, is the giving of God's favor. Here are three components of a blessing from Isaac's blessing of Jacob:

1. **Use appropriate physical touch.** As simple as a handshake – when it is appropriate and agreed upon by the other person, there is power in physical touch.
2. **Pray specific words of blessing over the person.** Don't just pray well-worn statements over them, but specifically apply the Word of God to the person and his or her life.
3. **Declare a hopeful future over the person.** God is for us, and our blessing should reflect God's love for the person and His favor for his or her future.

Seize the moment and be a person of blessing. Take time today to call someone or visit someone and give them this gift of faith, hope, and love. Be a hope-bearer in the person's life!

Dr. Jerry D. Ingalls

GENESIS 28
TRUST GOD TO KEEP HIS WORD!

Have you ever wondered what motivates people to do what they do?

In a previous episode of the patriarchs' soap opera, we watched Isaac unknowingly bless Jacob because of Rebekah's plot of deception to put her favored son ahead of Esau. They were discovered quickly, and Esau was very angry at Jacob – dangerously so.

When confronted, would their mother change her ways of plotting and deceiving?

Rebekah doesn't; rather, she protects Jacob from his angry brother by sending him off to find a wife back in her homeland, far away from danger. The episode ended with a smile on Rebekah's face as Isaac blessed Jacob before he departed in Genesis 28:3-4:

May God Almighty bless you and make you fruitful and multiply you, that you may become a company of peoples. May He also give you the blessing of Abraham, to you and to your descendants with you, that you may possess the land of your sojournings, which God gave to Abraham.

In Rebekah's eyes, her mission was accomplished. What was her motivation to do this?

A flashback scene from Rebekah's difficult pregnancy gives us the answer to this question. She was in great turmoil, and inquired of the Lord in Genesis 25:23, "The LORD said to her, 'Two nations are in your womb; and two peoples will be separated from your body; and one people shall be stronger than the other; and the older shall serve the younger.'"

Rebekah was motivated by God's prophecy that Jacob would rule over Esau, and worked to see the Word of God fulfilled in her family. Her meddling and deception were motivated by a noble desire to see God's will accomplished, but what a mess she caused in trying to help God do His job.

Seize the moment and trust God to keep His Word in His time and in His ways.

GENESIS 29
YOUR STORY FOR HIS SOVEREIGN GLORY!

The story of Jacob continues in Genesis 29. Rebekah sent her son away to protect him from Esau, but he went from the frying pan into the fire, as Rebekah's brother Laban took over where she had left off with the scheming.

Jacob fell in love with Laban's daughter, Rachel. Yes, she was his cousin, but don't judge them too harshly, as this was very common at that time and place. The real scandal was that, after Laban agreed to give Rachel, his youngest daughter, to Jacob in an arranged marriage following seven years of Jacob's labors, Laban tricked him and gave him Leah on his wedding night. He didn't realize it until it was too late, and Jacob was now married to the wrong woman.

Jacob got a taste of his own trickery. *Can't you hear Isaac laughing all the way back in the Promised Land?* I digress ...

Jacob agreed to work another seven years to receive Rachel as his bride.

If that isn't enough of a soap opera for you, this scandal was just heating up, as Rachel and Leah started to compete with one another on who could produce the most children.

Where was God in this story? Listen to Genesis 29:30-31, "Indeed [Jacob] loved Rachel more than Leah, and he served with Laban for another seven years. Now the LORD saw that Leah was unloved, and He opened her womb, but Rachel was barren."

This chapter ends with Leah conceiving four sons for Jacob – the first four tribes of Israel. What a scandal of God's grace!

In Genesis 30, the scandal will only intensify as these sisters pulled a play from Abraham and Sarah's playbook, throwing each of their handmaids into the mix. Hollywood has nothing on this story!

Seize the moment and walk in the mercy of God's grace upon your story. No matter the sordid details of your life, God can use your story for His sovereign glory.

GENESIS 30
THE DRAMA OF DUELING DECEIVERS!

As the patriarchs' saga continues, will Jacob be outwitted once again by his father-in-law Laban?

Genesis 30:33-34 captures the signing of an employment contract between Jacob and Laban:

> "So my honesty will answer for me later, when you come concerning my wages. Every one that is not speckled and spotted among the goats and black among the lambs, if found with me, will be considered stolen." Laban said, "Good, let it be according to your word."

This was the ongoing drama between the dueling deceivers. Both of their track records were speckled with dishonesty and spotted with deception.

Jacob had completed working 14 years for Laban's two daughters – Leah and Rachel – and now Jacob was seeking independence to provide for the future financial well-being of his growing family.

Laban eagerly agreed to the terms of this deal, and then acted in self-interest. He removed from the flocks that Jacob was tending all the sheep and goats that could breed to produce a greater flock for Jacob. In response, Jacob employed ancient practices of sympathetic magic to attempt to bring about better breeding results for his family's future.

The dueling deceivers took matters into their own hands!

Laban was trying to keep Jacob dependent on his wealth so that he could keep his daughters and grandchildren in his household. Jacob was attempting to break the yoke of Laban so he could take his family to the Promised Land of God.

Both were doing what was right in their own eyes!

Seize the moment and trust God with your family's future. As we will see in the next chapter, God honors His covenant with Abraham and rescues Jacob, not because of Jacob's righteousness, but because of God's faithfulness.

GENESIS 31
GOD'S INTERVENTION FOR HIS PEOPLE!

After six years under the new employment contract, Jacob had fled Laban. He did so in fear of Laban because of his twenty-year track record of deceitfulness. Jacob's instincts were correct, and Laban gave chase, but God, once again, intervened to protect the patriarch, not because Jacob earned it, but because of God's grace.

In Genesis 31:41-42, Jacob testified of God's righteousness and justice to Laban right before they made a covenant with God not to harm one another and to go their separate ways:

> These twenty years I have been in your house; I served you fourteen years for your two daughters and six years for your flock, and you changed my wages ten times. If the God of my father, the God of Abraham, and the fear of Isaac, had not been for me, surely now you would have sent me away empty-handed. God has seen my affliction and the toil of my hands, so He rendered judgment last night.

How did God intervene on behalf of Jacob the previous night?

Genesis 31:24 records, "God came to Laban the Aramean in a dream of the night and said to him, 'Be careful that you do not speak to Jacob either good or bad.'"

This was not the first time, nor would it be the last, that God used a dream to protect one of His chosen people. Apart from this dream, Laban would have not feared the God of Jacob and tempered his ambition to seize back what he still considered his own (Genesis 31:43).

Is God still in the business of intervening for His chosen people today?

Absolutely! Romans 8:34 reminds us of God's once for all intervention, "Christ Jesus is He who died, yes, rather who was raised, who is at the right hand of God, who also intercedes for us."

Seize the moment and pray for God's intervention in Jesus' name.

GENESIS 32
GOD MAKES A WAY HOME!

After narrowly escaping Laban's wrath, the soap opera immediately focused on Jacob's broken relationship with his twin brother Esau. It had been over twenty years since Jacob's betrayal of his brother, and he was heading back into the hornet's nest.

How does Jacob respond to this crisis? Will he finally trust the God who has provided and protected him time and time again? No, he didn't; Jacob schemed, once again, and this time he willingly put the lives of his women and children at risk to protect his own life.

Personally, I'm heartbroken. How low do the characters in this soap opera go?

But God … Genesis 32:26-28 records the conversation between Jacob and the God-man after a night of God's intervention in Jacob's story:

Then he said, "Let me go, for the dawn is breaking." But he said, "I will not let you go unless you bless me." So he said to him, "What is your name?" And he said, "Jacob." He said, "Your name shall no longer be Jacob, but Israel; for you have striven with God and with men and have prevailed."

God sent the God-man to wrestle with Jacob and to seize his attention. The way home for Jacob was not through his scheming and deception, but through God's mercy and grace.

The same is true for us today! God sent the God-man, His one and only Son Jesus Christ, to rescue us from our soap operas and give us a way home. Hebrews 4:16 teaches us the way home, "Therefore let us draw near with confidence to the throne of grace, so that we may receive mercy and find grace to help in time of need."

Seize the moment and trust Jesus with your burdens and fears. No matter how low the pit goes, it is never so deep that God can't rescue you from it. God's grace is your sufficiency (2 Corinthians 12:9).

GENESIS 33
CAPTURE THE MOMENT!

I am so happy and proud of Jacob in this triumphant scene. He wrestled with the God-man and God changed his name to Israel. But after all we have seen from Jacob, is a name change anything more than window dressing?

Yes! Jacob did the right thing in a difficult and dangerous situation. Jacob put his life in jeopardy to reconcile with Esau. Genesis 33:3-4 captures this touching scene:

> But he himself passed on ahead of them and bowed down to the ground seven times, until he came near to his brother. Then Esau ran to meet him and embraced him, and fell on his neck and kissed him, and they wept.

I feel like a proud father watching his child make an important decision and follow through with it. I want to capture this moment and celebrate it!

This is the promise of new creation from 2 Corinthians 5:17, "Therefore if anyone is in Christ, he is a new creature; the old things passed away; behold, new things have come."

Jacob was now Israel. His name was changed, and these are the first fruits of his new life.

Each of us needs to capture the moments of life transformation when we act more like Jesus. We will not live a perfect life once we become Christians, but we will have moments that capture the truth that we are a new creation in Christ.

Every believer in Christ is being transformed from the inside out, our sanctification through the Spirit (Philippians 2:12-13). We are a new creation, and a name change to Christian is not window dressing; it's the beginning of living a new life, our justification by grace (Ephesians 2:1-9).

Seize the moment and celebrate that God is making all things new and has already begun to fulfill that promise in each of our lives.

GENESIS 34
THE POWER OF OUR FAMILY OF ORIGINS!

How were you shaped by your childhood? The decisions of others impact who we become. That is never a defense for our own choices, as we each are accountable for our own decisions, but it does help us understand what influences us to think or act the way we do.

Jacob recently had a personal encounter with God, but, unfortunately, his kids have been shaped by a lifetime of watching Jacob deal with their grandfather, Laban, and their moms (Jacob's wives and their handmaids).

Should it be of any surprise to us that there are some troubles in this Brady Bunch?

The next installment of the patriarchs' soap opera came from Jacob's children, the new kids on the block in Shechem, where the family settled after Jacob's reconciliation with Esau. In a tragic turn of events, Jacob's daughter Dinah was deeply wronged by a man from Shechem. Genesis 34:13 records the brothers' initial words in their plot for vengeance, "But Jacob's sons answered Shechem and his father Hamor with deceit, because he had defiled Dinah their sister."

To our horror, their twisted plan for vengeance was not just against the man responsible for the crime, but against every man in the town. The scene turned gruesome and all they said in defense for their behavior was, "Should he treat our sister as a harlot?" (Genesis 34:31).

From deceit and trickery, the family moved to murder and mayhem.

The problem with generational sin is that, like all sin, it progresses with each successive generation. Until there is repentance based on an absolute standard of right and wrong, each generation justifies their behavior relative to the starting point of the previous generation's choices.

Seize the moment and repent today. Little ears are listening, and little eyes are watching. How is your life shaping the next generation?

GENESIS 35
THE WAY OF POWER PLAYS!

The world loves a good power play!

Jacob's oldest son, Reuben, made a power play after the death of Jacob's favored wife, Rachel. Whether this had to do with him being the first born of all Jacob's children, or simply the first born of Jacob's scorned first wife Leah, we don't know. But what we do know was that Jacob had just named Rachel's son, Benjamin; this was a powerful name meaning, "son of the right hand," and shortly after this Reuben made his move against his father.

Had Reuben finally had enough and took matters into his own hands? That appears to be the case as Genesis 35:19-22 records Reuben's powerplay:

So Rachel died and was buried on the way to Ephrath (that is, Bethlehem). Jacob set up a pillar over her grave; that is the pillar of Rachel's grave to this day. Then Israel journeyed on and pitched his tent beyond the tower of Eder. It came about while Israel was dwelling in that land, that Reuben went and lay with Bilhah his father's concubine, and Israel heard of it.

Why would he do this? In 2 Samuel 16:20-23, Absalom did the same exact power play in his rebellion against his father, King David. In both cases, the sons of these powerful men are marked forever by their failed attempts to seize power from their fathers.

We can learn from their failures and avoid making the same mistakes in our lives. God warns His people in 1 Peter 5:6-7, "Therefore humble yourselves under the mighty hand of God, that He may exalt you at the proper time, casting all your anxiety on Him, because He cares for you."

Seize the moment and trust God to be the one to raise you up. Power plays may be the way of corporations and politicians, but they should not be the way of God's people and of churches. Humble yourself and trust God to lift you up at the right time.

GENESIS 36
RUN THE RACE SET BEFORE YOU!

Do you remember Jacob's twin brother Esau? He was the son of the patriarch Isaac and his wife Rebekah, but he feels like a secondary character in the Bible – like an "also-ran" compared to Jacob.

Esau is important because he represents the fulfillment of God's promise to Rebekah. Listen to God's promise to her in Genesis 25:23, "Two nations are in your womb; and two peoples will be separated from your body."

Esau is important to God, and Genesis 36:9 records the purpose of this long chapter, "These then are the records of the generations of Esau the father of the Edomites in the hill country of Seir."

Yes, you've got it, Genesis 36 is forty-three glorious verses of genealogy of a people who don't even feel like the main point of the Bible, but they are important to God because God always keeps His promises.

God is investing significant time in the Bible to remind us about one of His beloved children. Esau's life was the fulfillment of the Genesis 17:6 prophecy to Abraham, "I have made you exceedingly fruitful, and I will make nations of you, and kings will come forth from you."

Did you notice the plural – nations and kings?

Esau was the king of the Edomites, and his brother Jacob, whose name was changed, is the father of Israel. Kings have come from the barren womb of Sarah because of God's miraculous power and covenant faithfulness.

God faithfully loves all His children. This chapter is not a waste of your time, because it practically demonstrates God's love for all people – even those who feel like "also-rans."

Seize the moment and run the race set before you! You may not feel like you're winning the race, but the victory comes by persevering to the finish line. Be faithful to the end because you never know how God is keeping His promises through you.

GENESIS 37
GROWING FAITH IN THE DEEPEST PITS!

Do you have a favorite Bible story?

Genesis 37 begins my favorite Old Testament story – the story of Joseph. This is a long story – one that will take us to the end of Genesis. It is my favorite story because I know how it ends. I don't envy Joseph for the events of his life, but I do deeply desire to live my life faithfully, like Joseph, trusting God no matter how dark the circumstances.

The story begins with Joseph as a teenager, seventeen years of age. God entrusted him with great responsibility at a young age – God gave Joseph dreams. Genesis 37:5 demonstrates this gift, "Then Joseph had a dream, and when he told it to his brothers, they hated him even more."

Joseph was young and inexperienced, and he didn't know how to steward this responsibility at first. In his youthfulness, he did not show discretion and his brothers hated him and were jealous. But Joseph remained the favored son of Israel.

Joseph had to fall from this position of privilege and power to become the man God would use to rescue the future nation of Israel.

Providentially, the formation process of the great people of faith very often starts at the bottom of a dark pit. Joseph's pit began with his brothers' plot for his downfall, found in Genesis 37:23-24a, "So it came about, when Joseph reached his brothers, that they stripped Joseph of his tunic, the varicolored tunic that was on him; and they took him and threw him into the pit."

Sometimes we dig our own pit, and other times we are thrown in the pit by others, but regardless of how we got there, never forget that great faith is most often developed in the deepest, darkest holes of life. This is the way we learn to trust in God more than we trust in ourselves.

Seize the moment and trust God no matter how deep or dark the hardships of your life. God is at work to tell a better story through your life.

GENESIS 38
JUDAH, TAMAR, AND JESUS!

Genesis 38 interrupts the story of Joseph to tell the story of Judah, one of Joseph's older brothers. Interestingly, it was Judah in Genesis 37:26-27 that saved Joseph's life, though he still sold him into slavery to the Egyptians. Ironically, in Genesis 46:28, Jacob chooses Judah to lead the entire family to Egypt where Joseph waited to save them all from the seven-year famine.

Did you know that Genesis 38 is important to understanding the genealogy of Jesus Christ? In Matthew 1:3 we read, "Judah was the father of Perez and Zerah by Tamar." Do those names mean anything to you?

Tamar was Judah's daughter-in-law, the disregarded widow of Judah's deceased first and second sons, Er and Onan; she was withheld from his third son, Shelah. Genesis 38:27-30 narrates the birth of these famous twins to Judah through Tamar:

> It came about at the time she was giving birth, that behold, there were twins in her womb. Moreover, it took place while she was giving birth, one put out a hand, and the midwife took and tied a scarlet thread on his hand, saying, "This one came out first." But it came about as he drew back his hand, that behold, his brother came out. Then she said, "What a breach you have made for yourself!" So he was named Perez. Afterward his brother came out who had the scarlet thread on his hand; and he was named Zerah.

Revelation 5:5 describes Jesus as "the Lion that is from the tribe of Judah." This is one of the triumphant names of Jesus, but have you recently read the story of Judah and Tamar in Genesis 38? Birthed through sordid details of this ancient story came the One who rescued all of humanity from their sins.

Seize the moment and trust God with your past, present, and future. Truly, our God gives beauty for ashes (Isaiah 61:3)! There is no life too far gone that God can't use it for His glory.

GENESIS 39
THE WITNESS OF HARD WORK AND HONESTY!

What are some of your greatest witnessing tools?

Genesis 39:2-3 narrates Joseph's integrous life as a slave:

> The LORD was with Joseph, so he became a successful man. And he was in the house of his master, the Egyptian. Now his master saw that the LORD was with him and how the LORD caused all that he did to prosper in his hand.

Joseph worked uncompromisingly hard for his master and was above reproach with all his master's possessions and affairs. In a scandalous turn of events, Joseph was framed and thrown into jail because he would not compromise his integrity; however, even in jail Joseph's hard work and honesty testified of his God.

Joseph had every reason to grumble or dispute, but instead he got back to work, and he brought glory to God! Genesis 39:22-23 testifies to Joseph's character in prison:

> The chief jailer committed to Joseph's charge all the prisoners who were in the jail; so that whatever was done there, he was responsible for it. The chief jailer did not supervise anything under Joseph's charge because the LORD was with him; and whatever he did, the LORD made to prosper.

I want to be like Joseph. He is an illustration of God's command to every believer from Philippians 2:14-15:

> Do all things without grumbling or disputing; so that you will prove yourselves to be blameless and innocent, children of God above reproach in the midst of a crooked and perverse generation, among whom you appear as lights in the world.

Seize the moment and shine brightly with your hard work and honesty. Whether you are working to financially support yourself or your family, or volunteering to make a difference in your community or church, never forget that you are there to shine as a witness of God's glory!

GENESIS 40
BE FAITHFUL WHEN FORGOTTEN!

Have you ever been forgotten? Maybe you were excluded, or passed over, or not recognized?

Everyone wants to feel included, to be remembered, and to be appreciated, but can you continue to live a faithful life even when you have been forgotten, passed over, or shelved?

In Genesis 40, Joseph was still in prison, and he approached two inmates – the chief cupbearer and the chief baker – who were looking especially dejected. Each had a dream the night before and they had no one to interpret the dream for them. Joseph faithfully replied to them in verse 8, "Do not interpretations belong to God? Tell it to me, please."

After interpreting both dreams, the chapter ends in Genesis 40:20-23:

Thus it came about on the third day, which was Pharaoh's birthday, that he made a feast for all his servants; and he lifted up the head of the chief cupbearer and the head of the chief baker among his servants. He restored the chief cupbearer to his office, and he put the cup into Pharaoh's hand; but he hanged the chief baker, just as Joseph had interpreted to them. Yet the chief cupbearer did not remember Joseph, but forgot him.

Joseph was correct in his dream interpretations, but his faithfulness was "rewarded" by being forgotten by the chief cupbearer. As we will see in the next chapter, it would be two long years before the cupbearer kept his promise.

How do you think Joseph responded? Would Joseph remain faithful, even though he had been forgotten and left in a prison for two more years?

How would you respond? Would you be bitter, or get better? That is always the choice!

Seize the moment and remain faithful to God, even if you feel shelved, forgotten, passed over, betrayed, or abandoned. Get better, not bitter!

GENESIS 41
WORK WITH CONFIDENT HUMILITY!

Can God use you to do great things for Him?

Joseph was still in prison, and the Pharaoh had a dream that no one could interpret for him. The chief cupbearer, having forgotten about Joseph in prison for the last two years, remembered and told Pharaoh about Joseph's ability to accurately interpret dreams. Pharaoh called for Joseph in Genesis 41:15-16:

> "I have had a dream, but no one can interpret it; and I have heard it said about you, that when you hear a dream you can interpret it." Joseph then answered Pharaoh, saying, "It is not in me; God will give Pharaoh a favorable answer."

This is the opportunity of a lifetime and Joseph seemingly deflected attention from himself. Our culture would have us update Joseph's resumé with something like this, "A reliable track record of interpretating dreams, including two successful contracts with high government officials in Pharaoh's court."

But that's not what Joseph did. Instead, Joseph showed confident humility! God responded by giving Joseph not only a right interpretation of Pharaoh's dream, but also wisdom on how to apply the dream to the nation. Pharaoh responded to Joseph's confident humility in verses 39-40:

> Since God has informed you of all this, there is no one so discerning and wise as you are. You shall be over my house, and according to your command all my people shall do homage; only in the throne I will be greater than you.

Joseph is a great illustration of Jesus' promise from Matthew 23:12, "Whoever exalts himself shall be humbled; and whoever humbles himself shall be exalted."

Humility is not thinking less of yourself, it is simply thinking of yourself less.

Seize the moment and walk in confident humility. Watch God work in ways that you could never make happen for yourself.

GENESIS 42
GRAPPLING WITH GUILT!

Do you grapple with guilt over something in your life?

Ten of Joseph's brothers had traveled to Egypt because they were starving in the famine. They found themselves bowing in front of the ruler of Egypt, who, unbeknownst to them, was their brother Joseph, who was giving them a chance to be free of their past sins. Genesis 42:21-22 captures the brothers' conversation during this confrontation:

> "Truly we are guilty concerning our brother, because we saw the distress of his soul when he pleaded with us, yet we would not listen; therefore this distress has come upon us." Reuben answered them, saying, "Did I not tell you, 'Do not sin against the boy'; and you would not listen? Now comes the reckoning for his blood."

The first thing that came to their minds was their guilt over Joseph. Isn't that interesting? Does your grappling with guilt cause you to feel smothered by feelings of condemnation, or do you experience God's invitation for a closer relationship with Him?

If you are in Christ Jesus, then you don't need to feel condemned; the Apostle Paul teaches us in Romans 8:1, "Therefore there is now no condemnation for those who are in Christ Jesus."

How you grapple with guilt either leads to life or death! Just like Joseph, Paul does not regret confronting the sin of his brothers! In 2 Corinthians 7:10, Paul discussed with the believers in Corinth a moment of confrontation he caused through a letter he wrote to them, "For the sorrow that is according to the will of God produces a repentance without regret, leading to salvation, but the sorrow of the world produces death."

You have a powerful choice when grappling with guilt: Choose life through a repentance without regret, leading to salvation!

Seize the moment and respond to the Holy Spirit's invitation for a closer relationship with God. Guilt, shame, conviction of sin, regret ... all such emotions are invitations for the ongoing work of your sanctification. God desires your freedom from sin!

GENESIS 43
TRUST GOD'S PROVIDENCE!

How do you respond to difficult circumstances in your life?

Genesis 43:1 tells us about the difficult circumstances that faced Jacob and his sons in the Promised Land, "Now the famine was severe in the land." We are reminded of the difficult circumstance that is the backdrop of this entire saga. The famine seemed to be the driving force behind this whole story.

In reality it was not the famine, but God! God did for His chosen people what they would not, and could not, do for themselves: God, using a famine, properly motivated them. Amazingly, this sounds very much like a story that Jesus taught, called the Parable of the Prodigal Son. What was it that finally caused the Prodigal Son to return to his father?

You guessed it: a famine! Luke 15:14 captures this easily missed, but critical detail in Jesus' parable, "Now when he had spent everything, a severe famine occurred in that country, and he began to be impoverished."

Jesus understands the importance of God's providence and builds it into His parable.

We often fret and complain about difficult circumstances, but instead shouldn't we examine each opportunity for God's providence? "Providence is the governing power of God that oversees His creation and works out His plans for it."[3]

In fact, providence is the finale of the Joseph saga as we learn from Genesis 50:20, "As for you, you meant evil against me, but God meant it for good in order to bring about this present result, to preserve many people alive."

Seize the moment and trust God for every circumstance in your life. You never know when God is doing for you what you cannot, or will not, do for yourself.

---

3 Gerald Bray, "Providence," in *Lexham Survey of Theology*, ed. Mark Ward et al. (Bellingham, WA: Lexham Press, 2018).

GENESIS 44
WHEN SAYING SORRY IS NO LONGER ENOUGH!

How do you know if someone is truly sorry for their past behaviors?

Genesis 44 captures a shining moment in the life of Judah. Joseph, the ruler of Egypt and Judah's long-lost brother, set his brothers up by placing his silver cup into Benjamin's bag as they prepared to leave Egypt.

Joseph did that because he had to know if his brothers were truly repentant of their past sins; words would not be enough. Before Joseph would reveal his identity to them, he had to know if his brothers had changed from the men who would sell a man into slavery, then lie about it and crush their father's spirit by faking his death.

What happens to a relationship when the word "sorry" has lost all its meaning?

The set-up worked! Listen to Judah's selfless plea to Joseph in verses 32-34:

For your servant became surety for the lad to my father, saying, "If I do not bring him back to you, then let me bear the blame before my father forever." Now, therefore, please let your servant remain instead of the lad a slave to my lord, and let the lad go up with his brothers. For how shall I go up to my father if the lad is not with me – for fear that I see the evil that would overtake my father?"

Little did Judah know that his willingness to sacrifice his own life to save his half-brother Benjamin, the youngest son of Jacob, was exactly the right response. His sacrificial love for his father's well-being was such a bright contrast – like night and day – from his past callousness.

Judah's shining moment demonstrated that he was a changed person and truly sorry for his past. The best way to show you are sorry is through your actions!

Seize the moment and walk in repentance. Are there people you need to make amends with from your life? Take steps today!

GENESIS 45
THE ABUNDANT GOD!

There is a great turn of events in Genesis 45. Joseph, the ruler of Egypt, overcome with emotion, announced to his brothers that he was their long-lost estranged brother. He offered reconciliation and then, in concert with Pharoah, showered gifts upon them. The brothers were being sent back to the Promised Land, not to stay, but to pick up their father and his household and to move everyone to Egypt, to the land of Goshen, for the five remaining years of famine.

Genesis 45:24 captures an interesting command by Joseph to his brothers, "So he sent his brothers away, and as they departed, he said to them, 'Do not quarrel on the journey.'"

This got my attention because Paul warned believers in a similar way after he gave the promise of the Fruit of the Spirit in Galatians 5:26, "Let us not become boastful, challenging one another, envying one another."

Why is it necessary to warn both Joseph's brothers and all Spirit-filled believers, against quarrelling, boasting, challenging, and envying upon receiving such blessings?

James 4:1-3 explains this human struggle:

What is the source of quarrels and conflicts among you? Is not the source your pleasures that wage war in your members? You lust and do not have; so you commit murder. You are envious and cannot obtain; so you fight and quarrel. You do not have because you do not ask. You ask and do not receive, because you ask with wrong motives, so that you may spend it on your pleasures.

Seize the moment and be generous with all that God has entrusted to you for your good, remembering that all that you have is from His gracious hand, for His glory. The secret to the abundant life is being generous with God's grace, lavishly poured out on you by Jesus Christ!

Dr. Jerry D. Ingalls

GENESIS 46
THE JOY OF A FAMILY REUNION!

What do you enjoy about family reunions? Is it the joy of seeing people you love whom you haven't seen in a long time?

Can you imagine what is must have been like for Joseph's father to be reunited with his son after nearly two decades of thinking that his son had been killed by a wild animal? His father was not only overjoyed that his son was alive, but he was journeying to see him face-to-face – what joy!

Genesis 46:29-30 captures the scene:

Joseph prepared his chariot and went up to Goshen to meet his father Israel; as soon as he appeared before him, he fell on his neck and wept on his neck a long time. Then Israel said to Joseph, "Now let me die, since I have seen your face, that you are still alive."

Can you put yourself in Israel's shoes? Getting your long-lost son back from the dead – what joy!

This makes me think of Easter Sunday – the excitement of those first believers who experienced the resurrection of Jesus in real time and not as a doctrinal statement thousands of years later.

Can you put yourself in the disciples' shoes? Getting your Lord back from the dead – what joy!

Jesus is alive! Whenever a person accepts Jesus as their Lord and Savior, there is a party in Heaven for that one lost family member who has been found. From death to life – what joy!

Jesus captured this scene in the Parable of the Prodigal Son found in Luke 15:22-24, "'Let us eat and celebrate; for this son of mine was dead and has come to life again; he was lost and has been found.' And they began to celebrate."

Seize the moment and celebrate whenever a lost person is found! Rejoice and throw a party in anticipation of Heaven being the biggest and most joyful family reunion ever – what joy!

GENESIS 47
EGYPT IS NOT YOUR HOME!

As we approach the end of Genesis, God's chosen people have finally found refuge from the famine in Egypt. The story now moves to Israel's final sojourning towards death.

Observe a significant moment in Genesis 47:29-31:

When the time for Israel to die drew near, he called his son Joseph and said to him, "Please, if I have found favor in your sight, place now your hand under my thigh and deal with me in kindness and faithfulness. Please do not bury me in Egypt, but when I lie down with my fathers, you shall carry me out of Egypt and bury me in their burial place." And he said, "I will do as you have said." He said, "Swear to me." So he swore to him. Then Israel bowed in worship at the head of the bed.

Israel made a request of Joseph that he not be buried in Egypt, but that he be returned to his own people in the land that God had promised them. This is a strategic request because Israel was reminding his sons that Egypt is not Israel's home! Joseph fulfilled his promise in Genesis 50:13, "For his sons carried him to the land of Canaan and buried him in the cave of the field of Machpelah before Mamre, which Abraham had bought along with the field for a burial site from Ephron the Hittite."

Joseph gets the import of this, and with his final words before death, made the same request of his brothers in Genesis 50:25. It would be four hundred years before the people of Israel would keep this promise during their exodus out of Egypt, when God rescued them from slavery.

Seize the moment and remember that Egypt is not your true Home – you are set free from sin through Jesus Christ as Paul said in Galatians 5:1, "It was for freedom that Christ set us free."

GENESIS 48
BLESSING THE NEXT GENERATION!

Are you willing to have your name become less so that God's will can be done through you?

Genesis 48:5 describes a powerful moment in the life of Joseph as his father Israel made Joseph's two sons his own, "Now your two sons, who were born to you in the land of Egypt before I came to you in Egypt, are mine; Ephraim and Manasseh shall be mine, as Reuben and Simeon are."

Amazingly, after the exodus from Egypt, and during the conquest of the Promised Land, Joseph's two sons each received a full inheritance of land. It is not the tribe of Joseph, but rather the tribes of Ephraim and Manasseh. As Israel explained to Joseph in Genesis 48:22, "I give you one portion more than your brothers."

Four hundred years later, we see this fulfilled in Numbers 1:32-35, "Of the sons of Joseph, namely, of the sons of Ephraim, ... their numbered men of the tribe of Ephraim were 40,500. Of the sons of Manasseh, ... their numbered men of the tribe of Manasseh were 32,200."

It was no longer Joseph's tribe who would be counted, but Ephraim's tribe and Manasseh's tribe. Joseph was willing to say, "They must increase, but I must decrease." To this day, look at a Bible map of the tribal allotments of land for Israel and you will see that the name of Joseph is not shown; rather, you will see Ephraim and Manasseh.

Over a thousand years later, John the Baptist followed Joseph's example and said about Jesus in John 3:30, "He must increase, but I must decrease."

Seize the moment and humble yourself so that the next generation may come to know Jesus Christ and be used by God to do great things for God's glory.

GENESIS 49
BLESSINGS AND CURSES!

Genesis 49 records the scene of Israel calling his twelve sons to his death bed so that he could bless them. Verse 28 summarizes, "All these are the twelve tribes of Israel, and this is what their father said to them when he blessed them. He blessed them, every one with the blessing appropriate to him."

The phrase that is revealing is that each one received, "the blessing appropriate to him."

When you read this chapter, you realize that for some of the sons this was a moment of honor and for others this was a moment of shame. Whereas Judah and Joseph were given a lion's share of Israel's good fortune, Reuben, Simeon, and Levi received curses. It must have been a painful moment as these three were remembered by their father for their worst moments of life.

Can you imagine being remembered forever for the worst decision of your life? What horror! The thought of that, for me, is deeply disturbing and it causes me to stop and ponder. Just like Jesus' teaching about the goats and the sheep in Matthew 25:31-46 when the sheep are blessed, and the goats are cursed, based on the actions of their lives.

Can you imagine your eternity being based on the actions of your life? We all fall short of the glory of God – not a single one of us meets God's righteous standards for Heaven (Romans 3:23)!

Praise God because eternal life is found in Jesus Christ and His finished work on the Cross, sealed with the Holy Spirit of promise. As Paul said in Ephesians 2:8-9, "For by grace you have been saved through faith; and that not of yourselves, it is the gift of God; not as a result of works, so that no one may boast" (cf. John 3:14-18).

Seize the moment and choose blessings through a life of faith in Jesus Christ. Life and death, blessings and curses, are before us every day.

GENESIS 50
A HAPPY ENDING!

I love it when stories have happy endings!

Joseph's life was epic; it was filled with great suffering, but every step of the way Joseph trusted God's providence, especially with the ending of his story.

After Joseph's father died, Joseph's brothers became insecure about how Joseph would treat them. In many ways, they saw their father as their security blanket, but it was in this dramatic moment that Joseph demonstrated that the forgiveness he had previously given his brothers in Genesis 45:4-15 was genuine. Joseph comforted his brothers with words of faith in Genesis 50:19-21:

> "Do not be afraid, for am I in God's place? As for you, you meant evil against me, but God meant it for good in order to bring about this present result, to preserve many people alive. So therefore, do not be afraid; I will provide for you and your little ones." So he comforted them and spoke kindly to them.

Joseph gave God all the glory for anything good that had come from his life, including how God used those worst moments of his life.

Genesis ends with Joseph's death in Egypt, but his final request to his brothers sets up the reader for the next book, the book of Exodus. On his death bed, Joseph asked to be buried in the Promised Land with his father. Little did Joseph know that, even though his story was coming to a happy ending, the epic story of the nation of Israel was about to dive deep into a very long and dark valley, as it would take over 400 years for Joseph's request to be fulfilled by Moses (Exodus 13:19).

Seize the moment and trust God for the happy ending of your story. Trust God for the ongoing epic story of His creation (Revelation 21-22).

EXODUS

EXODUS 1
THE POWER OF FEAR!

Fear is a powerful motivating force. I know this from personal experience. For example, when I was in the US Army Airborne School, I had moments of fear when I realized that I would not be landing in the airplane that I was flying in. But, as a 19-year-old West Point Cadet, my fear of the power of those in authority over me was greater than my fear of death.

What do you fear?

Fear can be used for good or evil. Egypt used it for evil to enslave the growing nation of Israel after the deaths of Joseph and his brothers. The new Pharaoh leveraged fear in Exodus 1:8-10:

> Now a new king arose over Egypt, who did not know Joseph. He said to his people, "Behold, the people of the sons of Israel are more and mightier than we. Come, let us deal wisely with them, or else they will multiply and in the event of war, they will also join themselves to those who hate us, and fight against us and depart from the land."

Pharaoh used fear to get his people to agree to enslaving a whole ethnic group of people. Furthermore, the Pharaoh's intensifying fear of the Hebrews caused him to command the murder of every male baby. He commanded the midwives do this in verse 16, but watch how they respond in verse 17, "But the midwives feared God, and did not do as the king of Egypt had commanded them, but let the boys live."

These women defied Pharaoh's evil order. They put their own lives at risk and faced the most powerful person in their world. Why? Because their fear of God was greater than the fear of their own death!

Seize the moment and put God first in every area of your life. The fear of the Lord has the power to cast out all other fear!

Dr. Jerry D. Ingalls

EXODUS 2
THE FORMATIVE YEARS OF A HERO!

Exodus 2 introduces us to Moses. He is the most revered man in Jewish history and one of the most honored men in the Bible. Moses was a hero!

Just as Exodus 1 sets the stage for the great deliverance of God's people, Exodus 2 gives the back story of the hero who would deliver His people from slavery. Just as Exodus 1 covers nearly four hundred years of Israel's history, Exodus 2 covers nearly eighty years of Moses' history.

The first forty years of Moses' life include his dramatic rescue as a baby placed in a wicker basket on the Nile River to escape Pharaoh's murderous edicts (1-9), his being brought into Pharaoh's household to be raised as a prince of Egypt (10), and his murder of an Egyptian and subsequent fleeing from Pharaoh's wrath into the wilderness (11-15). The second forty years capture Moses' life as a shepherd in the land of Midian and the beginning of his family (15-22).

The most important thing to realize about Moses is that he was formed in the crucible of God's passion to rescue His people from slavery, as explained in Exodus 2:23-25:

> Now it came about in the course of those many days that the king of Egypt died. And the sons of Israel sighed because of the bondage, and they cried out; and their cry for help because of their bondage rose up to God. So God heard their groaning; and God remembered His covenant with Abraham, Isaac, and Jacob. God saw the sons of Israel, and God took notice of them.

God's answer was Moses! Moses was formed into the man God could use to rescue His people through these eighty years of life experiences.

Seize the moment and trust God as He uses all your life experiences to form your character for His purposes and glory!

EXODUS 3
FRIEND OF GOD!

How do you treat your friends?

Exodus 3 tells the famous story of God's call of Moses at the burning bush. This is a magnificent story which captures a dynamic dialogue between God and Moses. Verses 13-15 highlight a significant exchange in the conversation:

Then Moses said to God, "Behold, I am going to the sons of Israel, and I will say to them, 'The God of your fathers has sent me to you.' Now they may say to me, 'What is His name?' What shall I say to them?" God said to Moses, "I AM WHO I AM"; and He said, "Thus you shall say to the sons of Israel, 'I AM has sent me to you.'" God, furthermore, said to Moses, "Thus you shall say to the sons of Israel, 'The LORD, the God of your fathers, the God of Abraham, the God of Isaac, and the God of Jacob, has sent me to you.' This is My name forever, and this is My memorial-name to all generations."

Wow! God revealed His personal name to Moses. This was unparalleled at this time in human history, but this would become the normative pattern of Moses' relationship with God. In Exodus 33:11, the Bible explains, "Thus the LORD used to speak to Moses face to face, just as a man speaks to his friend."

God invited Moses to be His friend and to go on His behalf to rescue His people from slavery and oppression.

Are you a friend of God?

Jesus followed His Father's example in John 15:15, "No longer do I call you slaves, for the slave does not know what his master is doing; but I have called you friends, for all things that I have heard from My Father I have made known to you."

Seize the moment and answer Jesus' invitation to be His friend and to go on His behalf to rescue His people from slavery and oppression.

Dr. Jerry D. Ingalls

EXODUS 4
STOP MAKING EXCUSES!

I remember when I first experienced God's call upon my life to be a pastor. I had a list of excuses, including bad choices from my past that I felt disqualified me, ongoing struggles in my life, and, the biggest one of all, my glaring inability to sing. Excuses, excuses!

I didn't realize it at the time, but I had joined a long list of people that spans thousands of years of history. What is the common denominator of this list of people? People who were called by God, but who made excuses for why they weren't qualified, or found reasons for why they were disqualified.

In Exodus 4:10-13, Moses made excuses to God, explaining why he couldn't be the right guy for the job:

Then Moses said to the LORD, "Please, Lord, I have never been eloquent, neither recently nor in time past, nor since You have spoken to Your servant; for I am slow of speech and slow of tongue." The LORD said to him, "Who has made man's mouth? Or who makes him mute or deaf, or seeing or blind? Is it not I, the LORD? Now then go, and I, even I, will be with your mouth, and teach you what you are to say." But he said, "Please, Lord, now send the message by whomever You will."

Audaciously, this conversation came *after* God had given Moses three supernatural signs of His endorsement:

1. The staff turning into a serpent.
2. His hand having leprosy and then being cleansed of it.
3. Turning water from the Nile into blood.

Moses tried to convince God that he was disqualified, but God wasn't buying it – because God has a whole different way of seeing things.

Are you currently making excuses for why God can't use you to do something?

Seize the moment and make yourself available to God, because God doesn't call the qualified, God qualifies the called!

EXODUS 5
COME UNDER RIGHT AUTHORITY!

Jesus made it very clear that living your life with great faith is to live your life under authority.

Under whose authority do you live your life?

Pharaoh gives us an interesting insight into the human condition – we only submit to the authority of that which we recognize. This plays out in the first interaction between Moses and Pharaoh in Exodus 5:1-2:

> And afterward Moses and Aaron came and said to Pharaoh, "Thus says the LORD, the God of Israel, 'Let My people go that they may celebrate a feast to Me in the wilderness.'" But Pharaoh said, "Who is the LORD that I should obey His voice to let Israel go? I do not know the LORD, and besides, I will not let Israel go."

It will take many more exchanges, and ten horrific plagues, to convince Pharaoh of his error in judgment about God's authority over him. Until that time, there would be significant loss of life and a great devastation to the Egyptian land and way of life.

It would take a great and divine compulsion for Pharaoh's heart to relinquish control. Because this God that Pharaoh did not know about and would not recognize as having any authority over his sovereign rule of Egypt, would demonstrate His ultimate sovereignty and absolute power over all things, with or without Pharaoh's approval.

The same is true in our own lives!

Seize the moment and accept God's sovereign rule of your life today – take on the easy yoke of Jesus Christ and come under the authority of God. His desire is for you to be free of Pharaoh, both from being one and from being under his heavy yoke of slavery.

Dr. Jerry D. Ingalls

EXODUS 6
THE HEAVY BURDEN OF DESPONDENCY!

Are there any heavy burdens weighing you down?

God desires to set you free from the burdens that are oppressing you and the anxieties that are enslaving you! God makes a profound promise to Moses for the Israelites in Exodus 6:5-7:

> Furthermore I have heard the groaning of the sons of Israel, because the Egyptians are holding them in bondage, and I have remembered My covenant. Say, therefore, to the sons of Israel, "I am the LORD, and I will bring you out from under the burdens of the Egyptians, and I will deliver you from their bondage. I will also redeem you with an outstretched arm and with great judgments. Then I will take you for My people, and I will be your God; and you shall know that I am the LORD your God, who brought you out from under the burdens of the Egyptians."

God was commanding Moses to free His people in what will forever be remembered as the first exodus! These are the words God gave to Moses to explain this to His beloved children, but they would not listen, as verse 9 explains, "So Moses spoke thus to the sons of Israel, but they did not listen to Moses on account of their despondency and cruel bondage."

The same is true today. People are living in despondency and under the cruel bondage of sin to such a point that many cannot hear God's gospel message of love and salvation through Jesus Christ.

Are there heavy burdens in your life causing you not to listen to God's invitation?

In Matthew 11:28, Jesus, the second Moses, invites you, "Come to Me, all who are weary and heavy-burdened, and I will give you rest."

Seize the moment and cast all your heavy burdens and anxieties onto Jesus and find rest from the tyranny of despondency and the cruel bondage of sin.

EXODUS 7
THE BATTLE BEGINS!

The first six chapters of Exodus have set the stage for the battle that had to happen between Moses and Pharaoh so that the people of God could be set free after centuries of Egypt's systematic slavery of the Israelites.

This battle would not be won with diplomacy, though words would be used, nor would this battle be won by armies, though Pharaoh would ultimately deploy his army. The battle belongs to the Lord, and God will fight and win it for His people in ways that go beyond human comprehension. God takes on Egypt's power using the ten plagues.

Listen to God's clear intent for the battle in Exodus 7:1-5:

Then the LORD said to Moses, "See, I make you as God to Pharaoh, and your brother Aaron shall be your prophet. You shall speak all that I command you, and your brother Aaron shall speak to Pharaoh that he let the sons of Israel go out of his land. But I will harden Pharaoh's heart that I may multiply My signs and My wonders in the land of Egypt. When Pharaoh does not listen to you, then I will lay My hand on Egypt and bring out My hosts, My people the sons of Israel, from the land of Egypt by great judgments. The Egyptians shall know that I am the LORD, when I stretch out My hand on Egypt and bring out the sons of Israel from their midst."

There is always something more going on in our circumstances than we can know or imagine, because God fights the battle for His glory and kingdom purposes!

God took on the pantheon of false gods in Egypt to demonstrate His power, and God took on the systemic slavery of Egypt, and stubborn pride of Pharaoh, to show His grace and compassion.

Seize the moment and trust God to fight your battles! God desires to demonstrate His power and presence in and through your life.

Dr. Jerry D. Ingalls

EXODUS 8
HOW TO SOFTEN A HARD HEART!

Have you ever felt your heart harden towards a situation or a person?

You know you should apologize to someone, but you don't want to. You know you should forgive someone, but you are not yet able to do so and truly mean it. Those are realities of a hard heart.

Exodus 8 covers three of the ten plagues: the plague of frogs (1-15), the plague of gnats (16-19), and the plague of flies (20-32).

How did Pharaoh respond to each of these three plagues?

Pharaoh promised to let the Israelites go if Moses gave them relief from the plague; Moses did this each time by interceding to God on behalf of Pharaoh. Amazingly, God responded to Moses' intercessions by taking away the plague.

Unfortunately, like many people, Pharaoh had another response after receiving relief from his suffering. He forgot and hardened his heart! Exodus 8:15 describes, "But when Pharaoh saw that there was relief, he hardened his heart and did not listen to them, as the LORD had said."

Obviously this did not surprise God, but why does it surprise us? This is an everyday struggle of the human condition – we so easily and quickly forget! Forgetting is one of the main reasons our hearts become hardened. That is why Peter says in 2 Peter 1:9, "For he who lacks these qualities is blind or short-sighted, having forgotten his purification from his former sins."

We must remember from what we have been saved! Because of grace and mercy, God has delivered us from death and darkness.

What has God delivered you from in the past? Are you thankful? Have you forgotten?

Seize the moment and soften your heart to God by remembering His grace and mercy towards you. You are forgiven and free because of the Cross of Jesus Christ. Make it a habit of your life to practice thankfulness and to remember daily.

EXODUS 9
FAVORITISM TO A FAVORED CHILD!

Every parent knows not to show favoritism. It causes jealousy and conflict between the kids, because people tend to act out when they feel like someone is getting treated better than they are. Just remember the story of Joseph and how his father's favoritism and special gifts brought great suffering upon him at the hands of his brothers.

There is an exception though. God, our heavenly Father, makes distinctions between those who belong to Him and those who do not. While every person can call upon God to be their Father, not everyone recognizes Him as the Creator, Redeemer, and Sustainer.

Exodus 9:4-6 overtly states how God makes distinctions between the Egyptians and the Israelites, and how God's plagues would impact them differently:

> "But the LORD will make a distinction between the livestock of Israel and the livestock of Egypt, so that nothing will die of all that belongs to the sons of Israel." The LORD set a definite time, saying, "Tomorrow the LORD will do this thing in the land." So the LORD did this thing on the next day, and all the livestock of Egypt died; but of the livestock of the sons of Israel, not one died.

In order to rescue His chosen people, God made a distinction between those who are His and those who are not. Why? Because, as we see in verse 16, God's motive is greater than one nation, "But, indeed, for this reason I have allowed you to remain, in order to show you My power and in order to proclaim My name through all the earth."

While God was working to rescue His chosen people from the Egyptians, His ultimate purpose was that, through them, all the children of the world would know His name and power. God accomplished this purpose through Jesus Christ.

Seize the moment and call upon God as your heavenly Father. He loves you! Jesus made the way for you to be His favored child!

Dr. Jerry D. Ingalls

EXODUS 10
LEGACY EVENTS!

What are the stories you tell the next generation? What legacy events from your life do you want talked about around the dinner table?

God adds the next generation to His motives behind His awesome display of power through the ten plagues. Not only is He rescuing the Israelites from Pharaoh, but He is also establishing a legacy event that will shape their new identity as God's people. God communicates this purpose to Moses in Exodus 10:1-2:

> Go to Pharaoh, for I have hardened his heart and the heart of his servants, that I may perform these signs of Mine among them, and that you may tell in the hearing of your son, and of your grandson, how I made a mockery of the Egyptians and how I performed My signs among them, that you may know that I am the LORD.

God is directing Moses to teach His people to remember the ten plagues and how He demonstrated His absolute sovereignty and ultimate power over Pharaoh and Egypt's pantheon of gods to rescue them from slavery and oppression. God was pointing out to them that this was not to be forgotten.

Are there moments from your life that should not be forgotten? Are there experiences with God, or events and situations from your past, that have shaped you into the person you are or have become defining moments for your family?

Seize the moment and reflect upon your life and the good that God has done for you. Write it down in a journal, or record you telling the story in your own voice. Plan a family gathering when you can share some of these stories with the next generation. Ask God to reveal to you the legacy events of your life and how He would like you to tell the future generations about His greatness through your story.

EXODUS 11
GOD MAKES A DISTINCTION!

Exodus 11:4-7 is a very important passage in this short chapter that warns of the final and most horrific plague:

> Moses said, "Thus says the LORD, 'About midnight I am going out into the midst of Egypt, and all the firstborn in the land of Egypt shall die, from the firstborn of the Pharaoh who sits on his throne, even to the firstborn of the slave girl who is behind the millstones; all the firstborn of the cattle as well. Moreover, there shall be a great cry in all the land of Egypt, such as there has not been before and such as shall never be again. But against any of the sons of Israel a dog will not even bark, whether against man or beast, that you may understand how the LORD makes a distinction between Egypt and Israel.'

There is a critical detail that is often missed in the teaching of the Passover: the tenth plague was a threat to "all the firstborn in the land of Egypt." That means both Israelites and Egyptians were in danger equally from this plague.

This time, and for all time forward, God makes a distinction between His people and other people by authorizing a specific way for them to be protected. The Israelites are no longer automatically protected, like they were in the first nine plagues, because now they must obey God's authorized way to be safe. As we will learn in Exodus 12, it was only through the blood of the Passover Lamb that God's people would be safe from His coming judgment.

The same is true today! Paul says in Romans 6:23, "For the wages of sin is death, but the free gift of God is eternal life in Christ Jesus our Lord."

Seize the moment and trust God for your protection from His coming wrath – believe in Jesus Christ for eternal life. God makes a distinction between those who are His and those who are not – it's called faith!

Dr. Jerry D. Ingalls

EXODUS 12
THE BLOOD OF THE PASSOVER LAMB!

Exodus 12 is a critical chapter to understanding both the religious and social identity of Israel as the people of God and their most important festival – the Feast of Unleavened Bread, commonly known as the Passover.

This chapter is not only important for the Jewish community, but also for Christians, as it lays a critical foundation to better understand our religious and social identity in Jesus Christ. Apart from understanding the Passover, it is impossible to fully understand why Jesus Christ had to die on the Cross of Calvary for the forgiveness of our sins, as the propitiation for God's wrath.

Listen to God's words from Exodus 12:12-13, as He summarizes His great deliverance of His people through the tenth plague:

> For I will go through the land of Egypt on that night, and will strike down all the firstborn in the land of Egypt, both man and beast; and against all the gods of Egypt I will execute judgments – I am the LORD. The blood [of the Lamb] shall be a sign for you on the houses where you live; and when I see the blood I will pass over you, and no plague will befall you to destroy you when I strike the land of Egypt.

This story, and the annual celebration of it, illuminates the importance of why Jesus is called the perfect Passover Lamb. As John the Baptizer said in John 1:29, "Behold, the Lamb of God who takes away the sin of the world!" John the Elder further explained in 1 John 1:7, "the blood of Jesus His Son cleanses us from all sin."

These are the precious declarations of our Christian faith, rooted in this ancient story from Exodus 12.

Seize the moment and know that your salvation has been won for you at a great cost – that cost was the precious blood of Jesus Christ, the perfect Passover Lamb, the Savior of the World.

EXODUS 13
GOD LEADS FOR GOD'S PURPOSES!

Who is leading your life, and to what end?

Exodus 13:17-18 enunciates an essential emphasis:

Now when Pharaoh had let the people go, God did not lead them by the way of the land of the Philistines, even though it was near; for God said, "The people might change their minds when they see war, and return to Egypt." Hence God led the people around by the way of the wilderness to the Red Sea.

God is the one leading the people, as we see in verse 21, "The LORD was going before them in a pillar of cloud by day to lead them on the way, and in a pillar of fire by night to give them light, that they might travel by day and by night."

God leads the Israelites out of Egypt and through the upcoming journey that would ultimately take forty years. Let's be honest: Moses, like any human leader, would have been fired if it took forty years to do what could be done in eleven days (Deuteronomy 1:2).

When we choose to follow God, it is always about the journey because the destination is already secured. God leads us so that we can learn to follow Him each step of the way. God's leadership always has a higher purpose than any person's leadership.

God's purpose is for you "to become conformed to the image of His Son" (Romans 8:29). That takes a long time and many twists along the way.

That's why I love it when people claim Romans 8:28 amid their situations, "God causes all things to work together for good to those who love God, to those who are called according to His purpose."

While what we want that to mean is that our lives will work out the way we want, God's purpose is to lead us closer to Him every step of the way.

Seize the moment and trust God on life's journey! Follow Jesus and He will make you become the best version of you to the glory of God.

Dr. Jerry D. Ingalls

EXODUS 14
EVERY CRISIS IS AN OPPORTUNITY!

Do you have a situation that is too big for you to tackle by yourself? Are you inviting God to fight this battle for you?

Exodus 14 narrates Israel's escape from Egypt after the Passover. Shortly after Israel's departure, Pharaoh forms his army to chase after, and capture, his escaping slaves. Verses 10-14 describe the Hebrews' response:

> They became very frightened; so the sons of Israel cried out to the LORD. Then they said to Moses, "Is it because there were no graves in Egypt that you have taken us away to die in the wilderness? Why have you dealt with us in this way, bringing us out of Egypt? ... But Moses said to the people, "Do not fear! Stand by and see the salvation of the LORD which He will accomplish for you today ... The LORD will fight for you while you keep silent."

In the urgency of this new crisis, the Israelites quickly forgot God's displays of power in the ten plagues and the Passover. They fell into despair and were willing to put themselves back into slavery without a fight.

Moses called them to trust God, who would fight the battle for them. In fact, three times we hear this phrase in Exodus 14: God declares "I will be honored through Pharaoh and all his army" (4, 17, and 18).

Where people saw only crisis and defeat, God saw victory through His people's faith! As we learn in 1 John 5:4, "This is the victory that has overcome the world – our faith."

Seize the moment and invite God into your circumstances. Through the eyes of faith, every crisis is transformed into an opportunity for God's glory.

EXODUS 15
WORSHIP IN SPIRIT AND TRUTH!

Have you ever written a song or poem about who God is and what God has done in your life?

Moses did! That is what Exodus 15:1-18 records. Let's highlight the first three verses, as well as the last two:

> I will sing to the LORD, for He is highly exalted; the horse and its rider He has hurled into the sea. The LORD is my strength and song, and He has become my salvation; this is my God, and I will praise Him; my father's God, and I will extol Him. The LORD is a warrior; the LORD is His name. ... You will bring them and plant them in the mountain of Your inheritance, the place, O LORD, which You have made for Your dwelling, the sanctuary, O Lord, which Your hands have established. The LORD shall reign forever and ever.

Moses is singing a new song! A song that he wrote after God demonstrated His miraculous power to rescue Israel through the ten plagues and the crossing of the Red Sea.

Moses' song praises God for who He is, what Has done in the past, and what He will do in the future. His song is filled with both faith and hope.

This is the heart of worship: to praise God for who He is, and to declare what God has done, is doing, and will do. When we do this, whether in a song, or poem, or dance, or some other medium of art and self-expression, we are worshipping God in spirit and truth.

Jesus explained in John 4:23-24, "An hour is coming, and now is, when the true worshipers will worship the Father in spirit and truth; for such people the Father seeks to be His worshipers. God is spirit, and those who worship Him must worship in spirit and truth."

Seize the moment and express your faith in a song, or poem, or art form today. Worship God in spirit and truth.

Dr. Jerry D. Ingalls

EXODUS 16
GOD'S POWERFUL PROVISION!

Have you ever had food or water insecurity? Do you know what it is like not to know where your next meal or drink will come from?

God had rescued the Israelites with powerful signs and wonders. There was no doubt of God's power because He had put it on display for all to know and see. But life went on from the big moments, and the ordinary needs of the daily journey into the desert started to become a reality – such as their daily need for food and water. When their needs weren't being met, the people grumbled against their leaders.

Moses and Aaron gave the grumblers God's answer in Exodus 16:6-7:

At evening you will know that the LORD has brought you out of the land of Egypt; and in the morning you will see the glory of the LORD, for He hears your grumblings against the LORD; and what are we, that you grumble against us?

God responded with awesome displays of His sufficiency. Quail covered the camp in the evening (13) and manna covered the ground in the morning (14-21). The people learned that they could trust God to take care of their ordinary day-to-day needs.

In fact, God provided for them this manna throughout their long desert journey, as told in verse 35, "The sons of Israel ate the manna forty years, until they came to an inhabited land; they ate the manna until they came to the border of the land of Canaan."

No matter the length of your journey through the difficulties of this life, Jesus invites you to pray, "Give us this day our daily bread" (Matthew 6:11).

Seize the moment and trust God for your daily bread! God cares for His children. He is our sufficiency! Ask Him today.

EXODUS 17
SPIRITUAL FRIENDSHIP!

We all need people around us. We need spiritual friends who hold up our arms by helping us in times when we are overwhelmed. They pray for us, come along side of us, and help in practical ways.

We see two new people in today's chapter in the ongoing saga of God's people: Joshua and Hur. While Joshua becomes a main character, Hur is only in this one scene, but will always be remembered as the "friend of Moses."[4]

Exodus 17:9-12 gives us a powerful image of spiritual friendship:

So Moses said to Joshua, "Choose men for us and go out, fight against Amalek. Tomorrow I will station myself on the top of the hill with the staff of God in my hand." ... So it came about when Moses held his hand up, that Israel prevailed, and when he let his hand down, Amalek prevailed. But Moses' hands were heavy. Then they took a stone and put it under him, and he sat on it; and Aaron and Hur supported his hands, one on one side and one on the other. Thus his hands were steady until the sun set.

Can you see this picture of spiritual friendship in your mind's eye?

While Joshua commanded the army in battle, Aaron and Hur were on either side of Moses. For whatever reason, the army fought to victory only when Moses was able to keep the staff of God raised up, but Moses physically couldn't keep the staff raised over his head. Aaron and Hur supported Moses and raised up his hands for him.

That is a beautiful picture of our need for spiritual friends. Who are the people who hold you up, pray for you, and help you in practical ways?

Seize the moment and help raise up the arms of the people in your life. You never know what victory will come from supporting another person.

---

[4] John D. Barry et al., eds., "Hur the Friend of Moses," *The Lexham Bible Dictionary* (Bellingham, WA: Lexham Press, 2016).

Dr. Jerry D. Ingalls

EXODUS 18
SHARE THE HEAVY LOAD!

Leadership can feel like a heavy burden of responsibility! There is something about that word that changes the weight of work. But being responsible doesn't mean you have to do it all yourself.

Moses was being crushed by the yoke of leading God's people. His father-in-law, Jethro, had a word of mentorship for Moses that changed Moses' life for the better. This same word has also changed my life for the better, and will transform any leader's life who will listen and learn, for the better.

Listen to selections from Exodus 18:17-21 as Jethro speaks to Moses:

The thing that you are doing is not good. You will surely wear out, both yourself and these people who are with you, for the task is too heavy for you; you cannot do it alone … You be the people's representative before God, and you bring the disputes to God, then teach them the statutes and the laws, and make known to them the way in which they are to walk and the work they are to do. Furthermore, you shall select out of all the people able men who fear God, men of truth, those who hate dishonest gain; and you shall place these over them as leaders of thousands, of hundreds, of fifties and of tens.

Jethro was teaching Moses the tried-and-true leadership principle of delegation. Good leaders don't try to do it all; they share the load. Moses learned it, Jesus modeled it, and Paul mobilized the church with it!

If you are a leader, then pray and ask God to show you how you can delegate and who to empower to serve alongside of you to fulfill the responsibilities of God in your life. If you are not currently in a leadership position, then pray and ask God where you can get involved to lend a helping hand. Leadership is a big job, but many hands make for light work!

Seize the moment and carry one another's burdens, and thereby fulfill the law of Christ (Galatians 6:2).

EXODUS 19
GOD'S PRESENCE PREPARES HUMAN HEARTS!

Have you ever had an encounter with the presence of God in a discernible way that deeply affected you for the rest of your life?

I did, and it was in a situation and place that forever directed my steps. The presence of God came upon me, and I responded to His grace. Later, I learned that the Spirit of God did this to prepare my heart to be His throne. God was purifying me with His consuming fire of holiness.

In Exodus 19, God is about to give His covenant with the Israelites through Moses. In order to prepare their hearts, He manifested His presence to them. The scene unfolds in Exodus 19:18-20:

> Now Mount Sinai was all in smoke because the LORD descended upon it in fire; and its smoke ascended like the smoke of a furnace, and the whole mountain quaked violently. When the sound of the trumpet grew louder and louder, Moses spoke and God answered him with thunder. The LORD came down on Mount Sinai, to the top of the mountain; and the LORD called Moses to the top of the mountain, and Moses went up.

Bible teachers call this event a theophany – an event where God reveals Himself in a way that people can discern. God revealed Himself to the Israelites because of His previously stated desire to make them "a kingdom of priests and a holy nation" (6).

God's presence prepares human hearts for God's purposes and glory!

Theophanies set the precedent for God's revelation of Himself to us in Jesus Christ. John testified to the incarnation in John 1:14, "The Word became flesh, and dwelt among us, and we saw His glory, glory as of the only begotten from the Father, full of grace and truth" (cf. Colossians 1:15; Hebrews 1:3).

Seize the moment and respond to the glory of God in your life. God's presence prepares your heart to be His throne. Pray that the Lord will prepare you to be His sanctuary, pure and holy, tried and true.

Dr. Jerry D. Ingalls

EXODUS 20
FROM GRACE FLOWS GOOD WORKS!

When my kids attended preschool, it was a big deal when they were the class line leader. It meant they got to go first. In the Christian life, there is always a designated line leader.

Grace goes first! The work of God precedes human efforts. God rescues us to live our lives for Him, solely by His choice, and apart from our merit.

It has always been this way. Exodus 20 is an important chapter in the Old Testament because it contains the giving of the Ten Commandments on Mount Sinai. The first words of the Decalogue are recorded in Exodus 20:2, "I am the LORD your God, who brought you out of the land of Egypt, out of the house of slavery."

Before God gives the Law, He reminds them that He is the One who rescued them. Grace led them out of Egypt, and across the Red Sea, and to Mount Sinai as a pillar of fire by night and cloud by day. Grace came first!

The Ten Commandments were not how the Hebrews came into a right relationship with God, but rather the signs of their freedom by the God who rescued them. They were the way of walking in His deliverance from their slavery to sin for the glory of God.

The same principle of grace is true for us today in Christ! Paul explains this clearly in Ephesians 2:8-10:

> For by grace you have been saved through faith; and that not of yourselves, it is the gift of God; not as a result of works, so that no one may boast. For we are His workmanship, created in Christ Jesus for good works, which God prepared beforehand so that we would walk in them.

God's grace frees us *from* sin, *for* good works!

Seize the moment and rest in the unforced rhythms of grace. Invite Jesus to lead your life today. "It is for freedom that Christ set us free" (Galatians 5:1).

EXODUS 21
THE LAW OF RETALIATION!

Have you ever wanted to get even with someone?

Immediately following the giving of the Ten Commandments to Moses in Exodus 20, God started giving His new people the covenant code. The covenant code is the body of Law within God's covenant with Israel. It is the content of what Moses called the "book of the covenant" (Exodus 24:7) and it would take the next three chapters to record it.

Exodus 21:23-25 captures the legal precedence of the code, "But if there is any further injury, then you shall appoint as a penalty life for life, eye for eye, tooth for tooth, hand for hand, foot for foot, burn for burn, wound for wound, bruise for bruise."

This passage "illustrates the principle of lex talionis, the idea that punishment must be meted out in exact equivalence to the crime (see Lev 24:17–22; Deut 19:18–19)."[5]

It is the law of retaliation, and it was prominent throughout ancient law, but Jesus transformed the covenant code by replacing the legal precedent behind it – from retaliation to generosity!

Jesus gives the transformative way of the New Covenant in Matthew 5:38-41:

You have heard that it was said, "An eye for an eye, and a tooth for a tooth." But I say to you, do not resist an evil person; but whoever slaps you on your right cheek, turn the other to him also. If anyone wants to sue you and take your shirt, let him have your coat also. Whoever forces you to go one mile, go with him two."

Seize the moment by retaliating against your enemy with generosity and kindness! The next time you want to get even with someone, stop and thank God that He didn't give you what you deserve, but gave you grace!

---

[5] John D. Barry et al., *Faithlife Study Bible* (Bellingham, WA: Lexham Press, 2012, 2016), Ex 21:24.

Dr. Jerry D. Ingalls

EXODUS 22
FROM EXCLUSION TO EMBRACE!

What motivates you to be kind and accepting of other people?

The covenant code continues in Exodus 22 with personal property rights and sundry laws. Exodus 22:21 gives reason to why we are to be kind and accepting of other people, "You shall not wrong a stranger or oppress him, for you were strangers in the land of Egypt."

The Israelites were commanded by God to have empathy with strangers. They were to be sensitive to the feelings of exclusion because they, too, were once strangers. God is commanding them never to forget their humble beginnings, in a tangible way.

This motivation is carried over into the New Testament. In 1 Peter 2:9-10, we learn that the identity of every new covenant believer is defined by God's embrace:

> But you are a chosen race, a royal priesthood, a holy nation, a people for God's own possession, so that you may proclaim the excellencies of Him who has called you out of darkness into His marvelous light; for you once were not a people, but now you are the people of God; you had not received mercy, but now you have received mercy.

God reminds us of our humble beginnings in a tangible way: we are to embrace the outsiders to the faith because we, too, were once excluded from the fellowship of God. Paul explains what Jesus did for us in Ephesians 2:13, 19:

> But now in Christ Jesus you who formerly were far off have been brought near by the blood of Christ. … So then you are no longer strangers and aliens, but you are fellow citizens with the saints, and are of God's household.

Seize the moment and remember from what you were saved so that you may have the empathy to move from excluding strangers to embracing them as fellow citizens, people for whom Jesus gave His life on the Cross.

EXODUS 23
SACRED TIME!

What is your most precious commodity?

You have heard it said that the way you spell love is T-I-M-E. Time is the most precious gift we can give to someone because it is something that we cannot produce. We all have a finite amount of time and how we spend it shapes our lives and proclaims our belief system.

Time is sacred, and God built this deeply into the covenant code. Listen to Exodus 23:10-12:

> You shall sow your land for six years and gather in its yield, but on the seventh year you shall let it rest and lie fallow, so that the needy of your people may eat; and whatever they leave the beast of the field may eat. You are to do the same with your vineyard and your olive grove. Six days you are to do your work, but on the seventh day you shall cease from labor so that your ox and your donkey may rest, and the son of your female slave, as well as your stranger, may refresh themselves.

God declared time as "holy" by sanctifying the seventh day in Genesis 2:3. He built His covenant code upon this truth. In Exodus 23, God was reminding His people of this foundational truth of their faith. He commanded it as the fourth commandment in Exodus 20:8-11, and then instituted it in the covenant code.

God designed us to find our rest only in Him, so He established a holy rhythm of life. God even built this into the collecting of the manna in Exodus 16:22-30, so that they would not have to work on the seventh day but rather could learn to trust Him and rest in His provision. God is sufficient!

Seize the moment and sanctify time by investing it in your worship of God. How you work and rest proclaims your faith in God!

EXODUS 24
PEOPLE OF THE BOOK!

God's people are people of the book! How are you investing time, energy, and resources into your study of the Bible?

God's people have been commanded to people of the book ever since Moses recorded the Old Covenant. From Exodus 24:3-4 & 8, observe Moses and the people after receiving the covenant code from God:

> Then Moses came and recounted to the people all the words of the LORD and all the ordinances; and all the people answered with one voice and said, "All the words which the LORD has spoken we will do!" Moses wrote down all the words of the LORD. Then he arose early in the morning, and built an altar at the foot of the mountain with twelve pillars for the twelve tribes of Israel. ... [After sacrificing young bulls as peace offerings to the LORD] Moses took the blood and sprinkled it on the people, and said, "Behold the blood of the covenant, which the LORD has made with you in accordance with all these words."

The people sealed their commitment to be a people of the book through the "blood of the covenant." While in the Old Covenant this was done through animal sacrifices, in the New Covenant our commitment is sealed through the blood of the perfect Passover Lamb, our High Priest and only Mediator with God, the Lord Jesus Christ.

Paul explains the importance of our commitment to the book in 2 Timothy 3:16-17, "All Scripture is inspired by God and profitable for teaching, for reproof, for correction, for training in righteousness; so that the [person] of God may be adequate, equipped for every good work."

Seize the moment by reading, reflecting upon, and responding to God's Word today! We have an exciting journey ahead of us as we walk through the Bible one chapter at a time. Invest time in God's Word daily.

EXODUS 25
GIVING IS AN AFFAIR OF THE HEART!

Giving has always been an affair of the heart! Whether it's our time, talents, or tangible resources, our giving is a product of God's work in our hearts.

In Exodus 25, God started to show Moses the patterns of all that Moses was commanded to lead the Israelites to build: the tabernacle and all its furniture. Specifically described in this chapter are the ark of the covenant, the table of showbread, and the golden lampstand.

Just these three items alone would take extraordinary amounts of resources to construct. Just like with the bread and water to nourish the Israelites, would God cause the necessary resources to appear like dew on the desert floor, or flow from the desert rocks?

No, this time God would work a miracle from His people. God's instruction to Moses in Exodus 25:2 was to "Tell the sons of Israel to raise a contribution for Me; from every man whose heart moves him you shall raise My contribution."

This time, God does not provide by causing the water to burst forth from a hard rock; instead, God provides by moving upon the hearts of His people!

Generous givers are people whose hearts have been moved upon by God to provide for His work – to build on Earth as it is in Heaven, according to the pattern of all that God has revealed to us!

How has God worked on your heart?

Paul commands in 2 Corinthians 9:7, "Each one must do just as he has purposed in his heart, not grudgingly or under compulsion, for God loves a cheerful giver."

Seize the moment and ask God to purpose your heart to be the way He provides for His will to be done on Earth as it is in Heaven! Giving is an affair of the heart!

Dr. Jerry D. Ingalls

EXODUS 26
DESIGNED BY GOD FOR GOOD WORKS!

Did you know that you are uniquely designed by God for good works?

Exodus 26 is a very detailed chapter, as it lays out the instructions for the building of the tabernacle, which was Israel's approved house of worship until the temple was built by King Solomon much later in their history. The tabernacle was Israel's portable sanctuary during their wanderings in the desert and throughout their conquest of the Promised Land.

This is important to know because the tabernacle had to be disassembled and reassembled every time Israel would make or break camp, which turned out to be quite often. The tabernacle was an ornate, sacred place, and a well-built sturdy place.

This required skilled workers — master craftsmen and craftswomen. Listen to an example of this from Exodus 26:1, "Moreover you shall make the tabernacle with ten curtains of fine twisted linen and blue and purple and scarlet material; you shall make them with cherubim, the work of a skillful workman."

Again, we read from Exodus 35:25, "All the skilled women spun with their hands, and brought what they had spun, in blue and purple and scarlet material and in fine linen."

Paul speaks this over every New Covenant believer's life in Ephesians 2:10, "For we are His workmanship, created in Christ Jesus for good works, which God prepared beforehand so that we would walk in them."

When we use what we have for God's glory, there is no insignificant work! Even the smallest job is for the glory of God, and that makes it of great importance!

Seize the moment and use all that you have – your education and vocational training, your athletic abilities and hobbies, your good looks and charming personality, for the glory of God! God designed you for this very purpose.

EXODUS 27
FORM FOLLOWS FUNCTION!

Have you ever noticed when something is different than before, it jumps out at you?

In Exodus 27, we learn that there is more than one way to build an altar. There are very specific details laid out for its construction, such as in verse 1, "And you shall make the altar of acacia wood, five cubits long and five cubits wide; the altar shall be square, and its height shall be three cubits."

This is different than the last time God gave instructions on how to build an altar. After Moses had received the Ten Commandments, God commanded him in Exodus 20:24-25:

> You shall make an altar of earth for Me, and you shall sacrifice on it your burnt offerings and your peace offerings, your sheep and your oxen; in every place where I cause My name to be remembered, I will come to you and bless you. If you make an altar of stone for Me, you shall not build it of cut stones, for if you wield your tool on it, you will profane it.

Do we make the altar out of acacia wood, or out of uncut fieldstone?

Both! For the altar in today's chapter, its functionality required it to be easily carried around, as it was a portable altar. Its function determined its form.

The same is true in our lives! We are now the temple of the Holy Spirit and we, too, are to offer appropriate sacrifices to God upon the altar of our lives (Romans 12:1). Each of us has been uniquely shaped for God's glory based upon the function God had in mind for our lives. We are different by design – coming in unique shapes and sizes, which God intended for good works that bring Him glory!

Seize the moment and discover how God designed you. Find true freedom, peace, and contentment by walking in the good works for which God designed you, for His glory alone.

Dr. Jerry D. Ingalls

EXODUS 28
HOLY TO THE LORD!

Believers in Jesus have been clothed in righteousness; we have taken off the soiled clothing of sin and put on the new garments of salvation. This kind of language is anchored in today's chapter of Bible reading.

Exodus 28 is all about the ornate garments the priests of the old covenant were required to wear to be a minister of God. Verse 4 summarizes the importance of putting on the right garments:

> These are the garments which they shall make: a breastpiece and an ephod and a robe and a tunic of checkered work, a turban and a sash, and they shall make holy garments for Aaron your brother and his sons, that he may minister as priest to Me.

They were not authorized to do their priestly duties without wearing priestly garments. The entire chapter is packed with intricate details that seem cumbersome, if not comical, by today's informal and relaxed standards in nearly every area of culture, including church life. An important detail is captured in Exodus 28:36-38:

> You shall also make a plate of pure gold and shall engrave on it, like the engravings of a seal, "Holy to the LORD." You shall fasten it on a blue cord, and it shall be on the turban; it shall be at the front of the turban. It shall be on Aaron's forehead.

Just as Aaron and his sons had to have "Holy to the LORD" visibly located on their foreheads to minister to God, we also must have the presence of the Holy One visibly in us.

Only that which is holy from the inside-out will bear the fruit of the Spirit for the world to see! One day, all of God's people "will see His face, and His name will be on their foreheads" (Revelation 22:4). Until that Day, abide in Jesus and bear much fruit, proving to be His disciple (John 15:8).

Seize the moment and live knowing that God will write His name on your forehead for all the world to see that you are "Holy to the LORD."

EXODUS 29
GOD'S DESIRE IS TO DWELL WITH HIS PEOPLE!

Have you ever wandered what God's desire is for your life?

In Exodus 29:43-46, God overtly stated His desire in establishing the tabernacle system, which included the priestly and sacrificial systems of the Old Covenant:

> I will meet there with the sons of Israel, and it shall be consecrated by My glory. I will consecrate the tent of meeting and the altar; I will also consecrate Aaron and his sons to minister as priests to Me. I will dwell among the sons of Israel and will be their God. They shall know that I am the LORD their God who brought them out of the land of Egypt, that I might dwell among them; I am the LORD their God.

God's desire is to dwell among His people. While this desire has not changed, the way we have access to His presence has been transformed by Jesus, once and for all.

Exodus 29 details the consecration and ordination of the priests who would mediate God's presence through the tabernacle system. This system was the only authorized way to the Father, and it was an elaborate and exacting process.

Then God sent His one and only Son, and established a new authorized way for the will of the Father to be fulfilled. Jesus declared in John 14:6, "I am the way, and the truth, and the life; no one comes to the Father but through Me."

Jesus' death atoned for the sins of those God desires to dwell among, and the infilling of the Holy Spirit causes His people to become His dwelling place. This is our salvation!

Seize the moment and thank Jesus for making a new way for you to experience God's desire for you and your life – to dwell with you!

Dr. Jerry D. Ingalls

EXODUS 30
THE SWEET AROMA OF HOME!

How does it make you feel when you walk into a place where one of your favorite meals has been cooking?

It smells like the sweet aroma of home! Smells are powerful and can invoke strong feelings of comfort and deep memories of association. God designed us this way on purpose.

Exodus 30 emphasizes the instructions for the altar of incense, the recipe for the incense, and the regulations for using it. Verses 6-8 talk about the purpose of the altar of incense:

> You shall put this altar in front of the veil that is near the ark of the testimony, in front of the mercy seat that is over the ark of the testimony, where I will meet with you. Aaron shall burn fragrant incense on it; he shall burn it every morning when he trims the lamps. When Aaron trims the lamps at twilight, he shall burn incense. There shall be perpetual incense before the LORD throughout your generations.

The tabernacle would have a unique smell, as the specific recipe of incense was not to be used except to worship God at His mercy seat (37-38). God intended our practices of worship to focus every part of our personhood on God.

Therefore, Paul commanded us in 1 Thessalonians 5:17 to, "pray without ceasing," and in Ephesians 5:12 to, "walk in love, just as Christ also loved you and gave Himself up for us, an offering and a sacrifice to God as a fragrant aroma."

God's desire is to make His home in our lives, and He has given us the recipe of heavenly home cooking that emanates the sweet aroma of our worship to the one true God!

Seize the moment and offer your life as a living sacrifice to God (Romans 12:1). Then you will give off the sweet aroma of Heaven as the fragrance of Christ to God (2 Corinthians 2:14-16).

EXODUS 31
THE IMPORTANCE OF REST!

When you hear the word sabbath, what comes to your mind?

God describes the importance of sabbath rest in His covenant code with Israel in Exodus 31:15-17:

> For six days work may be done, but on the seventh day there is a sabbath of complete rest, holy to the LORD; whoever does any work on the sabbath day shall surely be put to death. So the sons of Israel shall observe the sabbath, to celebrate the sabbath throughout their generations as a perpetual covenant. It is a sign between Me and the sons of Israel forever; for in six days the LORD made heaven and earth, but on the seventh day He ceased from labor, and was refreshed.

The word sabbath simply means to stop. In Genesis 2, God's stopping on the seventh day of creation was the first thing in all His creative efforts that He declared holy; it was a time, not a thing, or a place!

In Hebrews 4:9-11, we see the importance of the Sabbath reiterated to New Covenant believers:

> So there remains a Sabbath rest for the people of God. For the one who has entered His rest has himself also rested from his works, as God did from His. Therefore let us be diligent to enter that rest, so that no one will fall, through following the same example of disobedience.

Taking a day of rest has always been an important rhythm of God's creation. Our culture, and the Western church, ignore this rhythm at great cost to our well-being: spiritually, physically, mentally, and relationally! Sabbath is not a work of salvation, but a gift for the saved. Delight in God's grace and find rest for your soul (Matthew 11:28-30).

Seize the moment by taking out your personal calendar to prioritize one full day of Sabbath each week to experience the rest of God.

Dr. Jerry D. Ingalls

EXODUS 32
PATIENCE IS KEY TO SPIRITUAL GROWTH!

Has your impatience ever caused problems?

Exodus 32 is a dumpster fire caused by impatience! The Israelites have been rescued from generations of slavery, but they have complained to Moses for most of the caravan out of Egypt to their current location at Mount Sinai. Moses provided strong leadership along the way, and now is on the top of the mountain receiving the Law from God. The people, led by Aaron, had to wait for him to return, but, as with most of us, waiting was not their strength!

It all began in Exodus 32:1, with the uncertainty, and the fear of the unknown, that nearly always comes about when we have to wait:

Now when the people saw that Moses delayed to come down from the mountain, the people assembled about Aaron and said to him, "Come, make us a god who will go before us; as for this Moses, the man who brought us up from the land of Egypt, we do not know what has become of him."

The devastation and death of this moment of impatience is horrifying! Their impatience led to a great act of covenant unfaithfulness, with Aaron making a golden calf and the people participating in idol worship. Because they were unable to wait with patience and trust God, and Moses, they pressed upon one of their own, Aaron, to give them what they wanted.

Patience is essential to spiritual growth! When you don't know what God is doing, fill the gap with trust and patience. This takes faith in God and the courage to wait upon Him.

Later in their history, King David wrote these words in Psalm 27:14, "Wait for the LORD; Be strong and let your heart take courage; Yes, wait for the LORD."

Seize the moment and wait with patience, remembering that God has promised to bring to completion that which He began (Philippians 1:6). Wait on God and trust His timing (Isaiah 40:26-31)!

EXODUS 33
FRIEND OF GOD!

Would you consider yourself a friend of God?

Friends know one another, listen to each other, and like one another. Friends share common interests and passions that keep them moving in the same direction.

Exodus 33:9-11a states that Moses related to God as a friend:

Whenever Moses entered the tent, the pillar of cloud would descend and stand at the entrance of the tent; and the LORD would speak with Moses. When all the people saw the pillar of cloud standing at the entrance of the tent, all the people would arise and worship, each at the entrance of his tent. Thus the LORD used to speak to Moses face to face, just as a man speaks to his friend.

In James 2:23, another Old Testament character was called a friend of God, "The Scripture was fulfilled which says, 'And Abraham believed God, and it was reckoned to him as righteousness,' and he was called the friend of God" (cf. 2 Chronicles 20:7; Isaiah 41:8).

Is such a lofty title, and intimate relationship, exclusive to these two rock stars of the faith?

Jesus Christ invites you to know and relate to God as a friend in John 15:14-15:

You are My friends if you do what I command you. No longer do I call you slaves, for the slave does not know what his master is doing; but I have called you friends, for all things that I have heard from My Father I have made known to you.

I love God, and I know He loves me! We spend a lot of time together and listen to one another. In the easy yoke of Jesus, I am partnering with Jesus in the work that God is passionate about. God has made His home in me and I have made my home in Him. That sounds like friendship to me.

Seize the moment and live your life as a friend of God!

Dr. Jerry D. Ingalls

EXODUS 34
THE CHARACTER OF COVENANT RENEWAL!

How do you rebuild trust with another person?

Exodus 34 records the covenant renewal between God and Moses, which came after the people's impatience had led to idol worship – a significant breach of trust between God and His chosen people. As God rebuilt that which the people had broken – His relationship with them – He proclaimed His character to His rebellious children, in verses 6-7:

Then the LORD passed by in front of him and proclaimed, "The LORD, the LORD God, compassionate and gracious, slow to anger, and abounding in lovingkindness and truth; who keeps lovingkindness for thousands, who forgives iniquity, transgression and sin; yet He will by no means leave the guilty unpunished, visiting the iniquity of fathers on the children and on the grandchildren to the third and fourth generations."

Again, in verse 14, God established His law based on His character, "for you shall not worship any other god, for the LORD, whose name is Jealous, is a jealous God."

You rebuild trust with another person by establishing your character and living according to it – you demonstrate integrity. In the above passages, God described Himself as compassionate, gracious, slow to anger, abounding in lovingkindness and truth, faithful and forgiving, just to the guilty and righteous alike, and jealous for His people.

God desires covenant renewal with His people; His character compels Him to pursue that which was lost! Luke 19:10 declares that this was the mission of Jesus Christ, "For the Son of Man has come to seek and to save that which was lost." God demonstrated His own integrity in the sending of His Son Jesus Christ to rescue His beloved children from the penalty of sin.

Seize the moment and return to God. Trust His character by turning to Him and seeking His face today.

EXODUS 35
REST IS A PRIORITY!

Taking time to rest is an important part of your mental and spiritual health, as well as your physical well-being. So much of experiencing Jesus' promise of abundant life is learning to live in rhythm with God's plan for work and rest (John 10:10).

Exodus 35 is a significant chapter, as the description of the work on the tabernacle begins. God wants to make one thing perfectly clear to His people: rest is a priority! In verses 1-2, God reminds His people to work with a new ethic and no longer as the slaves of Egypt:

> Then Moses assembled all the congregation of the sons of Israel, and said to them, "These are the things that the LORD has commanded you to do: For six days work may be done, but on the seventh day you shall have a holy day, a sabbath of complete rest to the LORD; whoever does any work on it shall be put to death."

It should not surprise us that this is God's first reminder to all the congregation. God leads off with grace because good works are meant to flow out of relationship with God, not to earn favor with God. Paul taught this to New Covenant believers in Ephesians 2:8-10:

> For by grace you have been saved through faith; and that not of yourselves, it is the gift of God; not as a result of works, so that no one may boast. For we are His workmanship, created in Christ Jesus for good works, which God prepared beforehand so that we would walk in them.

Seize the moment and prioritize God's grace in your life by setting apart a weekly day for rest. It's a gift; not a burden! Your well-being is dependent on you living in the unforced rhythms of God's grace in every area of your humanity: work, play, and rest.

Dr. Jerry D. Ingalls

EXODUS 36
GOD PROVIDES FOR WHAT GOD PROMISES!

Have you ever heard a church leader tell the congregation to stop giving?

Exodus 36:4-7 captures an important moment as God's people provide in abundance for the building of the tabernacle and all that God commanded:

> And all the skillful men who were performing all the work of the sanctuary came, each from the work which he was performing, and they said to Moses, "The people are bringing much more than enough for the construction work which the LORD commanded us to perform." So Moses issued a command, and a proclamation was circulated throughout the camp, saying, "Let no man or woman any longer perform work for the contributions of the sanctuary." Thus the people were restrained from bringing any more.

Can you imagine something like this happening today?

Based on this passage, I believe every local church can prayerfully discern the following two things to experience a moment such as this: (1) We are to know specifically what God has commanded us to do; and (2) We are to know how we are invited to bring about the completion of that work.

Do you know what God has called your local church congregation to accomplish?

Do you know how you can help accomplish that work?

These are important questions. In answering them, God's Spirit can both compel us and restrain us in our giving and doing. Whether it's a "yes" or a "no," it should be the outworking of God's will in and through our lives. As Paul said in 2 Corinthians 5:14a, "For the love of Christ controls us." In and through us, God always provides for that which God promises to do!

Seize the moment and trust God every step of the way with your giving and doing. Join Jesus in glorifying God by accomplishing all that the Father has given you to do with your life (John 17:4).

EXODUS 37
AN IMPORTANT PUZZLE PIECE!

Do you like to put together jigsaw puzzles? What happens when you have spent hours putting together an intricate puzzle only to find out that there is a piece missing?

The picture is not complete when even one piece is missing!

In Exodus 37, we read of intricate, detailed work that is necessary for the completion of the tabernacle and all its furniture. Verses 1-2 provides an excellent example of the required craftmanship:

Now Bezalel made the ark of acacia wood; its length was two and a half cubits, and its width one and a half cubits, and its height one and a half cubits; and he overlaid it with pure gold inside and out, and made a gold molding for it all around.

Throughout this chapter, you hear the refrain, "He made...", which references Bezalel, the chief craftsmen. He was responsible to take all the detailed instructions from Exodus 25 up to this point and use all the materials provided by God through the people to oversee the work.

The reality is that it took an army of craftswomen and craftsmen, as well as a community of generous givers, to bring this project to completion. The tabernacle of God and all its furniture would not have been made to specification if it wasn't for every single person coming together.

The same is true in the church today regarding our ability to accomplish anything. We often reference the leader of a ministry, the teacher of a Sunday School class, or the missionary overseeing a mission, but it takes every single piece of the puzzle to get the job done!

As Paul says in Ephesians 4:16, "According to the proper working of each individual part, causes the growth of the body for the building up of itself in love."

Seize the moment and find your unique place in the church, because without you the picture is not complete. You are an important and valuable member of the body of Christ (Romans 12:4-5; Ephesians 4:16)!

Dr. Jerry D. Ingalls

EXODUS 38
BUILD UP THE NEXT GENERATION!

What is the most important legacy we leave behind from our ministry efforts?

Exodus 38 continues to tell the story of the completion of the tabernacle and all its furniture and all that it took to pull off this major construction project. Building campaigns are significant undertakings, and important to the community of God's people, but do you know what is more important? Building up the next generation!

Exodus 38:21-23 makes a subtle, but very important, observation of the ministry of God's people:

> This is the number of the things for the tabernacle, the tabernacle of the testimony, as they were numbered according to the command of Moses, for the service of the Levites, by the hand of Ithamar the son of Aaron the priest. Now Bezalel the son of Uri, the son of Hur, of the tribe of Judah, made all that the LORD had commanded Moses. With him was Oholiab the son of Ahisamach, of the tribe of Dan, an engraver and a skillful workman and a weaver in blue and in purple and in scarlet material, and fine linen.

This was a multi-generational project:

- Ithamar was the son of Aaron the priest, who worked with Moses in the deliverance and rescue of God's people.
- Bezalel was the son of Uri, the son of Hur, who held up Moses' arms as he held up the staff of God.
- Oholiab was the son of Ahisamach, of the tribe of Dan, one of the twelve sons of Israel.

Whether you are conducting a major construction project, hosting a church picnic, or serving the local community, be sure to do it in such a way as to build up the next generation.

Seize the moment and invite the next generation to partner with you in whatever ministry task you are called to do. May all that we do equip the next generation to live for Jesus.

EXODUS 39
THE WORK OF GOD!

Leadership can be a daunting task. Making decisions and feeling responsible for something can feel overwhelming, especially when the work is being done in the name of Jesus.

Exodus 39:42-43 gives a helpful overview of how to accomplish a big project:

> So the sons of Israel did all the work according to all that the LORD had commanded Moses. And Moses examined all the work and behold, they had done it; just as the LORD had commanded, this they had done. So Moses blessed them.

First, Moses spent time with God and then clearly communicated the Word of God to the people. All spiritual leaders must have healthy spiritual rhythms in their own lives; this allows them to separate from the demands and expectations of other people, in order to attend to their top responsibility: to sit at Jesus' feet and listen well (Luke 10:38-42). Spiritual leaders clearly communicate what they have received from God so that the members of God's community can take their next steps.

Next, the people are to discern the Word from the Lord and take practical steps toward doing what the Word of God calls them to do together as members of the body of Christ. The work of God gets accomplished as the people rally together, focused on God's Word, doing what each person is gifted and called to do (Romans 12:6-8).

Finally, spiritual leaders bless the people for obeying the Word of the Lord. While our greatest reward is Heaven, God calls us to speak words of love and encouragement to one another as we work together to accomplish what God would have us to do as a community.

Seize the moment and use words of love and encouragement to build up your community of faith, and those around you. God's work gets done when we each listen to Jesus and work together as the one body of Christ.

EXODUS 40
THE VEIL THAT SEPARATED!

Have you ever had a barrier between you and another person?

Exodus 40 describes the tabernacle being assembled "just as the LORD had commanded Moses." That refrain was repeated often because the people of Israel could not have access to God outside of following the prescribed way; therefore, great detail was recorded and insisted upon in the assembly of, and worship at, the tabernacle.

Exodus 40:20-21 captures an important detail of the holy of holies (most holy place), the inner chamber for God in the tabernacle:

> Then he took the testimony and put it into the ark, and attached the poles to the ark, and put the mercy seat on top of the ark. He brought the ark into the tabernacle, and set up a veil for the screen, and screened off the ark of the testimony, just as the LORD had commanded Moses.

The veil was not only functional, but it was also symbolic – there was a barrier between man and God. It was commanded in Exodus 26:33b, "the veil shall serve for you as a partition between the holy place and the holy of holies." While God sought to be with His people, access to Him was severely limited and highly formalized so that only the high priest could enter the most holy place once per year to make atonement for sin.

Jesus Christ came to give us direct access to the Father. Hebrews 10:19 declares this truth, "Therefore, brethren, since we have confidence to enter the holy place by the blood of Jesus."

This access happened at the time of Jesus' death. Jesus' crucifixion removed the veil because Jesus atoned for sin once for all. As Mark 15:38 records from that day, "the veil of the temple was torn in two from top to bottom."

Seize the moment and seek God's presence. He has made a way for you through the shed blood of Jesus Christ!

LEVITICUS

LEVITICUS 1
A COSTLY SACRIFICE!

Are you a good gift giver?

Leviticus 1:2-4 begins the teaching on the ancient sacrificial system:

When any man of you brings an offering to the LORD, you shall bring your offering of animals from the herd or the flock. If his offering is a burnt offering from the herd, he shall offer it, a male without defect; he shall offer it at the doorway of the tent of meeting, that he may be accepted before the LORD. He shall lay his hand on the head of the burnt offering, that it may be accepted for him to make atonement on his behalf.

The burnt offering was the costliest sacrifice the Israelites were commanded to make. It was to happen morning and evening. It required the burning of an entire animal carcass from the people's herds or flocks; it could not be a wild animal. It had to be a male without defect.

These details matter because God required a costly sacrifice! King David expressed this in 2 Samuel 24:24, "I will not offer burnt offerings to the LORD my God which cost me nothing."

The burnt offering was not only a sacrifice for the atonement of sin, but also of thankfulness and worship to God. It was a gift given to God, with the goal of it being accepted by God, who would then look with favor upon the one making the sacrifice.

While we no longer sacrifice animals, we are commanded to live so that our lives are accepted by God. Because we no longer need to go through a formal sacrificial rite every morning and evening to have atonement for our sins, we are invited to live in constant communion with Jesus Christ, the unblemished Lamb of God, who has made atonement for our sins, once and for all.

Seize the moment and give good gifts to God, starting with yourself every morning and evening; consecrate all that you have to the Lord.

LEVITICUS 2
THE COVENANT OF SALT!

Have you heard someone say that a certain person was worth his or her weight in salt?

That idiom speaks of a person having great value, being competent and worthwhile, excellent in what they do, and worthy of his or her wages.

Salt has always been an important commodity in trade, but did you know that it has also had importance in worship? Leviticus 2 teaches us about the grain offering, and verse 13 highlights this point, "Every grain offering of yours, moreover, you shall season with salt, so that the salt of the covenant of your God shall not be lacking from your grain offering; with all your offerings you shall offer salt."

With salt being a valuable preservative in ancient times, it symbolized the enduring nature of a covenant. Evidence of this is found in Numbers 18:19:

> All the offerings of the holy gifts, which the sons of Israel offer to the LORD, I have given to you and your sons and your daughters with you, as a perpetual allotment. It is an everlasting covenant of salt before the LORD to you and your descendants with you.

Furthermore, King David received his kingdom from God by a covenant of salt. Listen to 2 Chronicles 13:5, "Do you not know that the LORD God of Israel gave the rule over Israel forever to David and his sons by a covenant of salt?"

Therefore, we need to pay special attention to Jesus' words in Matthew 5:13a, "You are the salt of the earth." Through the shed blood of Jesus Christ on the Cross of Calvary you have entered a better and eternal way with God – the everlasting covenant of salt.

Seize the moment and live as one who has been salted with grace and truth. May you live at peace with God, yourself, and one another (Mark 9:50).

LEVITICUS 3
THE PEACE OFFERING!

Do you like to invite your friends or family to join with you to share a meal?

There is something about sharing food that draws you closer to people, especially when you have provided the meat, or a portion of the meal, for others to enjoy.

Leviticus 3 describes the regulations for the peace offering, also known as the fellowship offering. Based on the original Hebrew word, it has also been called the "well-being offering." While there is some ambiguity around the meaning, there is no confusion about its purpose.

We see the purpose of a peace offering in Leviticus 3:16, "The priest shall offer them up in smoke on the altar as food, an offering by fire for a soothing aroma." The peace offering was the primary type of sacrifice that provided meat for the people, unlike the sin and guilt offerings which could only be eaten by the priests, and the burnt offering which was to be completely consumed by fire on the altar. With the fat and blood consumed on the altar, and the priest receiving his portion (Leviticus 7:28-34), the rest of the meat would go back to the worshiper to be consumed within one or two days of making the peace offering (Leviticus 7:15; 19:6-8).

While giving thanks to God, the peace offering provided an acceptable way to slaughter a sacrificial animal for food (Leviticus 7:11-36). What a wonderful way to prepare for a time of fellowship around the table with your loved ones. The peace offering provided for a way to pass the peace on to your friends and family and invite everyone over to celebrate God's provision.

Peace offerings provided food for fellowship, which increases well-being. Don't we all feel better after sharing some good food with good friends?

Seize the moment and organize a time of celebration with your loved ones. If you are able, provide the meat and pass the peace.

LEVITICUS 4
IGNORANCE IS NO EXCUSE!

Have you ever heard someone say, "ignorance is no excuse?"

The law is an objective standard by which our actions are measured. If a police officer pulls you over for speeding, and you say you didn't know that the speed limit on I-70 went from 70 to 55 in the Indianapolis area, the police officer would still hold you accountable to the law.

Leviticus 4 teaches about the sin offering, specifically for sins that were committed unintentionally by the people. This truth is found in Leviticus 4:2, 13, 22, and 27:

> If a person *sins unintentionally* in any of the things which the LORD has commanded not to be done ... Now if the whole congregation of Israel commits error and the matter *escapes the notice of the assembly*, ... When a leader sins and *unintentionally* does any one of all the things which the LORD his God has commanded not to be done, ... Now if anyone of the common people sins *unintentionally* in doing any of the things which the LORD has commanded not to be done. [italics added]

Unintentional sin is a real issue. Sometimes we sin without intent. We simply fall short in our thoughts, speech, activities, and relationships. Sometimes these unintentional sins are not even things we do, but things we *don't* do.

While it is true that ignorance is no excuse, praise God that even when we don't know to ask for forgiveness of a particular sin, Jesus' blood "cleanses us from all sin" (1 John 1:7). This is God's truth and grace!

Seize the moment and seek God daily for a clear conscience through the forgiveness of your sins. Be at peace with God, and with yourself, because you are forgiven and set free from sin to live for God!

LEVITICUS 5
THE POWER OF WORDS!

Have you ever been in trouble because you made a promise you couldn't keep?

Leviticus 5 discusses the guilt offering and gives practical examples of the kinds of sins that would require it to purify the person. We see a relevant example in verses 4-5:

> Or if a person swears thoughtlessly with his lips to do evil or to do good, in whatever matter a man may speak thoughtlessly with an oath, and it is hidden from him, and then he comes to know it, he will be guilty in one of these. So it shall be when he becomes guilty in one of these, that he shall confess that in which he has sinned.

Thousands of years ago, if you made an empty promise, regardless of your intent being good or evil, and it was brought to your attention, then a sin offering was required for your purification.

Perhaps the person simply did not realize the implications of their promise, or maybe circumstances changed and the person could no longer fulfill it. No matter – the law said that an unfulfilled oath caused a person to be guilty.

Words have power! Words flow from a person and carry the power to build up and to tear down, to bind together or to loosen apart. Therefore, we must be wise with how we use our words, especially when making commitments and promises to people and communities.

Proverbs 18:21 teaches, "Death and life are in the power of the tongue, and those who love it will eat its fruit." The Bible is filled with wisdom for our words, and we should listen to and obey God's Word with how we use our words.

Seize the moment and be wise with the words you use when making promises! Death and life are in the power of your tongue, and with today's technology, in the power of your fingertips.

LEVITICUS 6
EARTHEN VESSELS!

What is the purpose of our bodies in this life?

Leviticus 6:28 describes what happens to the vessels used to prepare the offering to God, "Also the earthenware vessel in which [the sin offering] was boiled shall be broken; and if it was boiled in a bronze vessel, then it shall be scoured and rinsed in water."

Anything the animal sacrifice touched became holy. Everything that it touched became set apart for God. The priestly garments had to be cleansed from any blood defilement, the fat and blood had to be completely consumed in the fire, the meat portions were specifically allocated to the priests, and even the cooking vessels had to be either destroyed or thoroughly cleansed.

What struck me was that the temporary vessels made from clay had to be broken after being made holy, whereas the permanent vessels made from metal had to be scoured and washed thoroughly. While there are lots of practical reasons this was commanded, the connection with our bodies being the temples of the Holy Spirit is unmistakable.

Paul spoke of our bodies as earthen vessels in 2 Corinthians 4:7, "But we have this treasure in earthen vessels, so that the surpassing greatness of the power will be of God and not from ourselves." Again, Paul wrote in 2 Timothy 2:20-21:

> Now in a large house there are not only gold and silver vessels, but also vessels of wood and of earthenware, and some to honor and some to dishonor. Therefore, if anyone cleanses himself from these things, he will be a vessel for honor, sanctified, useful to the Master, prepared for every good work.

Seize the moment and use your body as an earthen vessel for God's glory. One day, you will receive a new resurrected body that will never be broken again.

LEVITICUS 7
A WORKER'S WAGES!

Every generation seeks to apply the Word of God to our contemporary cultures in timely and practical ways. One such discussion is that of the role of paid church workers.

God's Word is the foundation for all church discussions, including this ongoing conversation. Leviticus 7:7-9 communicates that a priest is worth his wages:

> The guilt offering is like the sin offering, there is one law for them; the priest who makes atonement with it shall have it. Also the priest who presents any man's burnt offering, that priest shall have for himself the skin of the burnt offering which he has presented. Likewise, every grain offering that is baked in the oven and everything prepared in a pan or on a griddle shall belong to the priest who presents it.

The sacrificial system was essential to providing for the priests and the tabernacle (temple) workers because these people were without land allotment to farm and subsist. Since God chose them to focus their work efforts on tending to the faith and practices of His people, He built into the Law that their wages came from their work.

In the church today, there are men and women – priests, pastors, ministry leaders, church and parachurch workers, and missionaries serving around world – whose chosen vocation has the same exclusive purpose of tending to the faith and practices of God's people. These people work hard and are worthy of their wages. Those wages are no longer through the Levitical sacrificial system, but they are still flowing through the sacrifices of God's covenant people.

As Paul reemphasized in 1 Timothy 5:18, "For the Scripture says, 'You shall not muzzle the ox while he is threshing,' and 'The laborer is worthy of his wages.'"

Seize the moment and give generously to God's work. Pray for and financially support the laborers you know who are tending to the faith and practices of God's people.

Dr. Jerry D. Ingalls

LEVITICUS 8
FILLED UP FOR GOD'S WORK!

Have you attended an ordination service in your faith tradition?

I will never forget my own ordination. I served in full-time pastoral ministry in various areas of ministry responsibility throughout my seminary Master of Divinity degree program, while walking through the ordination and mentorship process in my local church and denomination.

I was filled up and ready to be poured out. The ordination service was more than an acknowledgement of that nearly six-year process, it was the seal upon it. When the stole was placed over me and hands were laid upon me, the Holy Spirit filled me up to overflowing.

Leviticus 8 captures the formal beginning of the priesthood and sacrificial system, and a significant part of it is the seven-day ordination service of Aaron and his sons. The emphasis is upon the priestly clothing, ordination offering, and the purification rites. Let's focus on verse 33, "You shall not go outside the doorway of the tent of meeting for seven days, until the day that the period of your ordination is fulfilled; for he will ordain you through seven days."

The Hebrew translated, "he will ordain you" literally means, "he will make full with a sufficient quantity." To ordain the priest was for God to fill up that person to sufficiency. Through an intricate process, the people set apart their priests as consecrated and purified vessels, then God filled them up for His ministry. The ordination is God's work, not man's work!

In Ephesians 5:18, Paul invites all New Covenant believers to "be filled with the Spirit." As a follower of Jesus, you, too, like the priests of old, are ordained to be a vessel of God's glory, filled up with the Holy Spirit to walk in God's good works. This is God's grace!

Seize the moment and be filled with the Holy Spirit. Trust God to pour out your life for His glory!

LEVITICUS 9
CONFIRMATION FROM GOD!

Have you ever received a confirmation that you were doing a good job? A simple example would be when your boss praises or rewards your work.

Leviticus 9 narrates the inaugural sacrifices for worship at the tabernacle by Aaron and his sons after their seven-day ordination service. The sacrificial system of God's people had begun.

Leviticus 9:22-24 records God's confirmation to the leaders that they sacrificed to Him correctly, and to the people that they were now walking in His ways:

> Then Aaron lifted up his hands toward the people and blessed them, and he stepped down after making the sin offering and the burnt offering and the peace offerings. Moses and Aaron went into the tent of meeting. When they came out and blessed the people, the glory of the LORD appeared to all the people. Then fire came out from before the LORD and consumed the burnt offering and the portions of fat on the altar; and when all the people saw it, they shouted and fell on their faces.

This was not a one-time occurrence. Later in Israel's history, in 1 Kings 18:38-39, God confirmed Elijah's ministry and called the people back from their false worship of Baal:

> Then the fire of the LORD fell and consumed the burnt offering and the wood and the stones and the dust, and licked up the water that was in the trench. When all the people saw it, they fell on their faces; and they said, "The LORD, He is God; the LORD, He is God."

Seize the moment and worship by giving yourself to God as a living and holy sacrifice. May you experience the confirmation of God's consuming fire through the activation of His Holy Spirit in you.

LEVITICUS 10
RESPONSIBLE LIVING!

Is there anything in your life that keeps you from being available to God for His service?

Leviticus 10:1-2 makes a sudden transition from the inauguration of the sacrificial system to the tragic deaths of two newly ordained priests:

> Now Nadab and Abihu, the sons of Aaron, took their respective firepans, and after putting fire in them, placed incense on it and offered strange fire before the LORD, which He had not commanded them. And fire came out from the presence of the LORD and consumed them, and they died before the LORD.

Were the two sons of Aaron not authorized to offer the incense? Did they make a mistake in their methods through the type of incense, the time they offered it, or the source of the flame?

If you keep reading, you get some further insight on this incident because God issues a new command to the priests in verses 8-9:

> The LORD then spoke to Aaron, saying, "Do not drink wine or strong drink, neither you nor your sons with you, when you come into the tent of meeting, so that you will not die – it is a perpetual statute throughout your generations."

Prior to this horrific event, alcohol was not mentioned. Now, God makes it clear that, while drinking alcohol was not wholesale prohibited for His people, it was forbidden while fulfilling priestly duties. This would be emphasized again in Ezekiel 44:21.

In Ephesians 5:18, Paul discusses alcohol for New Covenant believers, who are all God's priests today, "And do not get drunk with wine, for that is dissipation, but be filled with the Spirit." The prohibition is not against alcohol usage, but against drunkenness and irresponsibility. The Bible calls us to being of sound mind, body, and soul, not intoxicated by anything, so that we can live our lives holy and whole.

Seize the moment and live a sober and responsible life! Be available to serve God effectively, at any time of the night or day.

LEVITICUS 11
THE HOLINESS OF FOOD!

Is food important to you? How do you view food?

Leviticus 11 records a significant part of the Levitical Law – its dietary restrictions. God presents His purposes as He finished giving the dietary restrictions in verses 44-45:

> For I am the LORD your God. Consecrate yourselves therefore, and be holy, for I am holy. And you shall not make yourselves unclean with any of the swarming things that swarm on the earth. For I am the LORD who brought you up from the land of Egypt to be your God; thus you shall be holy, for I am holy.

A significant part of the people's holiness in the Levitical Law was focused on food. God prescribed for them dietary restrictions as a part of their spiritual life. A major part of covenant faithfulness was demonstrated by who was invited to the dinner table and what was eaten. These became major points of contention between Jesus and the religious leaders of His day.

In today's culture, most people I know have a very different view of food consumption. We have either a utilitarian or hedonistic view of food, not a holistic one. Many have lost their connection with the rhythms of working the earth and raising animals for food. Today, we simply go to the store, purchase what we need, and find no relationship between that and our worship of the Sovereign God.

God calls us to a larger view of food; even though Jesus has freed us from the dietary restrictions (ref. Matthew 15:11; Acts 10:9-16), we are still called to view our time around the table as a central and holy part of our lives – a time of communion with God and table fellowship with others.

Seize the moment and reconsider the importance of food, and your time at the dinner table to celebrate God's work of deliverance, so that we can be His set apart people, called to the ministry of reconciliation.

Dr. Jerry D. Ingalls

LEVITICUS 12
THE SACRED BEAUTY OF MOTHERHOOD!

How do we honor and protect the mothers of our communities?

A society that does not place a high value on motherhood is destined to fail. A culture that does not seek to protect the esteemed role of mothers will perish. One of the ways we attempt to do this is with maternity leave for working moms, which allows them to stay home with their newborn babies for a length of time. This is not a new concept!

Leviticus 12 describes the purification process for mothers after giving birth to their children. This chapter prescribes a time of purification for the mother to remain at home with the child – 33 days for a boy and 66 days for a girl. While there are reasons for this, some of which revolve around the sacredness of blood as the life source, already established as an essential reality to the sacrificial system, one good reason is that nothing was asked of the mother for this length of time except to nurse and care for her baby, while resting from her labor.

After this length of time, verses 6-7 commanded every mother to go to the tabernacle and make a sacrifice to God:

When the days of her purification are completed, for a son or for a daughter, she shall bring to the priest at the doorway of the tent of meeting a one year old lamb for a burnt offering and a young pigeon or a turtledove for a sin offering. Then he shall offer it before the LORD and make atonement for her, and she shall be cleansed from the flow of her blood. This is the law for her who bears a child, whether a male or a female.

Seize the moment and honor life by protecting the sacred beauty of motherhood. Make space for new parents to bond with their babies.

LEVITICUS 13
PROTECT THE PUBLIC HEALTH!

Is public health important to you?

Leviticus 13 is all about the public health. It explains how to ensure the community's safety from contagious skin diseases. While the English word used to translate the original Hebrew is leprosy, modern scholars believe that it originally included a multitude of skin diseases.

When a person had symptoms, he would go to the priest, who was tasked with diagnosing the wound through the size and location of the diseased area, including the color of the skin and the hair in it. The priest decided if the person needed to be quarantined. If so, the infected person would go to isolation for seven days before reexamination. To be declared clean of the contagion, the marks could not have spread, and must have visibly healed over the course of fourteen days of quarantine.

From Leviticus 13:45-46, focus on the lengths God's Word went to protect the public health:

> As for the leper who has the infection, his clothes shall be torn, and the hair of his head shall be uncovered, and he shall cover his mustache and cry, "Unclean! Unclean!" He shall remain unclean all the days during which he has the infection; he is unclean. He shall live alone; his dwelling shall be outside the camp.

It is so painful to read these words as I write this devotion during the COVID-19 pandemic, when we have had to experience the quarantine of ourselves, and of so many of our friends and family. Truly, these are difficult and dark days!

God's Word is always relevant, even though it was written thousands of years ago in such a different cultural context. God's Word is applicable to our personal lives, and for the common good!

Seize the moment and trust God for every area of your life. Let us pray for the public health and that we will be a part of seeing our communities thriving to the glory of God.

LEVITICUS 14
GOD MAKES A WAY!

Leviticus 14 continues the teaching on infectious skin diseases with the cleansing of people, clothing, and materials. The Levitical Law took infectious diseases seriously with 116 verses in these two chapters. By contrast, the teaching on childbirth was a total of eight verses in chapter 12. As I am writing this devotion during the COVID-19 pandemic, it doesn't surprise me that people would write so much about an infectious disease.

Verses 30-32 make a way for people with limited resources to be able to get the care they need:

> He shall then offer one of the turtledoves or young pigeons, which are within his means. He shall offer what he can afford, the one for a sin offering and the other for a burnt offering, together with the grain offering. So the priest shall make atonement before the LORD on behalf of the one to be cleansed. This is the law for him in whom there is an infection of leprosy, whose means are limited for his cleansing.

God's Word makes a way for people of different means to have access to these cleansing rites. The Word of God intentionally protects against human greed and corruption by accommodating for all people to have access to the priests and the sacrificial system.

The New Testament speaks to this issue and protects all people's access to the Christian faith and practices of the church. James 2:9 states, "But if you show partiality, you are committing sin and are convicted by the law as transgressors."

God desires for His people to reflect His heart so that all would have access to Him and His healing work of cleansing and forgiveness through the shed blood of Jesus Christ. As Paul said in Romans 2:11, "For there is no partiality with God."

Seize the moment and ask God to give you His heart for people, so that all people can respond to the gospel.

LEVITICUS 15
PERSONAL MATTERS MATTER!

Do your personal matters matter to God?

Yes! Leviticus 15 covers the most intimate issues of the human body and relationships. As I write this devotion for such a diverse group of people, allow me to generalize this chapter by simply saying, "Personal matters matter!" In other words, you should be concerned about what you think, say, and do, regardless of whether other people know.

Leviticus 15:31 summarizes why your personal matters matter to God, "Thus you shall keep the sons of Israel separated from their uncleanness, so that they will not die in their uncleanness by their defiling My tabernacle that is among them."

To be defiled is to be unclean and no longer suited for God's presence. In biblical history, the tabernacle was the place of God's presence on Earth, and the mediation of His presence was dependent on the Levitical Law and its intricate systems of priests and sacrifices.

In this delicate system, one person could shut it all down! One person could impact the life of the community. It is important we realize how our personal decisions affect others. We are not islands unto ourselves!

Today, we are the priests of God, and Jesus has made the atoning sacrifice "once for all" (Hebrews 10:10). We are made clean by Him; we are now the temples of the Holy Spirit and have become the dwelling places of God in this world (1 Corinthians 6:19-20).

Peter further explains the importance of your cleansing in 2 Peter 1:4, "For by these He has granted to us His precious and magnificent promises, so that by them you may become partakers of the divine nature, having escaped the corruption that is in the world by lust."

Personal matters still matter to God because you are His visible presence to the world He loves.

Seize the moment and walk in purity with God and with other people.

LEVITICUS 16
THE ATONEMENT OF SIN!

Leviticus prescribed an intricate system of priests, daily sacrifices, dietary restrictions, weekly sabbaths, and annual festivals to make atonement for sin.

Atonement describes both the covering of human guilt and the turning away of God's wrath. It communicates the biblical concept of reconciliation, which is at the heart of God in giving the Levitical Law in the first place.

Leviticus 16:32-34 prescribed the annual festival known as Yom Kippur, which is the Day of Atonement:

So the priest who is anointed and ordained to serve as priest in his father's place shall make atonement: he shall thus put on the linen garments, the holy garments, and make atonement for the holy sanctuary, and he shall make atonement for the tent of meeting and for the altar. He shall also make atonement for the priests and for all the people of the assembly. Now you shall have this as a permanent statute, to make atonement for the sons of Israel for all their sins once every year.

The reconciliation of relationship between God and humanity is why Jesus Christ came and fulfilled the Levitical Law; through the one nation of Israel, all the nations can be restored under the rightful rule of God's Messiah, who provides, once for all, atonement of sin (Hebrews 7:27; 10:10).

Jesus Christ fulfilled the Day of Atonement in three ways:

1. Jesus is the priest who makes atonement (Hebrews 2:17; 9:1-15).
2. Jesus is the place of atonement (Romans 3:21-25).
3. Jesus is the sacrifice of atonement (1 John 2:2; 4:10; 1 Peter 1:17-19).

Praise God that it is through a relationship with Jesus Christ that we enter our relationship with God.

Seize the moment and trust Jesus Christ with your right relationship with God.

LEVITICUS 17
THE IMPORTANCE OF BLOOD!

Have you ever wondered why Christians talk so much about blood, and even sing songs about it?

The importance of blood is an ancient concept found in Leviticus 17:11 and 14:

> For the life of the flesh is in the blood, and I have given it to you on the altar to make atonement for your souls; for it is the blood by reason of the life that makes atonement. ... For as for the life of all flesh, its blood is identified with its life. Therefore I said to the sons of Israel, "You are not to eat the blood of any flesh, for the life of all flesh is its blood; whoever eats it shall be cut off."

Prior to the Levitical Law, Genesis 9:4 highlighted the importance of blood, "Only you shall not eat flesh with its life, that is, its blood." Verse 10 calls it, "lifeblood."

The ancients revered all blood as sacred, which is why the sacrifice of animals was an essential part of their holiness practices. As Hebrews 9:22 makes clear, "And according to the Law, one may almost say, all things are cleansed with blood, and without shedding of blood there is no forgiveness."

For this reason, Jesus Christ had to die on the Cross of Calvary – to atone for humanity's sin, once for all, by shedding the blood of the perfect Passover Lamb to fulfill the ancient covenant between God and humanity.

We remember the shed blood of Jesus Christ every time we gather at the table to drink from the cup of the New Covenant. We partake of the cup because Jesus said in Matthew 26:28, "For this is My blood of the covenant, which is poured out for many for forgiveness of sins."

Seize the moment and remember the sacrifice of Jesus Christ for the forgiveness of your sins and the cleansing of your unrighteousness.

LEVITICUS 18
LIVE PURE ON PURPOSE!

Leviticus 18 unapologetically dives deep into the intimate practices of people's private lives. In fact, the Bible teaches us that these most personal places of our lives demonstrate our true loyalties. God introduces this most sensitive conversation in verses 2-5:

> I am the LORD your God. You shall not do what is done in the land of Egypt where you lived, nor are you to do what is done in the land of Canaan where I am bringing you; you shall not walk in their statutes. You are to perform My judgments and keep My statutes, to live in accord with them; I am the LORD your God. So you shall keep My statutes and My judgments, by which a man may live if he does them; I am the LORD.

The prelude of this teaching on sexual purity is a call to covenant faithfulness to God. The motivation of God's heart is to protect His children and to establish a witness of His sovereign grace to those living in rebellion. God's desire is for His people to escape the corruption of the world and live pure on purpose.

Paul teaches living pure on purpose in 1 Corinthians 6:18-20:

> Flee immorality. Every other sin that a man commits is outside the body, but the immoral man sins against his own body. Or do you not know that your body is a temple of the Holy Spirit who is in you, whom you have from God, and that you are not your own? For you have been bought with a price: therefore glorify God in your body.

Paul emphasized it again in 1 Thessalonians 4:3, "For this is the will of God, your sanctification; that is, that you abstain from sexual immorality."

Seize the moment and live pure on purpose, for this is God's best for you and for His glory!

LEVITICUS 19
THE SECOND GREATEST COMMANDMENT!

Do you love your neighbor as yourself?

This concept comes from Jesus' teaching in Matthew 22:37-40, when Jesus responded to a lawyer's question about the most important commandment in the Levitical Law:

> And [Jesus] said to him, "'You shall love the LORD your God with all your heart, and with all your soul, and with all your mind.' This is the great and foremost commandment. The second is like it, 'You shall love your neighbor as yourself.' On these two commandments depend the whole Law and the Prophets."

Did you know that the second greatest commandment Jesus was quoting is found in Leviticus 19:18? This chapter captures the heart of Israel's moral teachings, which were anchored to their understanding of Yahweh's holiness, "You shall be holy, for I the LORD your God am holy" (2).

When you read verses 15-18 you learn the fullness of Jesus' teaching when He quoted verse 18 as the second greatest commandment:

> You shall do no injustice in judgment; you shall not be partial to the poor nor defer to the great, but you are to judge your neighbor fairly. You shall not go about as a slanderer among your people, and you are not to act against the life of your neighbor; I am the LORD. You shall not hate your fellow countryman in your heart; you may surely reprove your neighbor, but shall not incur sin because of him. You shall not take vengeance, nor bear any grudge against the sons of your people, but you shall love your neighbor as yourself; I am the LORD.

This teaches me that loving my neighbor is more than being nice and friendly; it is about justice, fairness, honesty, integrity, charity, and forgiveness. Loving your neighbor is the ministry of reconciliation.

Seize the moment and love others with the heart of God! Obedience to the second greatest commandment will change the world because it will first change you – love your neighbor *as yourself!*

Dr. Jerry D. Ingalls

LEVITICUS 20
THE ROOT OF THE ISSUE!

When I provide pastoral care for a person, which often is a combination of active listening, pastoral prayer, biblical counseling, and Christian discipleship, I am attempting to get to the root of the issue – not manage the bad fruit. This pairs well with a related concept: while catharsis provides short-term relief, transformation brings long-term victory.

Paul prescribed this treatment plan in Romans 12:2, "Do not be conformed to this world, but be transformed by the renewing of your mind, so that you may prove what the will of God is, that which is good and acceptable and perfect."

Leviticus 20:6-8 diagnoses the root of holiness issues as false worship:

As for the person who turns to mediums and to spiritists, to play the harlot after them, I will also set My face against that person and will cut him off from among his people. You shall consecrate yourselves therefore and be holy, for I am the LORD your God. You shall keep My statutes and practice them; I am the LORD who sanctifies you.

The previous verses address the false worship of Molech, which involved the Canaanite practice of child sacrifice, forbidding it by penalty of death. The chapter then lists many practices that flow from false worship that carried with them the death penalty, excommunication, or barrenness.

So often, churches have mutated Christianity into a laundry list of acceptable and forbidden activities, but that is not the heart of why Christ came. All our behaviors and activities flow out of our relationship with the God we truly serve. The God you worship will determine the fruit of your life because you are designed to reflect what you worship.

Seize the moment and worship Jesus in spirit and truth (John 4:24)! Jesus came to show you the heart of the Father and to bear the Fruit of the Spirit (Galatians 5:22-23).

LEVITICUS 21
HIGH STANDARDS FOR LEADERS!

Do you have high expectations of people who hold leadership positions in your church?

We all do! It is normal and right to desire for our leaders to have an integrity of faith and practice that manifests God's love throughout their lives – at home, in the church, and in the community. The problem is not in having high expectations of leaders, it is in failing to have grace and mercy for them when they fall short. I have yet to meet a leader who is fully qualified *all* the time.

Leviticus 21 focuses upon the priests and the high standards expected of them, and their families, by the Levitical Law. Without going into the details of those high standards, verse 6 summarizes them in this one statement, "They shall be holy to their God and not profane the name of their God, for they present the offerings by fire to the LORD, the food of their God; so they shall be holy."

Correspondingly, 1 Timothy 3:2-5 sets high standards for the New Testament church and its elders:

> An overseer, then, must be above reproach, the husband of one wife, temperate, prudent, respectable, hospitable, able to teach, not addicted to wine or pugnacious, but gentle, peaceable, free from the love of money. He must be one who manages his own household well, keeping his children under control with all dignity (but if a man does not know how to manage his own household, how will he take care of the church of God?).

Seize the moment and pray for the current and future leaders in your congregation. It is not surprising that few people are willing to serve as leaders in the church today as our culture moves away from biblical standards, but never forget that none of us are qualified to be members or leaders in the church except by God's grace.

LEVITICUS 22
GIVE YOUR VERY BEST!

When you give to God, how do you determine what is an acceptable offering?

While there are technical issues people love to focus on when it comes to giving money, never forget that God has a strategic purpose for inviting us to give. Leviticus 22:18-22 records God's command to His people to offer only acceptable sacrifices from the best of His provision:

> Any man of the house of Israel or of the aliens in Israel who presents his offering, whether it is any of their votive or any of their freewill offerings, which they present to the LORD for a burnt offering – for you to be accepted – it must be a male without defect from the cattle, the sheep, or the goats. Whatever has a defect, you shall not offer, for it will not be accepted for you.

God desires for us to give our very best to Him. God desires to be approached by people whose hearts are committed to giving back to Him the very best of what they have been entrusted to steward. It is not by accident that Jesus Christ, the only begotten Son of God, was called the Passover Lamb, a male without defect (1 Peter 1:19). Jesus willingly gave His *all*, so we must willingly approach God with our *all*.

God is after your heart, not your pocketbook! He doesn't need your money; He wants to bless you through your willingness to give Him your very best! As Paul teaches in Philippians 4:17, "Not that I seek the gift itself, but I seek for the profit which increases to your account."

Seize the moment and ask God to teach you how to give with a right heart so that He may find your giving acceptable in His sight and bring His increase to your life.

LEVITICUS 23
FIRST THINGS FIRST!

When you plan out your calendar, how do you protect first things first?

For example, if you asked me to meet with you on December 25, I hope you would fully expect me to say, "no." Why? Because that day is Christmas. We protect that day to celebrate the birth of Jesus Christ. It's a holy day!

For the ancients, the Levitical Law gave them direction on how to protect first things first on their annual calendar. Leviticus 23 clearly lays out their holy days:

1. The Passover (5).
2. The Feast of Unleavened Bread (6-8).
3. The Feast of First Fruits (9-14).
4. The Feast of Weeks, later known as Pentecost (15-22).
5. The Feast of Trumpets (23-25).
6. The Day of Atonement (26-32).
7. The Feast of Booths or Tabernacles (33-43).

God introduces these seven holidays in verses 2-4:

The LORD'S appointed times which you shall proclaim as holy convocations – My appointed times are these: For six days work may be done, but on the seventh day there is a sabbath of complete rest, a holy convocation. You shall not do any work; it is a sabbath to the LORD in all your dwellings. These are the appointed times of the LORD, holy convocations which you shall proclaim at the times appointed for them.

We must learn from God's rhythms of grace. Not only did God designate times of remembrance and celebration throughout the annual calendar, but He also instituted a protected day off every week. Until we realize that rest is God's idea for our good and His glory, we will continue to live in the tyranny of the urgent.

Seize the moment and protect first things first on your calendar today. This is a habit of grace because your life rhythms matter to God!

LEVITICUS 24
JUSTICE PROCLAIMS A PEOPLE'S VALUES!

Have you ever experienced an unfair situation where a person in a powerful position was not using the same standards for everyone? An easy example is when an umpire is not consistent with the size of the strike zone between the home and away teams. While this is upsetting in sporting events, it is unjust in legal systems.

Nations and people are characterized by how they handle justice, and whether it is fair and impartial. Because God knew that His reputation, and the sacredness of His name, was on the line based on how the Israelites would handle justice, God made a clear statement about justice for His people in Leviticus 24:22, "There shall be one standard for you; it shall be for the stranger as well as the native, for I am the LORD your God."

The justice of God must be consistently applied to all in His community, whether native born or strangers. Leviticus 24:10-23 provides a case study of this very issue, as a man born of an Israelite woman and an Egyptian father was put through the legal system for blaspheme – the misuse or cursing of God's hallowed name. The verdict is found in verse 16, "Moreover, the one who blasphemes the name of the LORD shall surely be put to death; all the congregation shall certainly stone him. The alien as well as the native, when he blasphemes the Name, shall be put to death."

Legal systems are an important part of any society because they define a people and the ideals they uphold as sacred. For the people of God, how we do justice defines the reputation of our God and declares the holiness of His name. Justice proclaims our values!

Seize the moment and exalt the name of Jesus by how you treat others with fairness and impartiality!

LEVITICUS 25
THE GIFT OF SABBATICAL!

I will never forget the love and support my family experienced when my local church worked with us to take a fully funded, three-month sabbatical in the fall of 2019. This was a gift of God's extravagant grace as I finished my tenth year as the Lead Pastor of FBC.

Leviticus 25:3-7 explains how all-encompassing the gift of sabbatical rest was intended to be for every aspect of the Israelite community:

Six years you shall sow your field, and six years you shall prune your vineyard and gather in its crop, but during the seventh year the land shall have a sabbath rest, a sabbath to the LORD; you shall not sow your field nor prune your vineyard. Your harvest's aftergrowth you shall not reap, and your grapes of untrimmed vines you shall not gather; the land shall have a sabbatical year. All of you shall have the sabbath products of the land for food; yourself, and your male and female slaves, and your hired man and your foreign resident, those who live as aliens with you. Even your cattle and the animals that are in your land shall have all its crops to eat.

Never forget that the rhythms of weekly sabbath, the sabbatical every seventh year, and the Jubilee every fiftieth year, were God's ideas first! It is still God's design for His people to be blessed by, and experience, His unforced rhythms of grace through rest.

Rest is part of God's rescue of His creation – from the rich landowners to the lowliest servants, He commands rest from their labors, as well as rest for the land to replenish and for the animals to be unburdened.

The fact that God's people have never been able to faithfully follow these commands demonstrates our desperate need for God's deliverance from the slavery caused by sin.

Seize the moment and prioritize God's rhythms of rest and work, in the easy yoke of Jesus.

Dr. Jerry D. Ingalls

LEVITICUS 26
THE BREAKING OF THE YOKE!

Leviticus 26 summarizes the blessings and curses of the Levitical Law, both of which are the promises of God. Verses 1-13 give the blessings for obedience, verses 14-39 promise the curses for disobedience, and verses 40-46 describe an opportunity for repentance.

Leviticus 26:12-13 is a critical passage to understand because it visually reminds the Israelites of what God did for them in the Exodus – the eternal grace He has extended to them in rescuing them from slavery:

> I will also walk among you and be your God, and you shall be My people. I am the LORD your God, who brought you out of the land of Egypt so that you would not be their slaves, and I broke the bars of your yoke and made you walk erect.

There is a contrast built into this everyday agricultural image of bearing a heavy burden – the oxen yoke. God broke the yoke of their slavery to Egypt and the burden of walking under Pharoah's oppression, so that they could walk upright with Him in covenant faithfulness. Thousands of years later, Jesus reminded a reprobate group of Israelites of God's promises in Matthew 11:30 utilizing this same agricultural imagery, "For My yoke is easy and My burden is light."

To walk in covenant faithfulness is to walk upright in the yoke of God's blessings, but to walk in disobedience to God's covenant is to be bowed down by the heavy yoke of slavery. That is why Paul said in Galatians 5:1, "It was for freedom that Christ set us free; therefore keep standing firm and do not be subject again to a yoke of slavery."

Seize the moment and take on yourself the easy yoke of Jesus Christ and experience the blessings of covenant faithfulness – rest for your soul! God has already broken the yoke of slavery for you; live in the freedom Christ has given you by walking in the new way of the Spirit (Romans 7:6).

LEVITICUS 27
EVERYTHING BELONGS TO GOD!

Did you know that nine dollars will go further than ten dollars when you give the first dollar to the Lord? This was a teaching principle I used with the brothers I ministered to in the men's recovery discipleship program at CityTeam Ministries in San Jose, California when they would receive their weekly ten-dollar stipend.

Leviticus 27:30-32 explains the ancient spiritual practice of tithing:

Thus all the tithe of the land, of the seed of the land or of the fruit of the tree, is the LORD'S; it is holy to the LORD. If, therefore, a man wishes to redeem part of his tithe, he shall add to it one-fifth of it. For every tenth part of herd or flock, whatever passes under the rod, the tenth one shall be holy to the LORD.

If a person wanted to redeem or purchase back part of the tithe for personal use, he must pay the value plus an additional 20%. Did you know that the principle of proportionate giving protects us from the presumption of ownership? While the tithe is no longer a legalistic mandate because we are under grace, it is a diagnostic tool of the Spirit for generous and sacrificial giving.

When you set apart as holy the first portion of what God has blessed you with, it demonstrates your awareness that everything given to you is a good gift from a perfect God (James 1:17). It is a proclamation of the truth that we own nothing! We are designed by God to steward and cultivate all His creation for His glory because everything belongs to God, as it has been from the beginning.

Seize the moment and give back to God what was never yours in the first place, and you will experience a new depth of freedom in your mind and heart.

NUMBERS

NUMBERS 1
A SET-APART PEOPLE!

Do you ever feel like you don't fit in with the world or its standards?

Numbers 1 records the census of Israel's warriors, who were the men twenty years of age or older and able to go to war (2-3). There were 603,550 fighting men listed in verses 20-46. If you add the rest of the Israelites, you have a very large camp.

But these numbers leave out a very important people – the Levites. Numbers 1:49-51 communicates a very different standard for the Levites, compared to the other tribes of Israel:

Only the tribe of Levi you shall not number, nor shall you take their census among the sons of Israel. But you shall appoint the Levites over the tabernacle of the testimony, and over all its furnishings and over all that belongs to it. They shall carry the tabernacle and all its furnishings, and they shall take care of it; they shall also camp around the tabernacle. So when the tabernacle is to set out, the Levites shall take it down; and when the tabernacle encamps, the Levites shall set it up. But the layman who comes near shall be put to death.

The Levites were a set-apart people on purpose – God's purpose!

The Levites, which included the priests, were set-apart; they were not counted for military service because they were to transport the tabernacle, and all that went with it, and ensure the proper observance of the Israelite religious system.

Additionally, the Levites were physically set-apart; they did not live out with the other tribes. They camped around the tabernacle to form a safety buffer around the sacred things of God to protect the community from the wrath of God (53).

Seize the moment and realize that, as a Christian, God has set you apart on purpose as His royal priesthood – "to offer up spiritual sacrifices acceptable to God through Jesus Christ" (2 Peter 1:5).

Dr. Jerry D. Ingalls

NUMBERS 2
JEHOVAH JIREH – MY GOD PROVIDES!

How do you provide for an army of 603,550 warriors?

The census had been completed and the camp of Israel was being organized by tribe. Numbers 2:2 states, "The sons of Israel shall camp, each by his own standard, with the banners of their fathers' households; they shall camp around the tent of meeting at a distance."

Both Numbers 1:46 and 2:32 state the census as yielding an army of 603,550 warriors, which excludes all the Levites, and all the women, children, and elderly men who would be unable to go to battle. The Israelite camp has been estimated to be over two million people. That's a lot of people traveling together through the desert!

Providing food and water would have been a major concern for their survival. Dr. Michael Heiser explains God's miraculous provision of manna, "The Israelites gathered an average of one omer (roughly two quarts) of manna each day (Exodus 16:16-17). This implies that 1 – 1.5 million gallons of manna appeared on the ground every day."[6]

This gives us the perspective we need to appreciate the miracle of God's provision. Listen to Exodus 16:12-13, when Jehovah Jireh responded to the food insecurity of His people:

"I have heard the grumblings of the sons of Israel; speak to them, saying, 'At twilight you shall eat meat, and in the morning you shall be filled with bread; and you shall know that I am the LORD your God.'" So it came about at evening that the quails came up and covered the camp, and in the morning there was a layer of dew around the camp.

Now that we know how big the camp was, all we can say is, "Wow! Jehovah Jireh – my God provides!"

Seize the moment and trust Jehovah Jireh for your daily bread!

---

6 Michael S. Heiser, "Large Numbers in the Exodus and Wilderness Journey," in *Faithlife Study Bible* (Bellingham, WA: Lexham Press, 2016).

NUMBERS 3
THE COST OF REDEMPTION!

Do you know what it means that you are redeemed?

An Old Testament illustration of redemption comes with the purchasing of all the firstborns of Israel through the tribe of Levi. Every firstborn of Israel rightfully became God's at the Passover event. Later, in Exodus 13:2, God reminded His people of His claim: "Sanctify to Me every firstborn, the first offspring of every womb among the sons of Israel, both of man and beast; it belongs to Me."

The firstborns should have died during the tenth plague, but instead were saved by the blood of the Passover Lamb and set apart as belonging to God.

God made a way for them to be redeemed; that is why the Levites weren't counted in the census. God explains the cost of redemption in Numbers 3:12-13:

> Now, behold, I have taken the Levites from among the sons of Israel instead of every firstborn, the first issue of the womb among the sons of Israel. So the Levites shall be Mine. For all the firstborn are Mine; on the day that I struck down all the firstborn in the land of Egypt, I sanctified to Myself all the firstborn in Israel, from man to beast. They shall be Mine; I am the LORD.

There were only 22,000 Levites (39), but 22,273 firstborn males of Israel needed redemption (41-43). What did God do about those additional 273 firstborns? He set a redemption price of five shekels per head (46-51). Redemption is never free!

There was a substitution for the redemption of every Israelite firstborn, just as Jesus Christ is our substitution for our redemption today. Paul says in 1 Corinthians 6:20, "For you have been bought with a price: therefore glorify God in your body."

Seize the moment and glorify God with your life! It's His anyway – surrender yourself to the One who purchased you back!

NUMBERS 4
GOD'S DIVISION OF LABOR!

Have you ever wished you had someone else's job, or life?

There were three Levitical clans – the Gershonites, Kohathites, and Merarites – with duties outlined in Numbers 4. Verse 49 summarizes their collective responsibility to the tabernacle system, "According to the commandment of the LORD through Moses, they were numbered, everyone by his serving or carrying; thus these were his numbered men, just as the LORD had commanded Moses."

Each clan was provided with detailed instructions of what they were responsible for in the administration of the Israelite religious system. This reminds me of Paul's words in Ephesians 2:10, "For we are His workmanship, created in Christ Jesus for good works, which God prepared beforehand so that we would walk in them."

In God's economy, every person has a purpose – good works to carry out! The earlier you learn what this is for your life, the sooner you will be content and happy.

For example, while Aaron and his sons were designated as the priests, and were allowed to touch and see the holy objects (5-14), it was the Kohathites who had the responsibility to transport them (15-20). God established a division of labor on purpose!

Even though both groups were working in the tabernacle system, they had very different jobs, which required each group to do their work precisely as commanded. Just like Aaron's two sons – Nadab and Abihu – were killed for offering "strange fire" upon the altar in Leviticus 10:1-2, so the Kohathites' job came with the death penalty if they were to touch or see the sacred things (e.g., 1 Samuel 6:19 and 2 Samuel 6:6-7).

Just as each clan of Levites had their own unique responsibilities, so do each of us. This is all for the glory of God and the orderliness of our worship. Don't get caught up in a desire for someone else's job or life, do what God has called you to do!

Seize the moment and walk in the good works of your unique life. Learn to be content in all circumstances (Philippians 4:11-13).

NUMBERS 5
THE IMPORTANCE OF RESTITUTION!

What happens when saying sorry is not enough?

Numbers 5:6-8 explains the command of paying restitution as part of a person's confession of sin:

> When a man or woman commits any of the sins of mankind, acting unfaithfully against the LORD, and that person is guilty, then he shall confess his sins which he has committed, and he shall make restitution in full for his wrong and add to it one-fifth of it, and give it to him whom he has wronged. But if the man has no relative to whom restitution may be made for the wrong, the restitution which is made for the wrong must go to the LORD for the priest, besides the ram of atonement, by which atonement is made for him.

Restitution is important because it is a sign of true brokenness over sin and of a sincere desire to get right with the person from whom you are seeking forgiveness. The root of the Hebrew word for restitution means "to turn back, return."

Restitution is yoked with our call to repent – the act of turning away from sin and turning back (returning) to God.

How do we know when a person is truly returning to faithfulness to God, and sincerely desiring to reconcile with the community of God's people? Is it enough to confess? Confession is the beginning, but it must be followed by life transformation – the active steps which demonstrate repentance.

Paying restitution, which requires you to go above and beyond the original offense, demonstrates that you are being transformed by the renewing of your mind (Romans 12:2). It is a sign and wonder of the Holy Spirit – to will and to work in you (Philippians 2:13).

Restitution invites the offended party to take the critical next step of offering forgiveness by accepting the restitution. This opens the door to future reconciliation.

Seize the moment and be a minister of reconciliation (2 Corinthians 5:18-20). Be reconciled today by giving or receiving restitution with grace.

NUMBERS 6
THE PRIESTLY BLESSING!

In Numbers 6:23-27, God gives Moses the priestly blessing for His people:

"Speak to Aaron and to his sons, saying, 'Thus you shall bless the sons of Israel. You shall say to them: The LORD bless you, and keep you; the LORD make His face shine on you, and be gracious to you; the LORD lift up His countenance on you, and give you peace.' So they shall invoke My name on the sons of Israel, and I then will bless them."

God responded dramatically to Aaron blessing the people in Leviticus 9:22-23, "Then Aaron lifted up his hands toward the people and blessed them, … When they came out and blessed the people, the glory of the LORD appeared to all the people."

When God's people do what He commands them to do, God responds with His presence and power. Today, we do this formally with the giving of the benediction at the end of a service. It is not simply a sending-out prayer; it is the giving of God's "priestly blessing."

Never forget that God is the one who blesses; we simply mediate the blessing to one another. In the same way, God is the only One who can save a single soul. We are commanded to mediate the gospel to people in loving word and generous deed, one person at a time.

God is the active agent of every blessing. That is what it means for God to "make His face shine on you" and "lift up His countenance on you." That is God giving you His attention and pouring out His blessings of grace and peace! Call upon the name of Jesus Christ through whom every promise of God is a "yes and amen" (2 Corinthians 1:20).

Seize the moment and seek the face of God in your life and He shall be found (Matthew 7:7-11).

NUMBERS 7
UNITY IN GIVING!

Numbers 7 records each of the twelve tribes of Israel giving the same dedicatory offerings. The leader of each tribe, on his prescribed day, over a twelve-day period, brought an identical offering to the priests. This demonstrated the unity of the twelve tribes as the one people of God in their common commitment to the Levites and the functioning of the tabernacle system.

While we find reading this chapter repetitive, the Israelites would have rejoiced in seeing each tribe's equal participation in the religious system. Without their unity and common commitment, Israel could not survive. As Jesus said in Mark 3:25, "If a house is divided against itself, that house will not be able to stand."

Interestingly, the offerings given to God were then disseminated based on a division of labor between the clans of Levites. Numbers 7:4-9 describes how the gifts of God's people were used to equip the religious workers to do their specific work in the tabernacle system:

> Then the LORD spoke to Moses, saying, "Accept these things from them, that they may be used in the service of the tent of meeting, and you shall give them to the Levites, to each man according to his service." So Moses took the carts and the oxen and gave them to the Levites. Two carts and four oxen he gave to the sons of Gershon, according to their service, and four carts and eight oxen he gave to the sons of Merari, according to their service, under the direction of Ithamar the son of Aaron the priest. But he did not give any to the sons of Kohath because theirs was the service of the holy objects, which they carried on the shoulder.

Seize the moment and give generously to the work of God, knowing that the resources you give will go where they are needed to do God's work.

NUMBERS 8
A LIVING SACRIFICE!

Christians are commanded to respond to the gospel of Jesus Christ in a very specific way – by presenting themselves to God as living sacrifices. Paul wrote this in Romans 12:1, "Therefore I urge you, brethren, by the mercies of God, to present your bodies a living and holy sacrifice, acceptable to God, which is your spiritual service of worship."

Do you understand what this would have meant to Paul and a Jewish audience?

The precedent for a group of people being a living sacrifice to God is found in Numbers 8:9-11:

> So you shall present the Levites before the tent of meeting. You shall also assemble the whole congregation of the sons of Israel, and present the Levites before the LORD; and the sons of Israel shall lay their hands on the Levites. Aaron then shall present the Levites before the LORD as a wave offering from the sons of Israel, that they may qualify to perform the service of the LORD.

A "wave offering" is a technical term in the sacrificial system for an offering presented to God but not put on the altar for consumption; it was, instead, given to the priest (Leviticus 7:30-34). In today's chapter, this term is being used in a peculiar way – a group of people are being offered to God, not for destruction, but for consecration and given to the priests for the work of the tabernacle.

Therefore, when Paul calls you, a Christ follower, to present yourself as a living sacrifice to God, he is calling you to participate in the ancient consecration rite of being a "wave offering." God is inviting you to live a set apart (holy) life for His purpose of redeeming you – "to offer up spiritual sacrifices acceptable to God through Jesus Christ" (1 Peter 2:5b).

Seize the moment and find your life through giving it as a living sacrifice to God.

NUMBERS 9
BE PATIENT IN DECISION MAKING!

How do you know when to make an allowance for something that isn't going exactly the way you thought it was supposed to go?

Moses demonstrated mature spiritual leadership in Numbers 9:6-8:

But there were some men who were unclean because of the dead person, so that they could not observe Passover on that day; so they came before Moses and Aaron on that day. Those men said to him, "Though we are unclean because of the dead person, why are we restrained from presenting the offering of the LORD at its appointed time among the sons of Israel?" Moses therefore said to them, "Wait, and I will listen to what the LORD will command concerning you."

Moses waited upon the Lord to give him the answer. According to Luke 5:16, Jesus Christ modeled this same pattern of listening for God, "But Jesus Himself would often slip away to the wilderness and pray."

Spiritual leaders cultivate a humble heart and a patient mind to wait upon the Lord to give direction. Moses could have quickly decided on this issue. These men were going to have to miss Passover this year because they were unclean – a clear-cut case. Instead, Moses waited on the Lord.

When discerning decisions, please cultivate a humble heart to wait upon the Lord, and a patient mind to listen for His voice. Just like in this situation, the Lord may disclose to you a new way forward. In Moses' case, God spoke to Him and set a secondary date for the observance of Passover one month later for not only these men, but for many others who would find themselves in similar situations in the future (9-14).

Seize the moment and learn to be dependent upon the Lord for your decision making; you never know how God will use your times of waiting upon Him to bless many!

NUMBERS 10
THE FIRST STEP!

Have you ever watched a baby take its first step?

It's a monumental moment in any person's life. Very often, the parents participate with eager excitement to support their child in this next step of his or her journey.

Numbers 10:33-36 narrates when the Israelites took their first step away from Mount Sinai as they finally broke camp after being there for about a year receiving the Ten Commandments and the Levitical Law, learning how to be the children of God:

> Thus they set out from the mount of the LORD three days' journey, with the ark of the covenant of the LORD journeying in front of them for the three days, to seek out a resting place for them. The cloud of the LORD was over them by day when they set out from the camp. Then it came about when the ark set out that Moses said, "Rise up, O LORD! And let Your enemies be scattered, and let those who hate You flee before You." When it came to rest, he said, "Return, O LORD, to the myriad thousands of Israel."

God, their loving parent, was fully present to them in this exciting moment, and they praised Him for His presence and power to lead them in their next faith step towards the Promised Land.

Moses' song of victory was expanded by King David in Psalm 68:1-7:

> Let God arise, let His enemies be scattered, and let those who hate Him flee before Him. ... Sing to God, sing praises to His name; lift up a song for Him who rides through the deserts, whose name is the LORD, and exult before Him. ... O God, when You went forth before Your people, when You marched through the wilderness, Selah.

Seize the moment and rejoice that your Heavenly Father holds your hand when you follow Him into your next faith step – God is with you, whether on your first or last step!

NUMBERS 11
THE OUTPOURING OF THE HOLY SPIRIT!

The most valuable resource in any church is people filled with the Holy Spirit.

In Numbers 11:27-29, Moses responds to a challenging leadership situation in a surprising way:

> So a young man ran and told Moses and said, "Eldad and Medad are prophesying in the camp." Then Joshua the son of Nun, the attendant of Moses from his youth, said, "Moses, my lord, restrain them." But Moses said to him, "Are you jealous for my sake? Would that all the LORD'S people were prophets, that the LORD would put His Spirit upon them!"

Moses' response foreshadowed the New Covenant and the Acts 2 Pentecost.

Moses was frustrated and exhausted because of the people's complaining (1-9). After praying for them, Moses went to God and complained about the heavy burden of leading the people that God had placed on him (10-15). God heard his prayer and responded to Moses in verses 16-17:

> Gather for Me seventy men from the elders of Israel, whom you know to be the elders of the people and their officers and bring them to the tent of meeting … and I will take of the Spirit who is upon you, and will put Him upon them; and they shall bear the burden of the people with you, so that you will not bear it all alone.

Even though Eldad and Medad weren't part of this gathered group of seventy elders to receive the Spirit (24-26), Moses saw no problem because he knew the more Spirit-filled people there were to help, the less he had to bear it all alone.

Joshua, the attendant of Moses, was jealous for Moses and wanted them restrained, but Moses saw an opportunity because "many hands make light work." The Holy Spirit makes the burden light when we work together.

Seize the moment and seek ways to help in your local church.

Dr. Jerry D. Ingalls

NUMBERS 12
HUMILITY IN THE FACE OF HURT!

Have you ever experienced a hurtful betrayal from someone you love and trust?

Numbers 12:6-8 reports God's words to Miriam and Aaron when they spoke against Moses:

If there is a prophet among you, I, the LORD, shall make Myself known to him in a vision. I shall speak with him in a dream. Not so, with My servant Moses, He is faithful in all My household; with him I speak mouth to mouth, even openly, and not in dark sayings, and he beholds the form of the LORD. Why then were you not afraid to speak against My servant, against Moses?"

God came to Moses' defense not only in these words, but also in a dramatic judgement against Miriam – she was struck with leprosy! God, being moved to compassion by Moses' prayer, healed her, but insisted that she experience a public consequence for her betrayal and sent her out of the camp for a seven-day quarantine.

Why was God lenient with Miriam and Aaron?

I don't think it was for their benefit, but, rather, because of Moses' character. I say this because verse 3 makes an important comment about Moses, "(Now the man Moses was very humble, more than any man who was on the face of the earth.)" This is possibly one of the most important things that can be said about a person in the Bible.

What will be remembered about you when you, or your family, are attacked, betrayed, or ridiculed?

Moses is remembered as the humblest person who ever lived. King David is remembered as a person after God's own heart (1 Samuel 13:14). Jesus described Himself as being "gentle and humble in heart" (Matthew 11:29). These are all character statements!

Seize the moment and remember that it is your character that is being put on display by how you handle difficult circumstances – show the world Jesus!

NUMBERS 13
CONFIRMATION BIAS!

Do you listen with *faith* or with *fear*?

That is an important question because of "confirmation bias." People naturally prefer and process information that confirms or strengthens their existing beliefs or values.

The nation of Israel was on the border of the Promised Land; in Numbers 13:1-2, God commanded Moses to send twelve men to spy out the land. After forty days, they brought back their report.

Caleb concluded the initial report with these faithful words in Numbers 13:30, "We should by all means go up and take possession of it, for we will surely overcome it." But the other spies replied with these fearful words in verses 31-33:

> "We are not able to go up against the people, for they are too strong for us." So they gave out to the sons of Israel a bad report of the land which they had spied out, saying, "The land through which we have gone, in spying it out, is a land that devours its inhabitants; and all the people whom we saw in it are men of great size. "There also we saw the Nephilim (the sons of Anak are part of the Nephilim); and we became like grasshoppers in our own sight, and so we were in their sight."

We are given two contrasting reports based on the same observations:

1. Caleb's report confirmed his faith that God would do what God promised to do – make the way into the Promised Land!
2. The other spies' sight was distorted by fear (33), and their report confirmed their fear that the giants of the land were too big to defeat.

Both were right. The giants were too big for the Israelites to defeat, but God! God is bigger than any giant, and God always makes a way for that which God promises!

Seize the moment and let your faith in God confirm the way of victory! "There is no fear in love; but perfect love casts out fear" (1 John 4:18).

Dr. Jerry D. Ingalls

NUMBERS 14
REMAIN FAITHFUL TO GOD'S CALL!

There are many Christians who need to pay attention to this important story found in Numbers 14, so they do not make the same mistakes as the Israelite congregation. In the same way, there are many pastors who need to learn from Moses' example of how to remain faithful to God, while executing their vocational calling to the people.

The fearful spies have incited a riot! The congregation has decided to fire Moses and replace him with a leader that will take them back to Egypt (1-4). How does Moses respond? Verse 5 describes what happened next, "Then Moses and Aaron fell on their faces in the presence of all the assembly of the congregation of the sons of Israel."

Moses and his associate went to prayer together. Caleb and Joshua tried to intervene, but the people picked up stones to kill them (10).

Moses responded in faith and not in fear! Numbers 14:17-19 records Moses' faithful petition to God on behalf of the people, even while they were in rebellion against him:

> But now, I pray, let the power of the Lord be great, just as You have declared, "The LORD is slow to anger and abundant in lovingkindness, forgiving iniquity and transgression; but He will by no means clear the guilty, visiting the iniquity of the fathers on the children to the third and the fourth generations." Pardon, I pray, the iniquity of this people according to the greatness of Your lovingkindness, just as You also have forgiven this people, from Egypt even until now.

Amen! We must remain faithful to God's call regardless of the challenges of our circumstances or the rebellion of people. Paul commands all Christians in 1 Thessalonians 5:16-18, "Rejoice always; pray without ceasing; in everything give thanks; for this is God's will for you in Christ Jesus."

Seize the moment and remain faithful in your daily walk with Jesus Christ – don't bail before the blessing!

NUMBERS 15
MEMORY JOGS!

Have you ever tied a piece of yarn around your finger to help you remember to do something?

We all need memory jogs or well-placed physical reminders to help us remember to do something. For example, a friend gave us a beautiful gift to put in our home as a reminder to pray for them. We associate that small sculpture with them, and every time I see it I pray for them.

Numbers 15:32-36 tells the story of a man who was punished for forgetting the sabbath. In verses 38-40, the Lord responded by giving the Israelites a new command so that they wouldn't forget Him and His Law:

Speak to the sons of Israel, and tell them that they shall make for themselves tassels on the corners of their garments throughout their generations, and that they shall put on the tassel of each corner a cord of blue. It shall be a tassel for you to look at and remember all the commandments of the LORD, so as to do them and not follow after your own heart and your own eyes, after which you played the harlot, so that you may remember to do all My commandments and be holy to your God.

God gave them a memory jog!

1. **Where was it located?** Memory jogs must be visible, and the blue tassels were located on the four corners of their garments (Deuteronomy 22:12).
2. **Why were they blue?** Memory jogs work by association and blue was used in the priest's wardrobe (Exodus 28).
3. **What was their purpose?** These blue tassels reminded them that they do not belong to themselves, but they are a "kingdom of priests and a holy nation" (Exodus 19:5-6).

Seize the moment and use well-placed memory jogs to remind you of who you are in Jesus – a dearly beloved child of God (1 John 3:1-3)!

Dr. Jerry D. Ingalls

NUMBERS 16
BEING CONSUMED!

What is consuming your emotions and your thoughts?

In Numbers 16, we find Israel stirred up like a hornet's nest after they were denied entrance to the Promised Land. The people were restless, irritable, and discontent! Their living conditions were rustic, the menu was monotonous, and the leadership just promised them forty more years of the same.

A perfect storm was brewing!

Korah, Dathan, and Abiram rebelled; in response, God consumed them and their households by opening the earth (1-34). Immediately, fire from heaven consumed the 250 men who had joined with the rebellion (35-40). The people were so stirred up that they even blamed Moses for these supernatural judgements and continued to grumble against him and Aaron (41-50). In response, God told Moses and Aaron to separate themselves from the congregation so that He could "consume them."

How would Moses and Aaron respond to a rebellious people so consumed with their circumstances that they had lost all perspective?

Numbers 16:45-48 narrates their faithful response:

They fell on their faces. Moses said to Aaron, "Take your censer and put in it fire from the altar, and lay incense on it; then bring it quickly to the congregation and make atonement for them, for wrath has gone forth from the LORD, the plague has begun!" Then Aaron took it as Moses had spoken, and ran into the midst of the assembly, for behold, the plague had begun among the people. So he put on the incense and made atonement for the people. He took his stand between the dead and the living, so that the plague was checked.

Today, a perfect storm is brewing! May all of God's people pray so that God "will hear from heaven, will forgive [our] sin and will heal [our] land" (2 Chronicles 7:14).

Seize the moment and remain calm in the consuming storm! Don't tell God how big your storm is, tell your storm how big your God is.

NUMBERS 17
STOP GRUMBLING!

Did you know that grumbling is no small matter to God?

Grumbling is an easy way to give the devil a foothold in your life, but the good news is that God has given us a way of victory to overcome it!

Numbers 17 describes God's effort to silence the grumbling of the Israelites against Moses and Aaron by clearly declaring His chosen leaders over Israel. Verse 5 implies that our grumblings aren't just against the people or circumstances themselves, but against the Sovereign God, Himself: "It will come about that the rod of the man whom I choose will sprout. Thus I will lessen from upon Myself the grumblings of the sons of Israel, who are grumbling against you."

God directed each tribal leader to turn in their rod (staff) which was their sign of authority to rule over their tribe. Next, God determined that the staff that sprouted would belong to His chosen leader over Israel. The conclusion was abundantly clear, as described in verse 8, "Behold, the rod of Aaron for the house of Levi had sprouted and put forth buds and produced blossoms, and it bore ripe almonds."

For dead wood to bud, blossom, and bear fruit was an articulate sign. There was no confusion! God shouted from Heaven that Moses and Aaron were the appointed leaders of God and, in doing so, was declaring that they should be trusted and followed.

Grumbling has always been a big deal to God, because it prevents God's people from living on mission. The answer for followers of Jesus is clear: STOP GRUMBLING!

Seize the moment and "do all things without grumbling or disputing; so that you will prove yourselves to be blameless and innocent, children of God above reproach in the midst of a crooked and perverse generation, among whom you appear as lights in the world" (Philippians 2:14-15).

NUMBERS 18
THE GIFT OF SERVICE!

Serving others is a sacred gift, not a job description!

In Numbers 18:5-7, God gave a sacred gift to Aaron and the Levites:

So you shall attend to the obligations of the sanctuary and the obligations of the altar, so that there will no longer be wrath on the sons of Israel. Behold, I Myself have taken your fellow Levites from among the sons of Israel; they are a gift to you, dedicated to the LORD, to perform the service for the tent of meeting. But you and your sons with you shall attend to your priesthood for everything concerning the altar and inside the veil, and you are to perform service. I am giving you the priesthood as a bestowed service...

The priesthood was a bestowed service – a gift from God! Aaron and his sons were given the gift of the priesthood, as well as the gift of the Levites to serve in the tabernacle system. Their very lives were given as a gift to the service of God.

Do you see opportunities to serve others as a gift from God?

I was recently talking to a friend who trains employees in customer service at a restaurant that is famous for their service. Many people learn to say the right things, but it is obviously not coming from their heart – they have the appearances of good service, but not the heart of a servant! They are fulfilling a job description, not accepting the divine gift of service.

Do you have the heart of a servant, or are you just going through the motions of your ministry?

Seize the moment and "whatever you do, do your work heartily, as for the Lord rather than for men, knowing that from the Lord you will receive the reward of the inheritance. It is the Lord Christ whom you serve" (Colossians 3:23-24).

NUMBERS 19
THE DANGER OF LEGALISM!

Are you familiar with Jesus' famous Parable of the Good Samaritan?

In Luke 10:30-37, Jesus answered a lawyer's question about the Law with this parable. Jesus taught us who our neighbor is by describing how a Samaritan, a person hated by the Jewish people, was the one who showed God's love to the dying Jewish man. To emphasize this point, Jesus' story included two Jewish elite, a Levite and a priest, who avoided the dying man.

Yes, there was a deep racial tension between the Jews and Samaritans that informed this story. It remains relevant to this very day that Jesus' parable uses this example to illustrate the profound impact of learning to "love your enemy" and "love your neighbor as yourself."

But there is more to the story, and that's the scandal of Jesus' parable!

Numbers 19:16 teaches what the Levite and priest were probably reciting to themselves when they responded to the man who was left for dead by moving away from him to the other side of the road: "Anyone who in the open field touches one who has been slain with a sword or who has died naturally, or a human bone or a grave, shall be unclean for seven days."

These religious men, like the lawyer who was trying to trap Jesus with his questions, were putting the letter of the Law before the heart of God. Jesus came to return God's people back to the heart of God and the purpose of the Law – to deliver God's people from sin to live as God's image bearers.

Don't let your religion blind you to the heart of God; Jesus came to seek and to save that which was lost (Luke 19:10)!

Seize the moment and return to the heart of God by loving your neighbor as yourself, neither allowing racism nor religion to prevent you from being an image bearer of God. Love your neighbor as yourself.

Dr. Jerry D. Ingalls

NUMBERS 20
A EULOGY TO MIRIAM!

What do you want people to say about you in your eulogy?

Numbers 20 records the deaths of Moses' brother and sister, Aaron and Miriam. Miriam's death could easily be missed. The end of verse 1 briefly records, "Now Miriam died there and was buried there." *That's it!?!* While the story continues for Israel, this was the end of the journey for Miriam.

Miriam was brave and bold! She was the older sister of Moses and worked with her mom to place baby Moses in a wicker basket among the reeds in the Nile, saving him from certain death and placing him in a house of privilege (Exodus 2:1-9).

Miriam had a vibrant faith and loved to praise God! After Moses delivered Israel out of Egypt and across the Red Sea, Miriam led them in worship to God. Exodus 15:20-21 described the scene:

> Miriam the prophetess, Aaron's sister, took the timbrel in her hand, and all the women went out after her with timbrels and with dancing. Miriam answered them, "Sing to the LORD, for He is highly exalted; The horse and his rider He has hurled into the sea."

Miriam was not perfect, but she was forgiven and loved! Yes, Miriam gave in to her jealousy of Moses in Numbers 12, but Moses forgave her and prayed for her healing and restoration. Moses loved his big sister.

Miriam was chosen by God to do a great work! Micah 6:4 gives us God's final word about Miriam, "Indeed, I brought you up from the land of Egypt and ransomed you from the house of slavery, and I sent before you Moses, Aaron and Miriam."

Seize the moment and remember that your past failures, present hurts, and future fears don't need to stand in the way of your faithfulness to God or your fulfillment of God's calling on your life!

NUMBERS 21
A WAY OF SALVATION!

There is a way of salvation!

Numbers 21 is a travel log with three stories of military conflict (1-3, 21-35) and one story of God's righteous judgment against Israel for their grumbling and complaining, again.

But God... God made a way of salvation during His righteous judgment of their rebellion. Watch the scene unfold in verses 6-9:

> The LORD sent fiery serpents among the people and they bit the people, so that many people of Israel died. So the people came to Moses and said, "We have sinned, because we have spoken against the LORD and you; intercede with the LORD, that He may remove the serpents from us." And Moses interceded for the people. Then the LORD said to Moses, "Make a fiery serpent, and set it on a standard; and it shall come about, that everyone who is bitten, when he looks at it, he will live." And Moses made a bronze serpent and set it on the standard; and it came about, that if a serpent bit any man, when he looked to the bronze serpent, he lived.

Did you know that Jesus used this story to illustrate God's way of salvation through faith in Him? This is remembered in John 3:14-16:

> As Moses lifted up the serpent in the wilderness, even so must the Son of Man be lifted up; so that whoever believes will in Him have eternal life. For God so loved the world, that He gave His only begotten Son, that whoever believes in Him shall not perish, but have eternal life.

There is a righteous judgment for rebellion, but God made a way to salvation for those who would put their faith in Jesus lifted up on the Cross for the forgiveness of their sins.

Seize the moment and put your faith in Jesus Christ, crucified, risen, and coming again! Jesus has crushed the head of the serpent (Genesis 3:15)!

NUMBERS 22
WALK IN THE WAY OF JESUS!

Do you remember the Sunday School story of the man whose donkey talked to him?

The story of Balaam is told in Numbers 22-24. It's about a seer (an old word for prophet), named Balaam, who was hired under pressure by Balak, the king of Moab, to curse the Israelites.

Two supernatural events happened to Balaam on his way to Balak:

1. **An angel speaks!** God's anger arose against Balaam, so God sent the angel of Yahweh. A donkey saved Balaam's life. The angel testified to this in Numbers 22:33, "But the donkey saw me and turned aside from me these three times. If she had not turned aside from me, I would surely have killed you just now, and let her live."
2. **A donkey speaks!** Before Balaam knew the donkey was saving his life, he beat his donkey for being obstinate. As if preparing Balaam for God's rebuke from His angel, Numbers 22:28a states, "the LORD opened the mouth of the donkey."

Sounds like the beginning of a bad joke – a mad prophet, a talking donkey, and an angel are traveling down the road together… But this is no joke; rather, it is a real historic event used to warn us not to follow the way of corruption!

Peter compared false prophets and teachers to Balaam in 2 Peter 2:15-16:

Forsaking the right way, they have gone astray, having followed the way of Balaam, the son of Beor, who loved the wages of unrighteousness; but he received a rebuke for his own transgression, for a mute donkey, speaking with a voice of a man, restrained the madness of the prophet (cf. Jude 11-13).

Seize the moment and walk in the way of Jesus, the best way not to be led astray into the way of Balaam is to take on the easy yoke of Jesus Christ and learn to be like Him, gentle and humble in heart.

NUMBERS 23
TRANSFORMING A CURSE INTO A BLESSING!

People often turn blessings into curses, but God transforms curses into blessings!

In Joshua 24:9-10, Joshua gives God's perspective of what happened in the story of Balaam:

Then Balak the son of Zippor, king of Moab, arose and fought against Israel, and he sent and summoned Balaam the son of Beor to curse you. But I was not willing to listen to Balaam. So he had to bless you, and I delivered you from his hand.

In Numbers 23, that story unfolded as Balak brought Balaam to three strategic locations to look down upon Israel to curse them. **But God...** God met with Balaam and put a word in his mouth (4-5). Balak brought Balaam to curse, but in verses 7-10, God transformed it into a blessing:

How shall I curse whom God has not cursed? And how can I denounce whom the LORD has not denounced? As I see him from the top of the rocks, and I look at him from the hills; Behold, a people who dwells apart, and will not be reckoned among the nations. Who can count the dust of Jacob, Or number the fourth part of Israel? Let me die the death of the upright, and let my end be like his!

Afterwards, in verses 11-12, watch the confusion of Balak, the king of Moab, "'What have you done to me? I took you to curse my enemies, but behold, you have actually blessed them!' [Balaam] replied, 'Must I not be careful to speak what the LORD puts in my mouth?'"

When we meditate upon God's Word and prayerfully cultivate a mindset of awareness to God's presence, every moment is transformed into a providential opportunity to speak His Words and be a blessing to others.

Seize the moment and "bless those who curse you, pray for those who mistreat you" (Luke 6:28). God's Word never returns void (Isaiah 55:11)!

Dr. Jerry D. Ingalls

NUMBERS 24
THE STAR OF THE SHOW!

Everyone wants to be the star of the show, but there can be only One!

Surprisingly, Balaam realized that God was the star of the show. In Numbers 24:1, he demonstrates this discovery, "When Balaam saw that it pleased the LORD to bless Israel, he did not go as at other times to seek omens but he set his face toward the wilderness [the Israelite camp]."

In Numbers 24:17, God used Balaam's fourth and final oracle to point to the true star of the show, the coming of the Messiah, "I see him, but not now; I behold him, but not near; a star shall come forth from Jacob, a scepter shall rise from Israel, and shall crush through the forehead of Moab, and tear down all the sons of Sheth."

God used an ancient seer, saved from the angel of the Lord by a talking donkey, and paid by an enemy king to curse Israel, to proclaim the coming of the Messiah-King!

One Bible scholar explains the connection between Balaam's ancient oracle and the messianic prophecy of Jesus Christ this way:

> Numbers 24:17 was considered messianic in ancient Jewish thinking, but no one thought of a celestial sign when reading it. ... For Israelites, star language pointed to the Messiah-King. Numbers 24:17 is therefore the backdrop for interpreting some odd passages in Revelation.[7]

Jesus described Himself in Revelation 22:16, "I, Jesus, have sent My angel to testify to you these things for the churches. I am the root and the descendant of David, the bright morning star" (cf. Revelation 2:26-28).

Seize the moment and point to Jesus Christ with your life – He alone must shine brightly in and through you as the Star of the show!

---

[7] Michael S. Heiser, *The Bible Unfiltered: Approaching Scripture on Its Own Terms* (Bellingham, WA: Lexham Press, 2017), 218–219.

NUMBERS 25
A RIPPLE EFFECT!

What happens when you throw a small stone into a lake? It causes a ripple effect from the point of impact.

One of the things that makes Balaam's story confusing is that Numbers 22-24 tells the story of a man who heard from God and faithfully refused to curse Israel (as he was hired to do), but the ripple effect of his influence was still a plague of judgment.

Even though Balaam's name is not mentioned in Numbers 25, the impact of his story ripples into the Israelite community as described in Numbers 25:1-3:

> While Israel remained at Shittim, the people began to play the harlot with the daughters of Moab. For they invited the people to the sacrifices of their gods, and the people ate and bowed down to their gods. So Israel joined themselves to Baal of Peor, and the LORD was angry against Israel (cf. Psalm 106:28-31).

Israel was seduced to become unequally yoked with a foreign people and their god. This heavy burden crushed them as God's wrath turned against them in a righteous judgment of their false worship. God's plague killed 24,000 Israelites (4-9).

How do we know this was a ripple effect of Balaam's impact? Numbers 31:16 explains, "Behold, these caused the sons of Israel, through the counsel of Balaam, to trespass against the LORD in the matter of Peor, so the plague was among the congregation of the LORD."

Furthermore, Jesus used Balaam's name as a condemnation against the Church of Pergamum in Revelation 2:14:

> But I have a few things against you, because you have there some who hold the teaching of Balaam, who kept teaching Balak to put a stumbling block before the sons of Israel, to eat things sacrificed to idols and to commit acts of immorality.

Seize the moment and leave a positive, lasting impact on people's faith and faithfulness through the choices you make today.

Dr. Jerry D. Ingalls

NUMBERS 26
POSITIONED FOR FAITHFULNESS!

Forty years is a long time to wait! How many of you could tell me from personal experience what was happening forty years ago? Personally, I was Willow's age (7), and what I know about forty years ago comes from the stories I have been told.

The book of Numbers started with a census after the Exodus and numbered the fighting men at 603,550 (Numbers 1:17-40). Except for Caleb and Joshua, the two believing spies, all who were counted in the census would die in the desert as a judgment for their unbelief (Numbers 14:20-38).

Fast forward forty years and, upon the judgment at Peor, the last of the unbelieving generation were now dead and a new census was ordered in Numbers 26:1-4. Verses 63-65 summarize this significant moment in Israel's history, as the new generation stood on the cusp of God's promise:

> These are those who were numbered by Moses and Eleazar the priest, who numbered the sons of Israel in the plains of Moab by the Jordan at Jericho. But among these there was not a man of those who were numbered by Moses and Aaron the priest, who numbered the sons of Israel in the wilderness of Sinai. For the LORD had said of them, "They shall surely die in the wilderness." And not a man was left of them, except Caleb the son of Jephunneh and Joshua the son of Nun.

There were now 601,730 fighting men in Israel (51). Every person counted was either a youth during the last census, or not yet born. A new generation was positioned for faithfulness and all that they knew came from the previous generation's stories about God and His faithfulness through forty years of following God in the desert.

Seize the moment and position the next generation for faithfulness through the stories you tell them about God and *His* faithfulness.

NUMBERS 27
SUCCESSION OF AUTHORITY!

It can be difficult for a young pastor to follow a beloved pastor who had been at the church for a long time. In fact, most denominations don't even try it; they put an interim pastor in the position to help the congregation work through their grief. But in the best of situations, the outgoing pastor works with the congregation ahead of time to develop a succession plan.

Moses recognized that it was time for his congregation to start putting a succession plan in place so that he could help oversee the transition of his leadership role to a new leader who would carry out the mission and care for the people. Moses and God developed the succession plan together in Numbers 27:15-20:

> Then Moses spoke to the LORD, saying, "May the LORD, the God of the spirits of all flesh, appoint a man over the congregation, who will go out and come in before them, and who will lead them out and bring them in, so that the congregation of the LORD will not be like sheep which have no shepherd." So the LORD said to Moses, "Take Joshua the son of Nun, a man in whom is the Spirit, and lay your hand on him; and have him stand before Eleazar the priest and before all the congregation, and commission him in their sight. You shall put some of your authority on him, in order that all the congregation of the sons of Israel may obey him."

Moses wasn't the only leader in the Bible to create a succession plan. Jesus trained and empowered the Apostles who succeeded Him, and also gives the Holy Spirit to train and empower all who follow Him today.

Seize the moment and plan your succession; it is never too early to start passing on what was given to you to the next generation (2 Timothy 2:2).

NUMBERS 28
THE APPOINTED TIME!

Do you have a good theology of time? From the world, we learn that time is money: another day another dollar! Is that all it is – a utilitarian commodity used in bartering for economic goods?

From God's Word, we learn that all time, every moment, is a gift from God for our good and His glory!

Numbers 28 and 29 invest 71 verses to review the Jewish calendar and highlight not only their major festivals, but also the sacred rhythms of ordinary time. These two chapters are bookended together by a key theological concept that we find in Scripture: "at [the] appointed time!"

Numbers 28:2 starts, "You shall be careful to present My offering, My food for My offerings by fire, of a soothing aroma to Me, at their appointed time."

Numbers 29:39 ends, "You shall present these to the LORD at your appointed times, besides your votive offerings and your freewill offerings, for your burnt offerings and for your grain offerings and for your drink offerings and for your peace offerings."

What is your theology of time?

Ecclesiastes 3:1 gives us an important starting point to answer this question, "There is an appointed time for everything. And there is a time for every event under heaven."

Very powerfully, Paul says in Galatians 4:4-5, "But when the fullness of the time came, God sent forth His Son, born of a woman, born under the Law, so that He might redeem those who were under the Law, that we might receive the adoption as sons."

Every moment of your life is a providential opportunity to know God and to make Him known!

Seize the moment, because every moment is a gift of God – for your good and His glory! Embrace the appointed time of your life – it's a gift!

NUMBERS 29
HONOR HOLY DAYS!

Everyone loves a good holiday!

While some see holidays as a chance to sleep in, or eat extra, what we find in Numbers 28 and 29 is that there is more to the story – much more! The sacred rhythms of ordinary time are anchored by the observance of holy days, or what we call holidays.

Numbers 28 and 29 commanded the Israelites to keep the sacred rhythms of time, which included the daily sacrifices, the weekly Sabbaths, and the major festivals. Numbers 28 legislated the observance of Passover, also called the Feast of Unleavened Bread (16-25), and the Day of Firstfruits, which begins the Feast of Weeks (or Harvest), also called Pentecost (26-31). Numbers 29 legislated the observance of the Feast of Trumpets (1-6), the Day of Atonement (7-11), and the Feast of Booths (or Tabernacles) (12-38).

What was the common variable to all these holy days in the Jewish calendar?

Numbers 28:18 & 26 and Numbers 29:1 & 12 prescribe that "you shall do no laborious work." It is the same for all the festivals, except for the Day of Atonement, where further details are given. Numbers 29:7 explains, "you shall humble yourselves; you shall not do any work."

There it is! For a holiday to be a holy day, according to the testimony of God's ancient practices, God's people must humble themselves from their activity and abstain from work. This is not because work is evil. Please pay attention to the biblical motive for work found in Genesis 1:28 – work is God's idea to partner with Him in bringing His rule to the Earth. However, we, who were created as God's people to partner in His work, must also cease from striving and know that He is the One and only God (Psalm 46:10)! Our observance of holy days teaches us how to find rest in God by trusting Him to finish the work of making all things news (Revelation 21:5).

Seize the moment and find rest for your soul by living in the unforced rhythms of God's grace!

Dr. Jerry D. Ingalls

NUMBERS 30
THE IMPORTANCE OF COMMITMENTS!

Do you struggle to keep your commitments? Do people trust that your "yes means yes" and your "no means no?"

Numbers 30:2 establishes the foundational principle for the making and breaking of vows, "If a man makes a vow to the LORD, or takes an oath to bind himself with a binding obligation, he shall not violate his word; he shall do according to all that proceeds out of his mouth."

Any commitment made before God must be fulfilled. The remainder of Numbers 30 legislated the exceptions to this law of God because it differed for women, especially for daughters who were under their father's authority and wives who were under their husband's, but the principle stood: God honors our personal decision-making authority ("agency") to make commitments.

Practically speaking, when I assist couples in their preparation for their wedding day, or when I am helping a married couple with their marriage, I often say, "Once you said yes to one another on your wedding day, that person became God's will for your life, because God honors your vows." There is no reason to doubt this truth, find security and hope in it!

Jesus simplified the conversation in Matthew 5:33-37, "Again, you have heard that the ancients were told, 'You shall not make false vows, but shall fulfill your vows to the LORD.' But I say to you, … let your statement be, 'Yes, yes' or 'No, no'; anything beyond these is of evil."

God honors your "yes" and your "no" because God honors you! Both your "yes" and your "no" are gifts from the Sovereign God to give you authority in your own life. Simply stated, Jesus calls you to steward the responsibility of personal agency with integrity.

Seize the moment and live within the boundaries of your yes and your no, so that the world may see God's love and faithfulness in and through your life!

NUMBERS 31
WELCOME HOME THE WARRIORS!

I was a Captain in the US Army when 9/11 happened. I remember exactly where I was at Fort Carson, Colorado. For years to come, we sent warriors overseas to seek vengeance in the Global War on Terrorism.

We see something similar happening in Numbers 31. Moses was given his last leadership assignment when God commanded him in verse 2, "Take full vengeance for the sons of Israel on the Midianites; afterward you will be gathered to your people." The warriors accomplished the task and Balaam, along with every male, was destroyed (7-8).

After the warriors achieved vengeance for Israel, Moses taught the nation how to welcome home their warriors. These warriors had become ritually unclean from dealing with death, and they needed cleansing from the bloodshed so that they could reenter the camp physically and spiritually, as well as mentally and emotionally.

In Numbers 31:19-24, Moses and Eleazar established the ritual cleansing for the warriors so that they could come home, holy and whole:

> And you, camp outside the camp seven days; whoever has killed any person and whoever has touched any slain, purify yourselves, you and your captives, on the third day and on the seventh day. You shall purify for yourselves every garment and every article of leather and all the work of goats' hair, and all articles of wood. ... And you shall wash your clothes on the seventh day and be clean, and afterward you may enter the camp.

Every culture needs a way to welcome home their warriors! It is our job as a community to acknowledge that what they did was for us, and is a heavy burden on them; we must do what we can to cleanse them of that bloodshed so that they can reenter homes and workplaces, holy and whole.

Seize the moment and support veterans by showing them respect and helping them re-assimilate back home. Welcome home our warriors!

NUMBERS 32
MAKE NECESSARY COMPROMISES!

Have you ever had to make a compromise that was necessary to keep your family together?

Moses did! In Numbers 32, his worst fear was coming true as the younger generation appeared to be balking at the edge of the Promised Land. The sons of Reuben and Gad approached Moses and asked to take claim of the Transjordan, instead of crossing the Jordan River to enter Canaan, the Promised Land (1-5).

Not again?!

Moses escalated his rhetoric and judgment against them for what he saw as history repeating itself (6-15). Immediately, the tribal leaders clarified their intent to not forsake the Promised Land or mistrust God's provision, but to settle adjacently to it in the Transjordan for its excellent grazing grounds (16-19).

Moses had to make an impossible leadership decision! He accepted their plan and required a good-faith compromise. Numbers 32:28-30 demonstrates Moses' foresight to ensure this compromise was clarified between the tribes and his successors so that all parties would keep their end of the agreement:

> So Moses gave command concerning them to Eleazar the priest, and to Joshua the son of Nun, and to the heads of the fathers' households of the tribes of the sons of Israel. Moses said to them, "If the sons of Gad and the sons of Reuben, everyone who is armed for battle, will cross with you over the Jordan in the presence of the LORD, and the land is subdued before you, then you shall give them the land of Gilead for a possession; but if they will not cross over with you armed, they shall have possessions among you in the land of Canaan."

Moses knew a compromise was the necessary way to keep the family of God together and on mission to conquer the Promised Land.

Seize the moment and prayerfully seek for ways to maintain the unity of the church so that the mission is accomplished in your generation!

NUMBERS 33
THE PROMISE OF THE PROMISED LAND!

Do you know why God gave His people the Promised Land?

Numbers 33 is a historical lesson intended to embolden the Israelites as they received the command to enter and conquer the Promised Land. Verses 1-49 provide a thorough travel log from Egypt to their current location on the plains of Moab opposite Jericho, which would be their first military objective to get a foothold in Canaan (Joshua 6).

Numbers 33:50-53 records God's command to the Israelites at this historic moment:

> When you cross over the Jordan into the land of Canaan, then you shall drive out all the inhabitants of the land from before you, and destroy all their figured stones, and destroy all their molten images and demolish all their high places; and you shall take possession of the land and live in it, for I have given the land to you to possess it.

Just as in Egypt during the ten plagues, God was bringing His judgment upon evil and destroying the worship of false gods. God reminded the Israelites of His purposes at the beginning of the travel log in verse 4, "While the Egyptians were burying all their firstborn whom the LORD had struck down among them. The LORD had also executed judgments on their gods."

This has been, and always will be, God's intent for His people: to bring all the nations back to Himself and rescue them from the dominion of the lesser gods, and to bless the nations with His presence! God chose Abraham for this very reason; this is the promise for which we, the Church of Jesus Christ, have been called, "And in you all the families of the earth will be blessed" (Genesis 12:1-3; Galatians 3:29).

Seize the moment, because you have been blessed by God to be a blessing to all the nations! "And you shall be My witnesses ... even to the remotest part of the earth" (Acts 1:8).

NUMBERS 34
LEADERS ARE NOT THE POINT!

Do you get distracted by the personalities and preferences of your leaders?

The orders to conquer the Promised Land were given in Numbers 33, and the boundaries of conquest were established in Numbers 34:1-15. It is time to call forth the tribal leaders who will execute the commands of God.

In the remainder of Numbers 34, Moses named the leaders beginning with this statement in verses 17-19, "These are the names of the men who shall apportion the land to you for inheritance: Eleazar the priest and Joshua the son of Nun. You shall take one leader of every tribe to apportion the land for inheritance."

The Hebrew word for leader means, "one lifted up," and denotes a chieftain, sheik, or ruler. A leader is a person lifted above the rest. Every tribal leader in this list, except for Caleb, although strategically placed by God for this critical time, is a once-mention in the Bible. These leaders served as great military leaders, city planners, religious overseers, and community organizers in a time of great leadership need, but they will never be mentioned by name again.

Why? Because leaders are never the point! The leaders are "lifted up" to *lead*, not to be celebrated!

God gives leaders to His people to play their part in seeing His will done in and through His people. When people start focusing more on the leader than they do on the mission of God, then they will become disunified by their preferences and distracted by their personalities (e.g., 1 Corinthians 1:10-17).

God gives leaders to equip the people to walk in the unity of the Spirit, as the one body of Christ, to fulfill the purposes of God (Ephesians 4:11-16).

Seize the moment and listen to your leaders to stay on mission for God; keep your eyes fixed on Jesus Christ, the only Name worthy of faith!

NUMBERS 35
GOD PROVIDES FOR JUSTICE!

Before they entered the Promised Land, the Israelite leaders were required to make provision for justice; in fact, that is what Numbers 35 is all about.

First, in verses 1-8, God commanded each tribe to give the Levites some of their cities, and pasture lands around those cities, as places to live. This was a necessary provision because the Levites had no right of land ownership because their inheritance was the Lord, and service in the tabernacle (Numbers 18:23).

Second, in verses 6-34, God commanded the Israelites to give up six more cities (the "cities of refuge") to ensure effective justice in the land. Verses 10-15 explain God's provision for justice:

> When you cross the Jordan into the land of Canaan, then you shall select for yourselves cities to be your cities of refuge, that the manslayer who has killed any person unintentionally may flee there. … You shall give three cities across the Jordan and three cities in the land of Canaan; they are to be cities of refuge. These six cities shall be for refuge for the sons of Israel, and for the alien and for the sojourner among them; that anyone who kills a person unintentionally may flee there.

God loves justice! Deuteronomy 32:4 describes God this way, "The Rock! His work is perfect, for all His ways are just; a God of faithfulness and without injustice, righteous and upright is He." Psalm 89:14 proclaims of God, "Righteousness and justice are the foundation of Your throne; lovingkindness and truth go before You."

God not only provided for the Levites so that they would not have to live at the mercy of the other tribes of Israel, but God also provided places for justice to be preserved, and due process to be protected, to distinguish between deliberate and involuntary homicide.

Seize the moment and do justice, love kindness, and walk humbly with your God (Micah 6:8)!

NUMBERS 36
THE POLITICS OF INHERITANCE!

It pains me to see families fight over estate issues at the time of a death, but the politics of inheritance are real, especially when there is a transfer of property or wealth.

As we enter the final chapter of Numbers, a concern was expressed in the inheritance laws regarding the tribal allotments of land. Previously, in Numbers 27, Moses decreed that Zelophehad's daughters were allowed to inherit their father's property, because he had no sons (1-11). Now in Numbers 36, as they are about to enter the Promised Land, the question was raised: Would the tribe lose that daughter's allotment of the Promised Land forever if she were to marry outside the tribe (1-4)?

Even though Israel was one nation, each tribal leader was a prince over their own tribe and looked out for their people's best interest, which included protecting their allotments of the Promised Land.

Moses' decision in verses 6-9 legislated marriage to mitigate the politics of inheritance between the tribes of Israel and, therefore, decrease the chance of tribal infighting for the future:

> Every daughter who comes into possession of an inheritance of any tribe of the sons of Israel shall be wife to one of the family of the tribe of her father, so that the sons of Israel each may possess the inheritance of his fathers. Thus no inheritance shall be transferred from one tribe to another tribe, for the tribes of the sons of Israel shall each hold to his own inheritance.

Preserving the promises of God through the inheritance laws is essential to the covenants of God. In Galatians 3:29, Paul expresses this reality for New Covenant believers, "And if you belong to Christ, then you are Abraham's descendants, heirs according to promise" (cf. Galatians 4:7).

Seize the moment and accept your birthright through Jesus Christ – God's politics of inheritance allows you to enter His Kingdom as His child!

DEUTERONOMY

DEUTERONOMY 1
THE RIGHT PLACE AT THE RIGHT TIME!

When I teach people conflict resolution skills, I highlight the importance of saying the right thing at the right time and in the right place. Location and timing are key!

Deuteronomy is the last of the five books of Moses. It means "second giving," and is composed primarily of the final sermons of Moses, which he gave to the new generation on the eve of their entrance into the Promised Land.

Moses wanted to ensure that the young people who would enter the Promised Land were not ignorant of God and His ways; so, at 120 years old, he passionately recounted the story of Israel and gave them, for the second time, the Law of God.

Deuteronomy 1:1-5 begins the book by describing the situation:

These are the words which Moses spoke to all Israel across the Jordan in the wilderness … In the fortieth year, on the first day of the eleventh month, Moses spoke to the children of Israel, according to all that the LORD had commanded him to give to them.

The people listened attentively to Moses' words because they were facing the task that their fathers had forsaken forty years prior. This moment had loomed over them their entire lives!

This was the right place and the right time for Moses to confront them with what lay before them. In verse 37, Moses grieved that he was not allowed to enter the Promised Land with them, "The LORD was angry with me also on your account, saying, 'Not even you shall enter there.'"

This was his last chance – the right time and the right place – for Moses to fulfill God's call to the people he led faithfully, though not perfectly, for over forty years. He gave them his heart, yet again!

Seize the moment and pray about the right place and right time for you to communicate what is important to you to the people in your life!

DEUTERONOMY 2
GIVE THANKS TO GOD!

In remembering where we have come from to where we are now, no matter what may be facing us tomorrow, we have much to give thanks for because "God is good and His lovingkindness is everlasting" (Psalm 136).

Psalm 136 recounts the goodness of God to the nation of Israel; and after every historical episode you hear this refrain, "For His lovingkindness is everlasting."

Deuteronomy 2 retells a segment of the epic journey of the Israelites from Mount Seir to the Transjordan where two-and-a-half tribes would ultimately settle. It is a theological travel log with the aim of emboldening the younger generation to trust that God will keep His word and do His part in the conquest of the Promised Land.

The following are two promises for which they needed to trust God:

1. **Provision.** Moses recounted God's provision throughout their wanderings in the wilderness in verse 7, "For the LORD your God has blessed you in all that you have done; He has known your wanderings through this great wilderness. These forty years the LORD your God has been with you; you have not lacked a thing."
2. **Protection.** Moses detailed how God either gave them favor with the nations as they wandered through the desert, or He gave them the nations, as in verse 30, "But Sihon king of Heshbon was not willing for us to pass through his land; for the LORD your God hardened his spirit and made his heart obstinate, in order to deliver him into your hand, as he is today."

Don't just believe *in* God, *believe* God! God always provides for that which God promises. Give thanks for God's provision and protection!

Seize the moment and give thanks to God in every circumstance of your life, for His lovingkindness is everlasting (1 Thessalonians 5:18; Psalm 136).

DEUTERONOMY 3
ENTER THE REST OF GOD!

Have you entered the "rest" of God?

Deuteronomy 3 reviews the conquest of the land in the Transjordan that would give "rest" to God's people (20). To enter this rest, they had to march into battle first. Verse 1 recounts, "Then we turned and went up the road to Bashan, and Og, king of Bashan, with all his people came out to meet us in battle at Edrei."

The Promised Land was not a place of rest until the kingdoms that served false gods were removed from the area. Deuteronomy 3 references places such as Bashan and Mount Hermon, which are just names to us, but were commonly known as the ancient domains of evil. The ancient worldview of these geographic locations is significant for us to be able to grasp the depth of God's victories so that His people could enter His rest:

> Canaanite (Ugaritic) peoples, then, literally believed Bashan to be the gateway to the Underworld – the dwelling place of the dead. ... According to Jewish theology of the Second Temple period (from books like 1 Enoch), the sons of God (called "watchers") of Gen 6:1-4 descended to Mount Hermon in Bashan before carrying out the deeds described in Gen 6:1-4. Bashan and Hermon thus had sinister reputations.[8]

God conquered these ancient domains of evil so that His people could live free from evil influences. In the same way, Jesus defeated the domains of evil on the Cross. Paul proclaimed in Colossians 2:15, "When He had disarmed the rulers and authorities, He made a public display of them, having triumphed over them through Him."

Seize the moment and "be diligent to enter [God's] rest, so that no one will fall;" trust Jesus and His victory over evil (Hebrews 4:11).

---

[8] Michael S. Heiser, "Bashan and the Gates of Hell," in *Faithlife Study Bible* (Bellingham, WA: Lexham Press, 2016).

DEUTERONOMY 4
A CALL TO WHOLEHEARTED OBEDIENCE!

Are you living wholeheartedly?

Moses called the new generation to live with a wholehearted obedience to God. This call to obedience was in stark contrast to their parents' unbelief forty years prior, as they rebelled against God at every adverse circumstance.

Deuteronomy 4 summarizes the purpose of Moses' historical recap and provides a transition to the "second giving" of the Ten Commandments in chapter 5, and the Law in chapters 6-26. Deuteronomy 4:39-40 called forth the next generation to listen closely:

Know therefore today, and take it to your heart, that the LORD, He is God in heaven above and on the earth below; there is no other. So you shall keep His statutes and His commandments which I am giving you today, that it may go well with you and with your children after you, and that you may live long on the land which the LORD your God is giving you for all time.

God is faithful to His faithful! Because of His mercy, there remains a hope for those who have not been faithful, but who return to God with their whole heart. God's mercy is promised in verses 29-31:

But from there you will seek the LORD your God, and you will find Him if you search for Him with all your heart and all your soul. When you are in distress and all these things have come upon you, in the latter days you will return to the LORD your God and listen to His voice. For the LORD your God is a compassionate God; He will not fail you nor destroy you nor forget the covenant with your fathers which He swore to them.

Seize the moment and seek God with all of your heart and all of your soul! God is always faithful to respond to His people when they faithfully return to Him.

DEUTERONOMY 5
GOD'S WORD IS FOR OUR GOOD!

Do you believe that the Bible is God's Word, given to us, faithfully recorded by His people for our good?

In Deuteronomy 5:1-5, Moses legitimized and authorized the "second giving" of the Law by establishing it as a divine revelation from God, not as something he wrote:

> Hear, O Israel, the statutes and the ordinances which I am speaking today in your hearing, that you may learn them and observe them carefully. The LORD our God made a covenant with us at Horeb. The LORD did not make this covenant with our fathers, but with us, with all those of us alive here today. The LORD spoke to you face to face at the mountain from the midst of the fire, while I was standing between the LORD and you at that time, to declare to you the word of the LORD; for you were afraid because of the fire and did not go up the mountain.

This chapter lays the foundation for the next twenty-one chapters so that the new generation would know and remember that it was God who rescued them from slavery, gathered them at Sinai, and brought them through these last forty years to prepare them for this moment in time. To that end, it's interesting to note the addition of a phrase in verse 15 that is not part of the first presentation of the Ten Commandments:

> You shall remember that you were a slave in the land of Egypt, and the LORD your God brought you out of there by a mighty hand and by an outstretched arm; therefore the LORD your God commanded you to observe the sabbath day.

The new generation was being reminded that the God who gave these commandments is the One who rescued and delivered them from slavery – God's intentions are trustworthy, and His Law is good!

Seize the moment and trust God that all His ways are for your good!

DEUTERONOMY 6
TREASURE THE SHEMA IN YOUR HEART!

What do you treasure in your heart?

The Shema is the central confession of Judaism. It is found in Deuteronomy 6:4-5, at the beginning of the "second giving" of the Law, "Hear, O Israel! The LORD is our God, the LORD is one! You shall love the LORD your God with all your heart and with all your soul and with all your might."

In Mark 12:29-30, Jesus gives the Shema as the greatest commandment of the Law, "The foremost is, 'Hear, O Israel! The LORD our God is one Lord; and you shall love the LORD your God with all your heart, and with all your soul, and with all your mind, and with all your strength'" (cf. Matthew 22:37; Luke 10:27).

Did you know that Jesus was quoting Deuteronomy 6? We must frame our understanding of Jesus' teaching with a thorough reading of the Old Testament, which is why I am committing three years of my early mornings, day in and day out, to study and write these devotionals. It is my hope that you will treasure the Word of Truth in your heart, that you may not sin against God (Psalm 119:11).

Moses commanded this of the Shema in verses 6-9:

These words, which I am commanding you today, shall be on your heart. You shall teach them diligently to your sons and shall talk of them when you sit in your house and when you walk by the way and when you lie down and when you rise up. You shall bind them as a sign on your hand and they shall be as frontals on your forehead. You shall write them on the doorposts of your house and on your gates.

Seize the moment and make the Word of Truth prominent in your life, so that you may know it, apply it, and pray it throughout your day. This is the way of victory!

DEUTERONOMY 7
COVENANT PROMISES!

Have you ever been metaphorically stabbed in the back, in word or deed? I don't know about you, but I prefer to be told to my face if there is an issue so that I can either repent, seek clarification, or agree to disagree on an issue.

God told His covenant people that He would let them know quickly, and to their face, if He had an issue with them. So often, we think of the promises of God as only blessings, but the promises also come with warnings, as Moses explained in Deuteronomy 7:9-10:

> Know therefore that the LORD your God, He is God, the faithful God, who keeps His covenant and His lovingkindness to a thousandth generation with those who love Him and keep His commandments; but repays those who hate Him to their faces, to destroy them; He will not delay with him who hates Him, He will repay him to his face.

Did you hear the promises of God?

Every promise of God is right and true and in accordance with God's covenant character! God is faithful to those who keep His covenant, which, as we have previously learned, includes people who repent by returning to God after they have been disobedient. And for those who reject God and prove disloyal to His covenant, God will repay them to their faces (Psalm 31:23; 94:2).

God won't stab you in the back! You will stand before Him as Paul promised in 2 Corinthians 5:10, "For we must all appear before the judgment seat of Christ, so that each one may be recompensed for his deeds in the body, according to what he has done, whether good or bad."

Seize the moment and respond to all the covenant promises of God today; "draw near to God and He will draw near to you" (James 4:8)!

Dr. Jerry D. Ingalls

DEUTERONOMY 8
THE IMPORTANCE OF THE WILDERNESS!

Do you believe that wilderness times are an important part of your spiritual formation? The key is how we walk through such times, and if we walk alone.

Deuteronomy 8:3 was quoted by Jesus at a time of temptation during His forty days in the wilderness. Its original context was God's gracious warning to the new generation to obey all His commandments in light of how He dealt with the previous generation during their forty years of wilderness wanderings:

> He humbled you and let you be hungry, and fed you with manna which you did not know, nor did your fathers know, that He might make you understand that man does not live by bread alone, but man lives by everything that proceeds out of the mouth of the LORD.

In the three temptations, found in Matthew 4, Jesus quoted from the second giving of the Law each time. He started with this one, then referenced Deuteronomy 6:16, "You shall not put the LORD your God to the test," and concluded with verse 13, "You shall worship the LORD your God, and serve Him only"

God's motivation in both wilderness experiences was to prepare His people for their greater purpose – to teach them humility and absolute dependence on God. Moses declared God's love for Israel when He shared this purpose in Deuteronomy 8:16-17:

> In the wilderness He fed you manna which your fathers did not know, that He might humble you and that He might test you, to do good for you in the end. Otherwise, you may say in your heart, "My power and the strength of my hand made me this wealth."

Seize the moment and walk faithfully with Jesus through your wilderness wanderings, remembering that God is using these times to prepare you to do even greater works (John 14:12).

DEUTERONOMY 9
FAITHFUL IN REBELLION!

As a parent of three children, I care deeply that my children develop the character quality of faithfulness. I model faithfulness to my children by the way I love Jesus and serve His Church, as well as by the way I love and serve my wife and family. When I see rebellion in my children, I don't reject them for it; rather, in love, I discipline them. Rebellion will fester in their hearts and destroy their lives if I don't address it directly.

Moses' greatest fear for Israel was that they would rebel against God after His death, and this motivated his "second giving" of the Law, as given to us in Deuteronomy (ref. Deuteronomy 31:26-27). For over forty years, Moses had to deal constantly with the people's rebellion against God. He used the Hebrew word for rebelling eight times in Deuteronomy, three of those times in this chapter alone. In Deuteronomy 9:23-24, Moses addresses the people's rebellion directly:

> When the LORD sent you from Kadesh-barnea, saying, "Go up and possess the land which I have given you," then you rebelled against the command of the LORD your God; you neither believed Him nor listened to His voice. You have been rebellious against the LORD from the day I knew you (cf. 9:7-8).

God is faithful, even when we are not! His desire is for His children to reflect His faithfulness to the nations. How? Through our faith! John the Beloved teaches that our faith is our victory in 1 John 5:4, "For whatever is born of God overcomes the world; and this is the victory that has overcome the world – our faith."

Seize the moment and be faithful to God in the face of rebellion. It can feel very lonely to be faithful, but have faith; you are never alone – God is with you! Your faithfulness is the evidence of Jesus' victory.

DEUTERONOMY 10 FROM THE INSIDE OUT!

One way to rebel against a leader is to do *only* exactly what they tell you to do. There is a significant difference between following the letter of the law and walking in the heart and intent of the commandments of God. A great rebellion is already happening if we are following with our actions but aren't trusting in our hearts!

God desires to have your whole heart, evidenced by the transformation of your life through the renewal of your mind. God wants His people to follow Him with all their heart, mind, body, and soul. Moses began the conclusion of his first sermon in the "second giving" of the Law with these words in Deuteronomy 10:12-16:

> Now, Israel, what does the LORD your God require from you, but to fear the LORD your God, to walk in all His ways and love Him, and to serve the LORD your God with all your heart and with all your soul, and to keep the LORD'S commandments and His statutes which I am commanding you today for your good? ... So circumcise your heart and stiffen your neck no longer.

Circumcision was the outward sign of the covenant, as commanded to Abraham in Genesis 17:9-14. Moses' words "circumcise your heart" is a call for the people to go beyond outward obedience to inward conformity to God's ways. Paul prays this for us in Ephesians 3:16, "that He would grant you, according to the riches of His glory, to be strengthened with power through His Spirit in the inner man." The circumcision of your heart is only possible through the indwelling of the Holy Spirit. It is God's work in you, from the inside-out!

Seize the moment and walk in a daily intimate relationship with Jesus that conforms you to His character and submits you to His will.

DEUTERONOMY 11
THE CHOICE!

The Bible calls every person who reads it to make the choice!

Moses introduced a phrase in Deuteronomy 11, which we will hear again in chapter 30 of his "second giving" of the Law, "I am setting before you a blessing and a curse." This is the choice that every single person must make after being confronted with the Word of God – to believe or not to believe, to submit or not to submit, to live by faith or by sight. Moses contrasted the choice in verses 26-28:

> See, I am setting before you today a blessing and a curse: the blessing, if you listen to the commandments of the LORD your God, which I am commanding you today; and the curse, if you do not listen to the commandments of the LORD your God, but turn aside from the way which I am commanding you today, by following other gods which you have not known.

Every generation must be confronted with the choice! Moses' successor, Joshua, had to do the same thing with the Israelites near the end of his life before he transitioned leadership to the elders. Joshua's famous words are recorded in Joshua 24:15:

> If it is disagreeable in your sight to serve the LORD, choose for yourselves today whom you will serve: whether the gods which your fathers served which were beyond the River, or the gods of the Amorites in whose land you are living; but as for me and my house, we will serve the LORD.

In the same way that Moses and Joshua called for the choice, so did Jesus Christ in His ministry, as in Luke 11:28, "blessed are those who hear the word of God and observe it" (cf. Matthew 7:24-27; John 14:15).

Seize the moment and build your life upon the rock of faith in Jesus Christ. Choose this day whom you will serve!

DEUTERONOMY 12
WORSHIP HABITS!

Have you ever had to change a long-established habit?

For athletes, it's one thing to learn a new skill, it is altogether another thing to break a bad habit.

In Deuteronomy 12:4-5 & 8, Moses made it clear that God was going to be breaking some bad habits of worship by establishing one central place of worship in the Promised Land:

> You shall not act like this toward the LORD your God. But you shall seek the LORD at the place which the LORD your God will choose from all your tribes, to establish His name there for His dwelling, and there you shall come. ... You shall not do at all what we are doing here today, every man doing whatever is right in his own eyes.

I can almost hear the people's response to Moses, "But we've always done it this way!"

The people of God were surrounded by the Canaanites who worshipped God in high places and on altars set about wherever they wanted. These were the worship practices of the ancient near eastern civilizations. God, like a good coach, was announcing to His athletes that it was time to break some bad habits.

Did you know that Jesus made the same kind of announcement when He came to bring all the nations back to God?

In response to a Samaritan woman's direct question about worship practices, Jesus replied in John 4:23-24 that it was no longer about being at a right location, but about having a sincere heart:

> But an hour is coming, and now is, when the true worshipers will worship the Father in spirit and truth; for such people the Father seeks to be His worshipers. God is spirit, and those who worship Him must worship in spirit and truth.

Seize the moment and worship God with a sincere heart. Wherever and whenever you worship God, do so full of spirit and truth.

DEUTERONOMY 13
LIFE OF DEVOTION!

As an athlete, I know what it is to live a life of devotion. As an All-American collegiate athlete, and when I was training for the 2000 Olympics, I was devoted to my sport. The danger with such a hyper-focus on sport, or anything, is that it shapes you. God designed us, on purpose, to be formed by that which has our devotion, which was meant to be Him alone! Therefore, I echo John, known for his passionate exposition of God's love, with these words from 1 John 5:21, "Little children, guard yourselves from idols."

The emphasis of Deuteronomy 13 is to protect the next generation from the dangers of idol worship. Three times, God commanded His people to put to death any person that tried to "seduce" their hearts away from Him:

1. A prophet or a dreamer of dreams (1-5).
2. A close family member, such as parent, child, or spouse (6-11).
3. The inhabitants of one of their cities (12-18).

God's solution to idolatry is a life of devotion to Him! That which seeks to seduce you from God needs to be removed, whether a person or a thing. God takes idolatry, and the false worship that arises from it, seriously because we are all susceptible to it. John Calvin explained, "The human mind is, so to speak, a perpetual forge of idols."[9]

The good news is that God gave us the solution to idolatry in Deuteronomy 13:3-4:

> For the LORD your God is testing you to find out if you love the LORD your God with all your heart and with all your soul. You shall follow the LORD your God and fear Him; and you shall keep His commandments, listen to His voice, serve Him, and cling to Him.

Seize the moment and love God by being faithful to Him! It is your life of devotion to God that protects you from being seduced by lesser things.

---

[9] John Calvin, *Institutes of the Christian Religion* (Bellingham, WA: Logos Bible Software, 1997), I.11.8.

Dr. Jerry D. Ingalls

DEUTERONOMY 14
A DEVOTED PARENT'S DESIRE!

"If your friends jumped off a bridge, would you do it too?"

There is a good chance that you have said it, or it's been said to you. This is a classic parenting question to teach your children to think for themselves and not go along with the crowd. The Bible says in 1 Corinthians 15:33, "Bad company corrupts good morals." Devoted parents care about who is influencing their children.

Deuteronomy 14:1a states, "You are the sons of the LORD your God." For the first time, God calls the Israelites His sons. As a devoted Father, He is commanding His children to be different. In this chapter, God tells His people to not grieve like the others (1-2), to not eat like the others (3-21), and to not do finances like the others (22-29). God was establishing a new community, which was to be different than the Egyptian culture they were rescued from, and the Canaanite culture that surrounded them.

God desires for His children to bring honor to the family name, so He set them apart! Verse 2 declares, "For you are a holy people to the LORD your God." The struggle is that kids, so often, just want to fit in with their friends. That is when devoted parents step in and ask ridiculous questions about jumping off bridges.

Why do devoted parents discipline their children? Because we love them and want only the best for them. Hebrews 12:10-11 explains the Father's discipline:

He disciplines us for our good, so that we may share His holiness. All discipline for the moment seems not to be joyful, but sorrowful; yet to those who have been trained by it, afterwards it yields the peaceful fruit of righteousness.

Seize the moment and trust that God's ways are for your good and His glory. God loves you like devoted parents love their children – He only wants the best for you!

DEUTERONOMY 15
CARE FOR THE POOR!

When different congregations come together as the one Church of Jesus Christ, it is usually for the sake of children or the elderly, or for the care of the poor and hungry. Until God completes all things on Earth as it is in Heaven, congregations agree that the poor will be amongst us (Matthew 26:11) and we must do something to care for them, even if we can't agree on how to alleviate their plight in a more sustainable way.

Deuteronomy 15 is the retelling of the Law for the Sabbath year, or sabbatical, which was to occur every seventh year for the sake of the poor and hungry. It was not only a time to let the land rest (Exodus 23:10-11), but also to cancel debts (Deuteronomy 15:2-11), and to free indentured servants and slaves (12-18). Just like the Sabbath, which occurred once per week, the sabbatical was a proclamation of God's rescue from slavery. This was to be a blessing to all, but overtly a benefit to the poor and hungry in their midst, as we see in verses 10-11:

> You shall generously give to him, and your heart shall not be grieved when you give to him, because for this thing the LORD your God will bless you in all your work and in all your undertakings. For the poor will never cease to be in the land; therefore I command you, saying, "You shall freely open your hand to your brother, to your needy and poor in your land."

God's justice is deeply connected to the care of the widow and the orphan, the poor and the oppressed, the sick and the hungry. God loves you and wants to bless you; therefore, God wants you to join with Him in caring for those who can't care for themselves.

Seize the moment and open your hand to the needy and the poor. Be God's hands to your community.

DEUTERONOMY 16
TELL GOD'S STORY ON THE HOLIDAYS!

What are the stories that define you as a part of a larger group of people to whom you belong? Within our American culture, we commemorate Thanksgiving and Memorial Day. Additionally, as Christians, we celebrate Christmas and Easter. We are shaped by the stories we tell on these days.

Deuteronomy, like Exodus and Numbers, teaches the importance of the feasts, with Deuteronomy 16 prescribing, once again, the three pilgrimage feasts. Verses 16-17 captures the priority of participation:

> Three times in a year all your males shall appear before the LORD your God in the place which He chooses, at the Feast of Unleavened Bread and at the Feast of Weeks and at the Feast of Booths, and they shall not appear before the LORD empty-handed. Every man shall give as he is able, according to the blessing of the LORD your God which He has given you.

The Feast of Unleavened Bread, in conjunction with the Passover, commemorates the exodus when God delivered His people from Egyptian slavery. The Feast of Weeks, also known as the Feast of Harvest or Pentecost, happens seven weeks after Passover, and not only celebrates the grain harvest, but has come to commemorate the receiving of the Law at Mount Sinai and the people's entrance into the Promised Land. The Feast of Booths, or Tabernacles, memorializes Israel's forty years of wilderness wanderings.

These national festivals required the nation to come together, and for the men of each family to bring a tribute. Like Christmas and Easter are designed to do, these festivals anchored the Israelite people in their common heritage and shared faith. By retelling the miraculous stories of God's direct activity in history, our corporate identity becomes deeply rooted in our shared faith.

Seize the moment and tell God's story through our holidays. Children, families, and communities are shaped by the stories we tell at the holidays we celebrate.

DEUTERONOMY 17
THE RULE OF A KING!

What rules over your life?

There is a short section in Deuteronomy 17 that has caused Bible students of the Old Testament to wonder about its timing: Were these seven verses about the establishment of a king original to Moses' second giving of the Law, or added later during the time of the monarchy in response to Solomon's sins, which led to the kingdom's division?

At the end of the time of Judges, in 1 Samuel 8:5, the great prophet Samuel was confronted by the people because they wanted a king, "like all the nations." In verse 7, God responded to Samuel about their request, "Listen to the voice of the people in regard to all that they say to you, for they have not rejected you, but they have rejected Me from being king over them."

God was not surprised! Likely, the people were invoking God's promise of Deuteronomy 17:14-15a when they made their request:

> When you enter the land which the LORD your God gives you, and you possess it and live in it, and you say, "I will set a king over me like all the nations who are around me," you shall surely set a king over you whom the LORD your God chooses, one from among your countrymen you shall set as king over yourselves.

The passage continued by establishing protections against a king's pride, self-reliance, and corruption (16-17), and the right administration of the kingdom by the king, as according to the Law of God (18-20). Regardless of the form of human government, it has always been God's will that His Word would rule over His people, from the inside out.

Seize the moment and meditate upon God's Word, day and night, and all that you do will be pleasing to God and prosper in His sight (Joshua 1:8).

Dr. Jerry D. Ingalls

DEUTERONOMY 18
THE WORD OF THE PROPHET!

How can we know God's will for our lives?

This was a significant question for the nation of Israel, as it is for us today. Israel had been rescued from Egypt and was now surrounded by the Canaanites. The people of the ancient Near East used a variety of illegitimate sources, from which Yahweh strictly forbade His people, as in Deuteronomy 18:9-11:

> When you enter the land which the LORD your God gives you, you shall not learn to imitate the detestable things of those nations. There shall not be found among you anyone who makes his son or his daughter pass through the fire, one who uses divination, one who practices witchcraft, or one who interprets omens, or a sorcerer, or one who casts a spell, or a medium, or a spiritist, or one who calls up the dead.

In direct contrast to these practices, God speaks through His chosen people, called prophets, such as He did with Moses. Moses prophesied of the coming Messiah, and His office of prophet, in Deuteronomy 18:15, "The LORD your God will raise up for you a prophet like me from among you, from your countrymen, you shall listen to him." The early church quoted this promise twice, in Acts 3:22 and Acts 7:37.

Jesus is the new Moses, and the fulfillment of the office of prophet. The first disciples of Jesus Christ declared it so in the Gospel of John 1:45, "We have found Him of whom Moses in the Law and also the Prophets wrote – Jesus of Nazareth, the son of Joseph." More than a prophet, Jesus is the Living Word, "In the beginning was the Word, and the Word was with God, and the Word was God" (John 1:1).

Seize the moment and know God's will for your life by trusting Jesus Christ and His Word (2 Peter 1:16-21).

DEUTERONOMY 19
YOU ARE SET FREE TO LOVE!

In Christ, you are set free to love! Jesus proclaims it in John 8:36, "So if the Son makes you free, you will be free indeed." Paul reinforced it in Galatians 5:1a, "It was for freedom that Christ set us free." Jesus did not come to abolish the Law; rather, Jesus came to fulfill the Law and set you free from sin so that you may live the commandments of God by grace, through the power of the Holy Spirit (Matthew 5:17-18; Romans 6:14-15).

While the Ten Commandments cannot save you, they have not ceased to be God's standard for living as His people. Deuteronomy 19:18-20 details how the ninth commandment, "You shall not bear false witness against your neighbor" (Deuteronomy 5:20; cf. Exodus 20:16), protects against miscarriages of justice:

> The judges shall investigate thoroughly, and if the witness is a false witness and he has accused his brother falsely, then you shall do to him just as he had intended to do to his brother. Thus you shall purge the evil from among you. The rest will hear and be afraid, and will never again do such an evil thing among you.

Does Jesus free you to lie, or give false testimony against your neighbor? Absolutely not! Does grace allow you to falsely accuse someone without bearing the responsibility for the damage you can do for perjury? May it never be!

As New Covenant believers, we are set free from sin to live God's way. That means we are to uphold the moral commandments of God because they demonstrate His character and desire for us to reflect Him to the world as His image bearers. The Law is not bondage, but your fleshly efforts to live according to it *apart from grace* are slavery.

Seize the moment and walk in the Spirit today. You are set free to love (Galatians 5:1-26)!

Dr. Jerry D. Ingalls

DEUTERONOMY 20
LIVE THE VICTORIOUS LIFE!

Do you ever struggle to live in the victory that God has promised you?

We join in His victory when we live our lives according to the promises of God. No matter your circumstances, the battle belongs to God! Moses commanded the religious leaders of Israel to remind God's people of this truth in Deuteronomy 20:2-4:

> When you are approaching the battle, the priest shall come near and speak to the people. He shall say to them, "Hear, O Israel, you are approaching the battle against your enemies today. Do not be fainthearted. Do not be afraid, or panic, or tremble before them, for the LORD your God is the one who goes with you, to fight for you against your enemies, to save you."

You may not be facing a literal battle today, but, whatever you are facing, have courage and trust God for His victory. The Bible teaches us that the victory we have, and the victory we live, is a vicarious one. That means it is a victory that is not of our own making or doing, but rather a victory that has been given to us through the life, death, and resurrection of Jesus Christ.

Living the victorious life is, and will always be, God's work of grace in us and through us for His glory. Let us be clear about this from the forefront: the battle belongs to God!

Paul declared our victory in 2 Corinthians 1:20-22:

> For as many as are the promises of God, in Him they are yes; therefore also through Him is our Amen to the glory of God through us. Now He who establishes us with you in Christ and anointed us is God, who also sealed us and gave us the Spirit in our hearts as a pledge.

Seize the moment and live the victorious life! Be an overcomer because "in all these things we overwhelmingly conquer through Him who loved us" (Romans 8:37).

DEUTERONOMY 21
AN UNSOLVED MURDER!

What happens to a community when there is an unsolved murder?

Deuteronomy 21:1-9 teaches the Israelite people how to deal with an unsolved murder. The elders of the city were to set apart an unworked heifer and take it to an unplowed valley, with running water, and offer it as a sacrifice. Then, the priests, who were responsible for settling disputes and administering justice, blessed the sacrifice, followed by the elders washing their hands over the dead heifer, reciting the prescribed words of verses 7-8, "Our hands did not shed this blood, nor did our eyes see it. Forgive Your people Israel whom You have redeemed, O LORD, and do not place the guilt of innocent blood in the midst of Your people Israel."

The conclusion of this section, verses 8-9, explains why they were to do this: "And the bloodguiltiness shall be forgiven them. So you shall remove the guilt of innocent blood from your midst, when you do what is right in the eyes of the LORD."

This sacrificial rite is for the expiation (or satisfaction) of the pollution to the land caused by the murder. In other words, it was to heal the land of the curse and absolve the people of their bloodguilt for the murder since there was no way to bring the murderer to justice. According to Numbers 25:33, "Blood pollutes the land and no expiation can be made for the land for the blood that is shed on it, except by the blood of him who shed it."

God made a way for the land to be liberated, and for the community to be set free of their bloodguilt. God did not want His people polluted in their hearts because justice could not be fulfilled. Injustice in a society creates insecurity; whereas, justice makes secure.

Seize the moment and ask God to cleanse our land and heal out hearts of any bloodguilt caused by unsolved murders or thwarted justice in our communities.

DEUTERONOMY 22
THE DANGER OF BEING UNEQUALLY YOKED!

Have you ever heard the phrase, "unequally yoked" and wondered what it meant?

Deuteronomy 22:10 is the beginning point of this conversation in the Bible, "You shall not plow with an ox and a donkey together." A yoke is an agricultural device used to combine multiple animals in the working of the fields. While it is no longer a common site in most modern-day farming, seeing animals yoked together would have been a six-day-per-week reality during Bible times. The command to not yoke two unequal animals was given to protect both animals from hurting one another, but especially to protect the weaker of the two.

The unequally yoked relationship is not only a dangerous partnership, but also an unproductive union. Just as the animals would not work together for the common reason they were yoked, unequally yoked people spend most of their time fighting against the yoke that seeks to bind them together, rather than working in harmony for the reason they were brought in union (2 Corinthians 6:14).

Jesus invites all who would follow Him to come into His yoke in Matthew 11:29-30, "Take My yoke upon you and learn from Me, for I am gentle and humble in heart, and you will find rest for your souls. For My yoke is easy and My burden is light." We are to learn from Jesus and become like Him in union with Him, working alongside of Him, day after day.

The yoke of Jesus is what transforms us into His image and unites us to His mission. His yoke is custom-made ("easy") for each of us, so that we are not crushed by His teachings and commandments. His yoke unites us with Him, the head, and one another as fellow members of His body. His burden is light because the Holy Spirit empowers our life together. All other yokes cause weariness and heavy burdens, and lead to divisions between people.

Seize the moment and find rest for your soul, and partnership with fellow believers, in the easy yoke of Jesus!

DEUTERONOMY 23
A SEASON OF GENEROSITY!

There are seasons of generosity! The Christmas season is a great example of this, as it is a time when people give gifts and make large donations to their churches and charities. Christmas is a time to remember Jesus Christ. As Paul said in 2 Corinthians 9:15, "Thanks be to God for His indescribable gift!" The season of Christmas reminds us to be generous, as God first gave to us (John 3:16; Romans 5:8; 1 John 4:19).

There are seasons of generosity built into the rhythms of creation! There are seasons of harvesting, both in the farmers' crops and out in the wild. I love it when I am out on a hike and come across wild berries. It is majestic to come across wild berries on the Appalachian Trail (AT). There is no desire to hoard them because you just eat as you walk and leave the rest for other hikers, with whom you are sharing the trail.

Like the hiking community on the AT, God's people are to share their harvest as a gift from God, remembering that all good gifts are from Him (James 1:17). In Deuteronomy 23:24-25, God commanded His people to be generous with their harvests, both those who raised the crop and those who were allowed to graze or glean from it:

> When you enter your neighbor's vineyard, then you may eat grapes until you are fully satisfied, but you shall not put any in your basket. When you enter your neighbor's standing grain, then you may pluck the heads with your hand, but you shall not wield a sickle in your neighbor's standing grain.

Seize the moment and be generous, in season and out, so that the world may know of God's great gift of Jesus Christ to the world – to you and me (1 John 3:16-18; 2 Corinthians 9:6-15)!

DEUTERONOMY 24
PROTECTING PRIORITIES!

Have you ever heard someone say, "Happy wife, happy life?"

While such a statement does not allow for an idolatrous view of marriage and family, it does call you to realize that right priorities make for a holy and healthy life. If you make the decision to get married, then you must protect and prioritize that relationship. If you and your spouse decide to have children, then you need to work together to figure out how to partner to prioritize the raising of those children. Neither marriage nor having children are required of you to live a holy life, but if you decide to follow either path, then you must accept the consequences of your decision by protecting and prioritizing the responsibilities those decisions require of you.

In Deuteronomy 24:5, Moses gave a command to protect and prioritize the importance of marriage and the family in God's design for society, "When a man takes a new wife, he shall not go out with the army nor be charged with any duty; he shall be free at home one year and shall give happiness to his wife whom he has taken."

This is an amazing teaching that demonstrates the power of shared priorities. But it also reveals how difficult it can be to protect your priorities when you live in a culture that doesn't share them, and even works against them. Don't allow busyness to rule your life and determine your priorities!

What decisions do you need to make to protect your priorities in your daily life? What boundaries must you put on your ambitions and calendars?

Jesus taught us to not let our worries of the future drive us to unfaithfulness in our priorities today. He taught in Matthew 6:33-34, "But seek first His kingdom and His righteousness, and all these things will be added to you. So do not worry about tomorrow; for tomorrow will care for itself. Each day has enough trouble of its own."

Seize the moment and protect your time and preserve your energy for the priorities of your life today!

DEUTERONOMY 25
GOOD STEWARDSHIP!

Some people treat their animals better than they treat people. Not so with the people of God! We are to treat our animals well, and people even better.

Deuteronomy 25:4 demonstrates God's love for all His creation, and how His people are to practically partner with Him, "You shall not muzzle the ox while he is threshing." The farmer must allow the ox to benefit from its labors and eat grain while it works.

This was not only a stewardship practice, but part of a larger stewardship principle that God's people were supposed to live as His partners in caring for the creation. As image bearers of God, we are fellow stewards of creation (Genesis 1:27-29; 9:1-3). We read in Proverbs 12:10a, "A righteous man has regard for the life of his animal." Loving care of animals is an important part of being a good steward of God's creation.

In the same way that God desires for His people to steward His creation by acting with kindness to animals, He commands His people to treat one another with even greater kindness and fairness. Paul said in Galatians 6:10, "So then, while we have opportunity, let us do good to all people, and especially to those who are of the household of the faith."

Yoking these concepts, Paul quoted Deuteronomy 25:4 in 1 Corinthians 9:9. In doing so, he connected the stewardship practice of financially providing for the laborers in God's harvest (Luke 10:2), with how the farmers were to care for their oxen as they worked to thresh the harvest. Then, with finality, Paul referenced Jesus' words from Luke 10:7 ("the laborer is worthy of his wages") in 1 Corinthians 9:14, "So also the Lord directed those who proclaim the gospel to get their living from the gospel."

Seize the moment and be a good steward of what God has entrusted to you! Care for God's people and the household of faith.

Dr. Jerry D. Ingalls

DEUTERONOMY 26
A FARMER'S LITURGY!

What are your rhythms of giving thanks to God? To demonstrate your dependency upon God as the giver of all good gifts (James 1:17), what words do you say, and what practical gestures of gratitude do you make?

Deuteronomy 26:1-19 records the farmer's liturgy for the giving of the annual tithe of their crop. The farmer was required to travel to a specified location with the first fruits of his crop in a basket, and present the offering to the priest, reciting verse 3, "I declare this day to the LORD my God that I have entered the land which the LORD swore to our fathers to give us." Upon the priest receiving it and placing it before the altar of God, the farmer would then repeat verses 5-10 before God:

> My father was a wandering Aramean, and he went down to Egypt and sojourned there, few in number; but there he became a great, mighty and populous nation. And the Egyptians treated us harshly and afflicted us, and imposed hard labor on us. Then we cried to the LORD, the God of our fathers, and the LORD heard our voice and saw our affliction and our toil and our oppression; and the LORD brought us out of Egypt with a mighty hand and an outstretched arm and with great terror and with signs and wonders; and He has brought us to this place and has given us this land, a land flowing with milk and honey. Now behold, I have brought the first of the produce of the ground which You, O LORD have given me.

God required rhythms of formal worship (liturgies) to remind them of His mighty deeds and to call them to a shared life of faith and purpose as His "treasured possession" (16-19).

Seize the moment and build rhythms of formal worship into your life! These are not meaningless religious rituals when you walk in faith with your God, and obey His Word. You are shaped by your life of devotion.

DEUTERONOMY 27
TAKE RESPONSIBILITY!

I was recently in a meeting, when someone suggested that we put a name next to each action item. If you want something to get done, then someone must take responsibility to bring the good idea to fulfillment.

Moses completed the second giving of the Law (12-26), and was about to lay out the blessings and curses of the Law (27-28). But first, a command was given by Moses and the elders, in Deuteronomy 27:1-3, that the people must publicly commit themselves to obeying the Law in a covenant renewal ceremony upon their entrance to the Promised Land:

> Then Moses and the elders of Israel charged the people, saying, "Keep all the commandments which I command you today. So it shall be on the day when you cross the Jordan to the land which the LORD your God gives you, that you shall set up for yourself large stones and coat them with lime and write on them all the words of this law, when you cross over, so that you may enter the land which the LORD your God gives you, a land flowing with milk and honey, as the LORD, the God of your fathers, promised you."

It is important that "the elders of Israel" were included in the giving of this charge with Moses, as it had been only Moses speaking prior to this. The answer for this addition was simple; Moses would not be with them when they entered the Promised Land so, just like with the pronouncement of Joshua as the next leader (Deuteronomy 3:28), the elders were put in a position of responsibility to ensure the covenant renewal ceremony happened upon their entrance.

Seize the moment and take responsibility for what needs to get done around your home, church, and community. Don't expect others to do what God lays on your heart to be done. Put your name next to the good works Jesus is asking you to do for God and His kingdom (Ephesians 2:10)!

Dr. Jerry D. Ingalls

DEUTERONOMY 28
THE CURSE OF AN IRON YOKE!

The Lord has given each of us a choice – blessings or curses! Moses gave us the promises of the covenant in Deuteronomy 27-28 as He closed out his second giving of the Law. After a litany of covenant curses in Deuteronomy 27:15-26 and 28:15-68, you can feel the heavy burden of disobedience to the covenant of God. To capture the consequences of disobedience, God gave His people the image of an iron yoke in Deuteronomy 28:47-48:

> Because you did not serve the LORD your God with joy and a glad heart, for the abundance of all things; therefore you shall serve your enemies whom the LORD will send against you, in hunger, in thirst, in nakedness, and in the lack of all things; and He will put an iron yoke on your neck until He has destroyed you.

Furthermore, Deuteronomy 28:65 connected the yoke imagery to the biblical theme of rest, "Among those nations you shall find no rest, and there will be no resting place for the sole of your foot; but there the LORD will give you a trembling heart, failing of eyes, and despair of soul." This would have been immediately contrasted with God's promise of rest for His people when they entered the Promised Land in Deuteronomy 25:19.

The yoke is an agricultural image that depicts a choice: God's people are either in the easy yoke of covenant blessings, where they have peace and find rest for their soul through a faithful relationship with God (Matthew 11:28-30), or they are in the hard yoke of covenant curses, where they find weariness and despair because of their rebellion against God (Jeremiah 28:13-14). The choice comes down to submission to God and His ways.

Seize the moment and find rest for your soul in the easy yoke of Jesus. It's your choice!

DEUTERONOMY 29
GOOD FRUIT OF COVENANT ROOTS!

It is my prayer for you that you will manifest the good fruit of your relationship with Jesus Christ. This has always been God's hope for His people. We are His image bearers.

Deuteronomy 29:14-18 taught His people about the importance of staying rooted in God's covenant:

> Now not with you alone am I making this covenant and this oath, but both with those who stand here with us today in the presence of the LORD our God and with those who are not with us here today …; so that there will not be among you a man or woman, or family or tribe, whose heart turns away today from the LORD our God, to go and serve the gods of those nations; that there will not be among you a root bearing poisonous fruit and wormwood.

Hebrews 12:11 & 15 contrast the fruit of those who are and are not rooted in God's grace:

> All discipline for the moment seems not to be joyful, but sorrowful; yet to those who have been trained by it, afterwards it yields the peaceful fruit of righteousness. … See to it that no one comes short of the grace of God; that no root of bitterness springing up causes trouble, and by it many be defiled.

The evidence of your relationship with God is either found in the peaceful fruit of righteousness, or the poisonous fruit of a bitter root. As Jesus Christ said in Matthew 7:20, "So then, you will know them by their fruits."

Seize the moment and bear the good fruit of abiding in the Vine of a personal relationship with Jesus Christ (John 15:1-16). May your life make evidence the fruit of the Holy Spirit: love, joy, peace, patience, kindness, goodness, faithfulness, gentleness, self-control (Galatians 5:22-23)!

Dr. Jerry D. Ingalls

DEUTERONOMY 30
THE CLOSENESS OF THE WORD!

Ignorance is not an excuse! This was drilled into me as a cadet at West Point, and as an officer in the US Army.

God, in His mercy and grace, according to Deuteronomy 30:11-14, has come close to us so that we may know Him and live to please Him:

> For this commandment which I command you today is not too difficult for you, nor is it out of reach. It is not in heaven, that you should say, "Who will go up to heaven for us to get it for us and make us hear it, that we may observe it?" Nor is it beyond the sea, that you should say, "Who will cross the sea for us to get it for us and make us hear it, that we may observe it?" But the word is very near you, in your mouth and in your heart, that you may observe it.

Paul quotes this passage in Romans 10:6-8 to emphasize the availability of Christ to all people, and then explains in verses 9-10:

> If you confess with your mouth Jesus as Lord, and believe in your heart that God raised Him from the dead, you will be saved; for with the heart a person believes, resulting in righteousness, and with the mouth he confesses, resulting in salvation.

Jesus came from Heaven to Earth to come close and invite us to follow Him. Jesus is the way, and the truth, and the life. God made Himself and His salvation visible and accessible so that people would come to Him. It is not for a lack of access that people are not saved, but for their refusal to accept Jesus Christ as the Savior.

Seize the moment and draw near to God by putting your faith in the life, death, and resurrection of Jesus Christ, the Living Word, who has come close to you. The victory of God is your faith (1 John 5:4)!

DEUTERONOMY 31
CONFIDENCE IN GOD!

As a military officer, I learned the importance of being confident, and instilling confidence in my soldiers. Confidence is critical to completing the mission.

Moses was 120 years old, he could no longer get around, and he was about to die. What does Moses do? In Deuteronomy 31:3-6, Moses seizes the moment to instill confidence in his people:

> It is the LORD your God who will cross ahead of you; He will destroy these nations before you, and you shall dispossess them. Joshua is the one who will cross ahead of you, just as the LORD has spoken. The LORD will do to them just as He did to Sihon and Og, the kings of the Amorites, and to their land, when He destroyed them. The LORD will deliver them up before you, and you shall do to them according to all the commandments which I have commanded you. Be strong and courageous, do not be afraid or tremble at them, for the LORD your God is the one who goes with you. He will not fail you or forsake you.

Confidence is a powerful motivator, but we must be wise and discerning regarding who or what receives the allegiance of our confidence. Moses was correct to put all his confidence in God. Yes, he called forth Joshua to lead in his place, and charged the priests and elders with their responsibilities, but it was God who was worthy of his confidence.

While I strive to be faithful as a pastor and call forth people to fulfill their callings faithfully in life, it is my ambition that people would put their confidence in Jesus. May you be strong and courageous in the face of your circumstances, because God is with you. He will not fail you or forsake you.

Seize the moment and put your confidence in Jesus! He alone is faithful and true (Revelation 3:14; 19:11).

DEUTERONOMY 32
GOD IS THE ROCK!

What is the most important part of a house? The foundation! If you don't lay a strong foundation, then, no matter what else you do, it is still unstable and insecure. The same is true for our lives.

Before his death, Moses wrote two songs: the Song of Moses (Deuteronomy 32) and the Blessings of Moses (Deuteronomy 33). In psalm-like fashion, these songs serve as memorials to the future generations of Israel. You hear Moses' purpose in writing them in Deuteronomy 32:2, "Let my teaching drop as the rain, my speech distill as the dew, as the droplets on the fresh grass and as the showers on the herb." He wants these songs to serve as a refreshment and a reminder to the future generations so that they may prosper as a people.

In the Song of Moses, God is called, for the first time, "the Rock!" This is found in Deuteronomy 32:3-4, "For I proclaim the name of the LORD; ascribe greatness to our God! The Rock! His work is perfect, for all His ways are just; a God of faithfulness and without injustice, righteous and upright is He." Moses described God as "the Rock," so that the future generations would build their lives and society on His unchanging nature and the stability of His righteous leadership.

Any nation that is not built on God will collapse under the weight of its people's instabilities and insecurities. Do not forsake God, because in doing so you weaken the foundation of your life and your society. Moses explicitly stated this in verses 15-18:

> But Jeshurun grew fat and kicked – You are grown fat, thick, and sleek – Then he forsook God who made him, and scorned the Rock of his salvation. They made Him jealous with strange gods; with abominations they provoked Him to anger. They sacrificed to demons who were not God, to gods whom they have not known, new gods who came lately, whom your fathers did not dread. You neglected the Rock who begot you, and forgot the God who gave you birth.

Seize the moment and build your life upon the Rock! Anchor deep into Jesus because He is the only sure foundation for your life (Matthew 7:24-27). Everything else is shifting sands.

DEUTERONOMY 33
THE TWO BLESSINGS OF THE TWELVE TRIBES!

How often do you pray a blessing over your family and loved ones?

It's been approximately 450-500 years between the two blessings over the twelve tribes of Israel. Moses' final demonstration of leadership was to bless the twelve tribes of Israel. Prior to this, the last recorded blessing of the tribes we have was from Jacob (Israel) himself, right before his death in Genesis 49:33, which says, "When Jacob finished charging his sons, he drew his feet into the bed and breathed his last, and was gathered to his people."

Jacob's blessing was prior to the exodus, and the over 400 years the Israelites would spend in Egypt. Moses led them out of slavery at the age of 80, then led them through their 40 years of wilderness wanderings, until this very moment when he blessed them, as recorded in Deuteronomy 33. Moses blessed the tribes, starting in verse 6 with Reuben, and ending with a beautiful blessing over all of Israel in verses 26-29:

> There is none like the God of Jeshurun [Israel], Who rides the heavens to your help, and through the skies in His majesty. The eternal God is a dwelling place, and underneath are the everlasting arms; and He drove out the enemy from before you, and said, "Destroy!" So Israel dwells in security, the fountain of Jacob secluded, in a land of grain and new wine; His heavens also drop down dew. Blessed are you, O Israel; who is like you, a people saved by the LORD, who is the shield of your help and the sword of your majesty! So your enemies will cringe before you, and you will tread upon their high places.

What a beautiful tradition that we should carry into our families and churches: the blessing of the generations!

Seize the moment and say a blessing over your family and the next generation today! There is no reason to wait 50 years, not to mention 500 years.

Dr. Jerry D. Ingalls

DEUTERONOMY 34
THE DIVINE GIFT OF WISDOM!

We all need wisdom to live our lives on mission for God and His glory, but do we realize that God is the only true source of wisdom?

After Moses blessed the twelve tribes, like Jacob did before he died, he went to the top of the mountain and looked out over Jericho and the beauty of God's Promised Land. His 120 years of sojourning upon the Earth was over, but the journey would continue for Israel as they were about to enter the Promised Land and seize Jericho.

The 40 years of wandering have finally come to an end! Deuteronomy 34:9-12 ends this chapter of Israel's history and begins another, as the leadership baton was passed from Moses to Joshua:

> Now Joshua the son of Nun was filled with the spirit of wisdom, for Moses had laid his hands on him; and the sons of Israel listened to him and did as the LORD had commanded Moses. Since that time no prophet has risen in Israel like Moses, whom the LORD knew face to face, for all the signs and wonders which the LORD sent him to perform in the land of Egypt against Pharaoh, all his servants, and all his land, and for all the mighty power and for all the great terror which Moses performed in the sight of all Israel.

Joshua was given the divine gift of wisdom to lead Israel into the Promised Land. We should pray, like Solomon did in 1 Kings 3:9, for wisdom to lead our families and churches. As we start the next chapter of our lives, let us ask God for His gift of divine wisdom, as commanded in James 1:5, "But if any of you lacks wisdom, let him ask of God, who gives to all generously and without reproach, and it will be given to him."

Seize the moment and seek wisdom from God and His Word!

JOSHUA

JOSHUA 1
BE STRONG AND COURAGEOUS!

The Bible is a history of God's work through real people, with real faith, in real history. When I teach someone how to memorize the order of the books of the Old Testament, I emphasize that the book of Joshua follows the five books of Moses (Genesis, Exodus, Leviticus, Numbers, and Deuteronomy), because Joshua assumed command of the Israelite nation after Moses' death, to fulfill God's promise to enter the Promised Land.

God charged Joshua with this task of leadership in Joshua 1:6-9:

Be strong and courageous, for you shall give this people possession of the land which I swore to their fathers to give them. Only be strong and very courageous; be careful to do according to all the law which Moses My servant commanded you; do not turn from it to the right or to the left, so that you may have success wherever you go. This book of the law shall not depart from your mouth, but you shall meditate on it day and night, so that you may be careful to do according to all that is written in it; for then you will make your way prosperous, and then you will have success. Have I not commanded you? Be strong and courageous! Do not tremble or be dismayed, for the LORD your God is with you wherever you go.

Including verse 18, God tells Joshua to be "strong and courageous" four times in in this opening chapter. People presume that God said this because of the long military campaign ahead, starting with Jericho; while that is true, the only real danger Joshua faced was the people's rebellion against God and His word. Joshua's primary duty and greatest challenge was leading the people spiritually. Without obedience to God, there could be no military victory, nor rest in the land (13-18; Hebrews 4:8-11).

Seize the moment and be strong and courageous to follow God!

JOSHUA 2
RAHAB'S TESTIMONY!

Testimonies about God are powerful and can move people to make important decisions.

In Joshua 2:9-11, Rahab the harlot gave a powerful testimony to the two Israelite spies, who had entered Jericho to scout the land:

> I know that the LORD has given you the land, and that the terror of you has fallen on us, and that all the inhabitants of the land have melted away before you. For we have heard how the LORD dried up the water of the Red Sea before you when you came out of Egypt, and what you did to the two kings of the Amorites who were beyond the Jordan, to Sihon and Og, whom you utterly destroyed. When we heard it, our hearts melted and no courage remained in any man any longer because of you; for the LORD your God, He is God in heaven above and on earth beneath.

Can you imagine how encouraging this must have been for the two spies to hear?

Upon return to Joshua, the two spies told him the whole story of Rahab, and the deal they made with her to redeem her and her household, but they also testified to her words, in verse 24, "Surely the LORD has given all the land into our hands; moreover, all the inhabitants of the land have melted away before us."

What God did through this Canaanite woman's testimony, even though Rahab didn't know it, was confirm His promise from Exodus 15:16, "Terror and dread fall upon them; by the greatness of Your arm they are motionless as stone; until Your people pass over, O LORD, until the people pass over whom You have purchased" (cf. Exodus 23:27). It had begun!

Seize the moment and share your testimony about God with people because you never know how God may use you to lead a person to make an important decision.

JOSHUA 3
CALL UPON THE LIVING GOD!

Do you need God to make a way for you through an impossible situation or difficult season?

There was a significant obstacle between Joshua and the Promised Land – the swelling Jordan River at harvest time (Joshua 3:15). God emboldened Joshua, in Joshua 3:7, by drawing his memory back to what He had done for Moses at the crossing of the Red Sea (Exodus 14), "This day I will begin to exalt you in the sight of all Israel, that they may know that just as I have been with Moses, I will be with you."

In response, Joshua encouraged the Israelites in verses 10-13:

By this you shall know that the living God is among you, ... Behold, the ark of the covenant of the Lord of all the earth is crossing over ahead of you into the Jordan. ... It shall come about when the soles of the feet of the priests who carry the ark of the LORD, the Lord of all the earth, rest in the waters of the Jordan, the waters of the Jordan will be cut off, and the waters which are flowing down from above will stand in one heap.

Joshua described God as the "living God" to testify of His active presence to make a way in an impossible situation. When you face obstacles in your life, the living God is with you!

Listen to Daniel 6:26b-27 and the powerful testimony of God's active presence when He rescues His people from impossible situations:

For He is the living God and enduring forever, and His kingdom is one which will not be destroyed, and His dominion will be forever. He delivers and rescues and performs signs and wonders in heaven and on earth, who has also delivered Daniel from the power of the lions.

Seize the moment and call upon the living God in your impossible situations.

JOSHUA 4
A MEMORIAL STONE!

What are the ways you memorialize God's saving work in your life?

Joshua 4:20-24 concludes the two-chapter focus on Israel's miraculous crossing of the Jordan River with Joshua's command to commemorate God's mighty hand bringing His people into the Promised Land:

> Those twelve stones which they had taken from the Jordan, Joshua set up at Gilgal. He said to the sons of Israel, "When your children ask their fathers in time to come, saying, 'What are these stones?' then you shall inform your children, saying, 'Israel crossed this Jordan on dry ground.' For the LORD your God dried up the waters of the Jordan before you until you had crossed, just as the LORD your God had done to the Red Sea, which He dried up before us until we had crossed; that all the peoples of the earth may know that the hand of the LORD is mighty, so that you may fear the LORD your God forever."

Joshua did not want the people to forget, so a man from each tribe was required to take a stone from the center of the Jordan River and carry it to Gilgal. The establishment of this memorial was costly, and it was strategically located in the foothold of the Promised Land. The message was clear: God did this!

The night before His crucifixion, Jesus established the commemoration of His own sacrificial death with the institution of the Lord's Supper in Luke 22:19, "And when He had taken some bread and given thanks, He broke it and gave it to them, saying, 'This is My body which is given for you; do this in remembrance of Me'" (cf. 1 Corinthians 11:23-26).

Seize the moment and routinely remember God's mighty hand which brings you into His promises through the Cross of Jesus Christ. This is the victory of God for you and me!

JOSHUA 5
WAIT UPON GOD'S PLANS!

The nation of Israel was now poised to take the Promised Land, but God had not yet revealed His battle plans to Joshua. Instead of revealing the plan, God ordered Joshua to circumcise the generation who had been born in the wilderness (2-8), and to celebrate the Passover on the "desert plains of Jericho" (9-10). Afterwards, the manna that had fed God's people for forty years unexpectedly stopped, and God's people were now dependent on God's provision of the Promised Land for their daily bread (11-12).

Can you imagine the burden of responsibility Joshua was experiencing?

Still with no plan, Joshua goes to look upon Jericho, a heavily fortified city prepared for a siege. Now, with his people in need of the food that this city's crops would provide, Joshua contemplates his next steps. In Joshua 5:13-15, God reveals His abundant provision:

> Now it came about when Joshua was by Jericho, that he lifted up his eyes and looked, and behold, a man was standing opposite him with his sword drawn in his hand, and Joshua went to him and said to him, "Are you for us or for our adversaries?" He said, "No; rather I indeed come now as captain of the host of the LORD." And Joshua fell on his face to the earth, and bowed down, and said to him, "What has my lord to say to his servant?" The captain of the LORD'S host said to Joshua, "Remove your sandals from your feet, for the place where you are standing is holy." And Joshua did so.

God's plan was to lead the battle! God's captain, with his sword drawn, was ready to lead Joshua and His people to victory. Can you imagine how relieved Joshua must have felt?

Seize the moment and wait upon God, His plans are for your good and His glory (Psalm 46:10-11)!

Dr. Jerry D. Ingalls

JOSHUA 6
ABSOLUTE TRUST!

Do you understand what it means to be a good soldier of Christ Jesus?

In today's story, Joshua exemplified what Jesus praises in the centurion (Matthew 8:5-13) and how Paul exhorts Timothy (2 Timothy 2:3-4). Joshua received the battle plan from the "captain of the LORD's host" (Joshua 5:14-15), and he executed it with great faith, even though it was unusual. God's plan would have been unlike anything Joshua had ever heard. God directed him in Joshua 6:3-5 to lead the army to walk around the city wall of Jericho for seven days, once per day for six days, and seven times on the seventh day. Upon completion of the seventh lap on the seventh day, the priests were to blow seven trumpets and the people were to shout out with a great shout. Then the wall of the city would fall flat.

I can only imagine how Joshua, an experienced military leader, could think of all the reasons this plan would not work. And if this was Joshua's burning bush moment, wouldn't he, like Moses, second guess and argue against every point of God's plan (Exodus 3:10-4:13)? But he doesn't! Joshua executes the word of God in verses 6-7:

> So Joshua the son of Nun called the priests and said to them, "Take up the ark of the covenant, and let seven priests carry seven trumpets of rams' horns before the ark of the LORD." Then he said to the people, "Go forward, and march around the city, and let the armed men go on before the ark of the LORD."

The battle for Jericho was a decisive victory that brought great glory to God, and fame to Joshua (27), all because Joshua believed God and acted with absolute trust in His Commander.

Seize the moment and, like a good soldier, believe God, submit to His authority, and obey His Word in your daily life.

JOSHUA 7
A STARTLING DEFEAT!

Have you ever held a grudge or lingered on a hurtful thought? I have hidden things in my mind and heart that are not of God, and they have caused me to become weak and discouraged.

Joshua 7 is a sad story that starts with the startling defeat of the army of Israel at Ai (1-5). There was no military reason for their defeat, especially after the amazing victory at Jericho. The defeat was a spiritual one.

Joshua leads the people back to God in verse 13:

Rise up! Consecrate the people and say, "Consecrate yourselves for tomorrow, for thus the LORD, the God of Israel, has said, 'There are things under the ban in your midst, O Israel. You cannot stand before your enemies until you have removed the things under the ban from your midst.'"

The defeat was caused by the sin of Achan, who coveted the spoils of war and greedily hid in his tent that which God forbade (16-26). What he thought would go unnoticed, and had justified in his mind and heart to help his family survive, caused great devastation to the nation.

The startling defeats often begin in our heads and hearts. Consecrate yourself to God and dedicate your heart and mind to Him by dwelling on thoughts that are worthy of praise (Philippians 4:8).

Psalm 139:23-24 teaches us the prayer of examen so that we don't fall into the same trap of Achan, "Search me, O God, and know my heart; try me and know my anxious thoughts; and see if there be any hurtful way in me, and lead me in the everlasting way."

Seize the moment and consecrate yourself to God. Invite the Holy Spirit to inspect and purify your heart and mind of anything that should not be there; surrender it to God.

JOSHUA 8
OBEY GOD!

Have you ever wondered why some things are permissible, while others are not? While I'm a rule-follower at heart, I do find it very interesting that, in my lifetime, I have watched things once called evil be deemed good, and that which used to be considered good become perceived as morally wrong. It can be confusing, especially if you are focused on our ever-changing culture.

The Israelites are facing the city of Ai after suffering a defeat because of the sin of Achan. Joshua has received a new battle plan from God. Joshua 8:1-2 captures a significant change in God's commands between the battles of Jericho and Ai:

> Do not fear or be dismayed. Take all the people of war with you and arise, go up to Ai; see, I have given into your hand the king of Ai, his people, his city, and his land. You shall do to Ai and its king just as you did to Jericho and its king; you shall take only its spoil and its cattle as plunder for yourselves. Set an ambush for the city behind it.

After the punishment of Achan, and the people's willingness to root the evil out of their camp, God promised to give them the city of Ai. This time the Israelites were allowed to take plunder. If only Achan had waited upon the Lord to provide the increase!

In 1 Samuel 15:22-23a, Saul justified his disobedience to God's battle plans, but Samuel explained what was most important:

> Has the LORD as much delight in burnt offerings and sacrifices as in obeying the voice of the LORD? Behold, to obey is better than sacrifice, and to heed than the fat of rams. For rebellion is as the sin of divination, and insubordination is as iniquity and idolatry.

Seize the moment and obey God! Submit yourself to His ways as a good soldier of Christ Jesus (2 Timothy 2:3-4).

JOSHUA 9
ASK GOD FIRST!

Have you ever been duped, swindled, hoodwinked, deceived, defrauded, or cheated?

Joshua and the leaders were hustled by the Gibeonites after Israel's victories at Jericho and Ai. A large coalition of neighboring peoples was forming against the Israelites to fight (1-2), when a caravan arrived at their camp. Joshua 9:4-5 describes what Joshua and the leaders found upon inspection, "worn-out sacks on their donkeys, and wineskins worn-out and torn and mended, and worn-out and patched sandals on their feet, and worn-out clothes on themselves; and all the bread of their provision was dry and had become crumbled."

Joshua and the leaders did their due diligence to inspect and to interview them. Everything seemed to line up with their story of being from far away, and the people persuasively flattered the Israelite military victories and God's miraculous powers. So, Joshua made a treaty with the Gibeonites.

The Israelite leaders seemed to have done everything they should have done to make an informed decision. However, in their action was their error; they were trusting in *themselves* to make the decision! Joshua 9:14 clearly states where they went wrong, "So the men of Israel ... did not ask for the counsel of the LORD."

Did Joshua get caught up in his role as a military commander and forget his spiritual responsibilities? Why did he forget to ask God?

When Joshua was commissioned for his leadership role in Numbers 27:18-21, he was commanded to inquire of God, "Moreover, he shall stand before Eleazar the priest, who shall inquire for him by the judgment of the Urim before the LORD." This was his primary responsibility, as it is for every spiritual leader – to pray and seek God in every decision!

Seize the moment and ask God first! Before you make any commitments or decisions, seek God in the Word, and through prayer.

JOSHUA 10
GOD HONORS INTEGRITY!

In Joshua 10:6-7, Joshua demonstrated the highest form of integrity in his sacrificial decision to uphold the treaty with the Gibeonites even though the Gibeonites made the treaty using deception (Joshua 9):

> Then the men of Gibeon sent word to Joshua to the camp at Gilgal, saying, "Do not abandon your servants; come up to us quickly and save us and help us, for all the kings of the Amorites that live in the hill country have assembled against us." So Joshua went up from Gilgal, he and all the people of war with him and all the valiant warriors.

Joshua faithfully responded and, in turn, God honored his integrity by giving him a successful military campaign, including the conquest of a substantial section of the Promised Land, as summarized in Joshua 10:41-43:

> Joshua struck them from Kadesh-barnea even as far as Gaza, and all the country of Goshen even as far as Gibeon. Joshua captured all these kings and their lands at one time, because the LORD, the God of Israel, fought for Israel. So Joshua and all Israel with him returned to the camp at Gilgal.

All this happened because Joshua let his yes be yes. Read Joshua 10, and you will be amazed at God's supernatural intervention to bring about the victory. But the most amazing miracle of this story is not in God sending the large hailstones (11), or the stopping of the sun and the moon (12-14), but, rather, the integrity of a man named Joshua to honor his promise and lead his army in the defense of Gibeon. God honored Joshua's integrity!

While many marvel at these supernatural events, and pray for God's direct activity in today's world, I pray that God's people would live with the integrity of Joshua.

Seize the moment and let your yes be yes (Matthew 5:37)! God will respond because He honors integrity!

JOSHUA 11
THE DEFEAT OF THE GIANTS!

Is there a "giant" from your past that needs to be defeated so that you can answer God's call upon your life?

Joshua 11:21-23 concludes the conquest of the Promised Land with the defeat of the giants – the Anakim:

> Then Joshua came at that time and cut off the Anakim from the hill country, from Hebron, from Debir, from Anab and from all the hill country of Judah and from all the hill country of Israel. Joshua utterly destroyed them with their cities. There were no Anakim left in the land of the sons of Israel; only in Gaza, in Gath, and in Ashdod some remained. So Joshua took the whole land, according to all that the LORD had spoken to Moses, and Joshua gave it for an inheritance to Israel according to their divisions by their tribes. Thus the land had rest from war.

This was a necessary conclusion to the conquest. Numbers 13:32-33 records how it was the Anakim who struck such a fear in the spies that they gave the bad report, causing the people to rebel against God, which led to their forty years of wilderness wandering:

> So they gave out to the sons of Israel a bad report of the land which they had spied out, saying, "The land through which we have gone, in spying it out, is a land that devours its inhabitants; and all the people whom we saw in it are men of great size. There also we saw the Nephilim (the sons of Anak are part of the Nephilim); and we became like grasshoppers in our own sight, and so we were in their sight."

In Deuteronomy 9:1-3, God spoke directly to the people's fear of the giants when they stood at the entrance of the Promised Land. God knew of their historical fear, and was pledging His protection, which he fulfilled in Joshua 11:21-23.

Seize the moment and do not fear any of the "giants" from your past. Trust God and watch Him win the victory in and through your life today.

JOSHUA 12
GET A LAY OF THE LAND!

Do you like maps? I do! Still, I get overwhelmed by all the locations in the Bible. Keeping it straight is like trying to remember the location of the 92 counties in Indiana, and I still get lost in Henry County!

Joshua 12 gives you a lay of the Promised Land. While verses 1-6 reviewed the land that Moses conquered to the east of the Jordan River, verses 7-24 cataloged the conquest of the western side of the Promised Land:

> Now these are the kings of the land whom Joshua and the sons of Israel defeated beyond the Jordan toward the west, from Baal-gad in the valley of Lebanon even as far as Mount Halak, which rises toward Seir; and Joshua gave it to the tribes of Israel as a possession according to their divisions (7).

Now, pull out a biblical map because verses 9-24 list the 31 cities and their kings that were defeated: 16 in the southern portion and 15 in the northern portion. Surprisingly, we find that these kings were like today's equivalent of a group of disjointed mayors who reigned over city-states with only local authority. In all, these 31 kings ruled over a land approximately 150 miles from north to south and 50 miles from east to west, averaging about 252 square miles per king. By comparison, Indiana has a maximum dimension of 250 miles north to south and 145 miles east to west with 92 counties in it; Henry County covers 392 square miles.

Imagine how much harder it would have been on Israel had these 31 kings forged an alliance and worked together, instead of only protecting their own local self-interest.

Seize the moment and take time to get a lay of the land in today's divided world. Pray!

JOSHUA 13
A BETTER INVESTMENT!

How are you investing for the future? In Joshua 13:14 & 33, it was emphasized that the Levites did not receive an inheritance of land:

> Only to the tribe of Levi he did not give an inheritance; the offerings by fire to the LORD, the God of Israel, are their inheritance, as He spoke to him. ... But to the tribe of Levi, Moses did not give an inheritance; the LORD, the God of Israel, is their inheritance, as He had promised to them.

History would prove that the inheritance of Levi, who did not receive land, was far better, and more secure, than that of the firstborn Reuben, of Gad, and of the half-tribe of Manasseh (7-32). Like Lot had done in Genesis 13:11, they chose as their own what appeared to be the best of the land, and, like Lot before them, there were consequences to their choice:

> Their territories had no natural boundaries to the east and were therefore constantly exposed to invasion by the Moabites, Canaanites, Arameans, Midianites, Amalekites, and others. And when the king of Assyria looked covetously toward Canaan, Reuben, Gad and the half-tribe of Manasseh were the first to be carried into captivity by the Assyrian armies (1 Chron. 5:26).[10]

While the Levites had no inheritance of land, their inheritance of the God of Israel could not be taken from them and would ultimately be the only source of hope for the nation of Israel. In Matthew 6:19-21, Jesus teaches His followers to make better investments:

> Do not store up for yourselves treasures on earth, where moth and rust destroy, and where thieves break in and steal. But store up for yourselves treasures in heaven, where neither moth nor rust destroys, and where thieves do not break in or steal; for where your treasure is, there your heart will be also.

Seize the moment by choosing to make a better investment!

---

[10] Donald K. Campbell, "Joshua," in *The Bible Knowledge Commentary: An Exposition of the Scriptures*, ed. J. F. Walvoord and R. B. Zuck, vol. 1 (Wheaton, IL: Victor Books, 1985), 356.

JOSHUA 14
CALEB, A WHOLEHEARTED MAN!

Are you willing to live wholeheartedly for God, even if you must wait a long time to receive God's reward for your faithfulness?

After forty-five years of waiting, Joshua 14:13-14 was a significant moment in the life of Caleb, the faithful spy who stood for God and received the promise to survive the forty years of wilderness wanderings, and to find rest in the inheritance of the Promised Land:

> So Joshua blessed him and gave Hebron to Caleb the son of Jephunneh for an inheritance. Therefore, Hebron became the inheritance of Caleb the son of Jephunneh the Kenizzite until this day, because he followed the LORD God of Israel fully.

Caleb was forty years old when he was sent out to spy the land. Upon returning, after forty days, he gave his faithful report to Moses in Numbers 13:30, "We should by all means go up and take possession of it, for we will surely overcome it." From their generation, only Joshua and Caleb were allowed to enter it. Even that promise took a long time to unfold, as Caleb reminded Joshua in Joshua 14:10-12, when he made his request for God's promise to be honored:

> Now behold, the LORD has let me live, just as He spoke, these forty-five years, from the time that the LORD spoke this word to Moses, when Israel walked in the wilderness; and now behold, I am eighty-five years old today. ... Now then, give me this hill country about which the LORD spoke on that day.

Though rejected by man, Caleb was accepted by God and continued to live a faithful life. Caleb was a wholehearted man who followed God fully! In Colossians 3:23, Paul exhorts us to do the same, "Whatever you do, do your work heartily, as for the Lord rather than for men."

Seize the moment and be a wholehearted person! Grow in your character as you learn to trust God through seasons of waiting upon Him.

JOSHUA 15
CALEB, AN 85-YEAR-OLD CHAMPION FOR GOD!

Caleb's story continued in Joshua 15, as Judah claimed their portion of the Promised Land. Not surprisingly, the land that Caleb was given required him to demonstrate, once again, the same faith that allowed him to give a faithful report forty-five years previously. Pay special attention to an important detail about the land Joshua entrusted to Caleb in Joshua 15:13-14:

> Now he gave to Caleb the son of Jephunneh a portion among the sons of Judah, according to the command of the LORD to Joshua, namely, Kiriath-arba, Arba being the father of Anak (that is, Hebron). Caleb drove out from there the three sons of Anak: Sheshai and Ahiman and Talmai, the children of Anak.

There be giants in the land! The "three sons of Anak" are most likely the same giants that the spies would have seen forty-five years prior, for which the unfaithful spies reported in Numbers 13:33, "There also we saw the Nephilim (the sons of Anak are part of the Nephilim); and we became like grasshoppers in our own sight, and so we were in their sight." Moses spoke of these same ones in Deuteronomy 9:2, "A people great and tall, the sons of the Anakim, whom you know and of whom you have heard it said, 'Who can stand before the sons of Anak?'"

Caleb was a rock star – an 85-year-old champion for God! But I want you to see one last detail; Caleb inspired the next generation with his faith. Othniel, who would become the first judge of Israel (Judges 3:9), took up Caleb's challenge to continue the conquest (15-17; cf. Judges 1:11-13). Caleb's life of faithfulness was contagious, and was passed on to Othniel (2 Timothy 2:2).

Seize the moment and walk faithfully with God! You never know who you will inspire to live like a champion for God.

JOSHUA 16
DESTROY SIN!

Is there something in your life that you are toying with, or tolerating, that you know you should remove or destroy today?

Joshua 16:10 says this about Ephraim's possession of the Promised Land, "But they did not drive out the Canaanites who lived in Gezer, so the Canaanites live in the midst of Ephraim to this day, and they became forced laborers" (cf. Judges 1:29).

This may not seem to be a big deal, but it was an act of disobedience to enslave the Canaanites in a city within the Promised Land. Moses' instruction from Deuteronomy 20:16-18 was to remove them from the land, "so that they may not teach you to do according to all their detestable things which they have done for their gods, so that you would sin against the LORD your God" (18).

Ephraim's disobedience to God may have seemed good at first, but it proved to be a fatal mistake for their future generations. Whether the Israelites had battle fatigue and simply could not remove them, or they were greedy and wanted a local workforce, their disobedience led to future compromise, as God warned, and conflict throughout the land.

Paul explained of spiritual warfare in 2 Corinthians 10:3-4, "For though we walk in the flesh, we do not war according to the flesh, for the weapons of our warfare are not of the flesh, but divinely powerful for the destruction of fortresses." We cannot toy with or tolerate any sin because, in time, it will become a stronghold for our destruction. While it may seem to be adding value or pleasure to your life at first, I promise you that it is not for your good in the long run.

Seize the moment and deal a decisive blow to sin in your life today!

JOSHUA 17
CULTIVATE A COURAGEOUS CONFIDENCE!

Where does the confidence to act courageously come from? Hebrews 11:1-2 provides the answer, "Now faith is the assurance of things hoped for, the conviction of things not seen. For by it the men of old gained approval."

Courage is not an absence of fear, but rather a trained mindset to act according to your faith in the face of fear. Joshua 17:16-18 spotlights Joshua's leadership skills as he directly dealt with the two tribes of Ephraim and Manasseh, the sons of Joseph, who complained after they received their allotments of the Promised Land:

> The sons of Joseph said, "The hill country is not enough for us, and all the Canaanites who live in the valley land have chariots of iron, both those who are in Beth-shean and its towns and those who are in the valley of Jezreel." Joshua spoke to the house of Joseph, to Ephraim and Manasseh, saying, "You are a numerous people and have great power; you shall not have one lot only, but the hill country shall be yours. For though it is a forest, you shall clear it, and to its farthest borders it shall be yours; for you shall drive out the Canaanites, even though they have chariots of iron and though they are strong."

What was the difference between Caleb, of the tribe of Judah, whose allotment of land included giants (the sons of Anak), and these two tribes, whose land included Canaanites with iron chariots? Caleb had cultivated an instinctual confidence trained by his faith in God!

Joshua's task as the leader of the people was to lead the people to live with this same kind of courageous confidence in God – "Be strong and courageous! Do not tremble or be dismayed, for the LORD your God is with you wherever you go" (Joshua 1:9).

Seize the moment and cultivate a courageous confidence by training yourself to respond to your fears with faith (1 Timothy 4:7-8).

JOSHUA 18
FULFILL YOUR RESPONSIBILITIES!

Procrastination is not the best strategy to getting a job done. Do you struggle with putting off a job because it requires time, energy, or money to get it accomplished? Is there a promise you need to keep, or a responsibility you need to fulfill, but keep putting it off?

Caleb is facing giants, while the tribe of Judah settles its allotment of land. The two tribes of Manasseh and Ephraim are mustering up the courage to deal with the Canaanites and their chariots of iron. With the two and a half tribes settling on the east side of the Jordan River, there are seven tribes left to settle the Promised Land. We will watch them do so in Joshua 18 and 19, with Joshua 18:1-3 setting the stage:

> Then the whole congregation of the sons of Israel assembled themselves at Shiloh, and set up the tent of meeting there; and the land was subdued before them. There remained among the sons of Israel seven tribes who had not divided their inheritance. So Joshua said to the sons of Israel, "How long will you put off entering to take possession of the land which the LORD, the God of your fathers, has given you?

Joshua knew that every day these seven tribes delayed in occupying the land, the people of the land would fortify their cities and prepare their defenses. As a military leader, his people's procrastination was slowly spelling disaster for all of them. As a spiritual leader, Joshua knew the people's procrastination was nothing short of disobedience to God. He had to act immediately to motivate a recalcitrant people to fulfill their responsibilities to God and to one another. God's promises call His people to action!

Seize the moment and fulfill your responsibilities! You will feel better, everyone around you will be blessed by your faithfulness, and God will be glorified. Prayerfully take a decisive step today!

JOSHUA 19
THE POSITION OF HONOR!

Joshua was a humble man – a servant leader! We see this clearly demonstrated in Joshua 19:49-50:

> When they finished apportioning the land for inheritance by its borders, the sons of Israel gave an inheritance in their midst to Joshua the son of Nun. In accordance with the command of the LORD they gave him the city for which he asked, Timnath-serah in the hill country of Ephraim. So he built the city and settled in it.

It is important to point out that Caleb's inheritance of land was the first to be given in Canaan (Joshua 14:6-15), whereas Joshua's inheritance was the last to be apportioned. The two faithful spies, the only remaining men of their generation allowed to enter the Promised Land, bookended the dividing of the Promised Land. Joshua could easily have taken the choice of the land for himself, but that was not the way of humility, taught to him by Moses (Numbers 12:3). Joshua chose to give the honored position to Caleb instead of demanding it for himself.

Jesus taught His disciples this lesson about humility in Luke 14:8-11:

> When you are invited by someone to a wedding feast, do not take the place of honor, for someone more distinguished than you may have been invited by him, and he who invited you both will come and say to you, "Give your place to this man," and then in disgrace you proceed to occupy the last place. But when you are invited, go and recline at the last place, so that when the one who has invited you comes, he may say to you, "Friend, move up higher"; then you will have honor in the sight of all who are at the table with you. For everyone who exalts himself will be humbled, and he who humbles himself will be exalted.

Seize the moment and put another person before yourself today. Be a servant leader, and, in doing so, follow the example of Jesus; you will be blessed for doing so (John 13:12-17).

Dr. Jerry D. Ingalls

JOSHUA 20
GOD IS OUR REFUGE!

Is your home a safe place? Are you a sanctuary for people to find peace and rest?

By God's grace, the nation of Israel had conquered and apportioned the Promised Land. It was time to ensure the protection of due process in God's special place through the establishment of the six refuge cities, three on either side of the Jordan River. Joshua 20:9 summarizes:

> These were the appointed cities for all the sons of Israel and for the stranger who sojourns among them, that whoever kills any person unintentionally may flee there, and not die by the hand of the avenger of blood until he stands before the congregation.

Interestingly, and to the confusion of modern-day scholars, there are no biblical accounts of this system of refuge cities being utilized, in those initial days of chaos in the time of the Judges, in the years of order under the monarchy, or even during the dark days of the divided kingdom. The closest allusion we have is from King David's words about refuge in God, not in any specific city, found in Psalm 46:1, "God is our refuge and strength, a very present help in trouble."

It is speculated that the system either worked so well, or so completely fell apart, that there was no reason to highlight it in the biblical account. Either way, it is widely agreed upon that the system foreshadowed God's grace granted to His people in Jesus Christ. Hebrews 6:18b reminds us that a believer's relationship with God through Jesus Christ grants us this grace, "we who have taken refuge would have strong encouragement to take hold of the hope set before us." In Romans 8:1, Paul declares for all who have found their refuge in Jesus Christ, "Therefore there is now no condemnation for those who are in Christ Jesus."

Seize the moment and flee from sin and death into the everlasting arms of Jesus Christ!

JOSHUA 21
GOD IS A PROMISE KEEPER!

Joshua 21:41-43 summarizes the fulfillment of an old promise:

> All the cities of the Levites in the midst of the possession of the sons of Israel were forty-eight cities with their pasture lands. These cities each had its surrounding pasture lands; thus it was with all these cities. So the LORD gave Israel all the land which He had sworn to give to their fathers, and they possessed it and lived in it.

The Levites did not receive an allocation of the Promised Land, like the rest of the tribes of Israel, but these priests and temple workers still needed homes to live in, places to raise their children, and pastureland to feed their animals (Numbers 18:20). So, God spoke to Moses, promising the Levites cities in Numbers 35:1-8.

It was up to Joshua to ensure that the promise was kept. Under his leadership, all the tribes have had their land allocated to them, the six refuge cities have been declared, the forty-eight Levite cities have been selected, and the tabernacle has been centralized at Shiloh. Joshua 21:44-45 captures this crowning moment's significance to the nation of Israel:

> And the LORD gave them rest on every side, according to all that He had sworn to their fathers, and no one of all their enemies stood before them; the LORD gave all their enemies into their hand. Not one of the good promises which the LORD had made to the house of Israel failed; all came to pass.

God is a promise keeper! While there was much work to do to settle the land, and, we know, there is much about their future that was not to be envied, God's people stopped at this moment in time, and this place in their history, to celebrate God's faithfulness to keep His promises.

Seize the moment and celebrate God's faithfulness to keep His promises to you! Like Joshua, play a part in God's plan by being a promise keeper yourself.

JOSHUA 22
GO TO THE PERSON!

How do you respond when someone does something you don't like, or don't agree with? Do you seek clarification from them?

The warriors from the tribes of Reuben and Gad, and the half-tribe of Manasseh, were ready to head home after a long military campaign. Their families had been left behind on the other side of the Jordan River, and they were ready to be reunited after fulfilling their obligations. Before they departed, Joshua reminded them that the greatest threat to the security of the Promised Land was from the enemy within – the unfaithfulness of God's people! Joshua commanded them with a succinct, six-point sermon found in the one verse of Joshua 22:5:

> Only be very careful to observe the commandment and the law which Moses the servant of the LORD commanded you, to love the LORD your God and walk in all His ways and keep His commandments and hold fast to Him and serve Him with all your heart and with all your soul.

Joshua knew that the unity of Israel would be quickly tested. Not only would the tribes be spread out throughout the Promised Land, and separated by such landmarks as the Jordan River, but they were going to have to trust one another to remain faithful to God and His Law. He was right! Even before the departing tribes crossed the Jordan, they built a large altar, which caused chaos back in the camp (10-34). Even though the situation was quickly resolved, because the leaders went to them and sought clarification for their actions, the congregation had been ready to go to war.

The tribes passed judgment on each other before checking anyone's motivations! Have you ever done that to someone?

Seize the moment and go to the person to seek clarification on what they did, and why they did it (Matthew 18:15). Fill the gap with trust until you know for sure.

JOSHUA 23
CLING TO GOD!

Is your relationship with God like a sticky note, that can be detached and reattached with ease, or is it like a piece of wood glued to the wall with super glue where separation is difficult and damaging?

Joshua, as he begins his farewell address, uses the phrase, "cling to," twice. In the positive, Joshua commands the people in Joshua 23:8, "But you are to cling to the LORD your God, as you have done to this day." In the negative, Joshua warns the people in verses 12-13:

> For if you ever go back and cling to the rest of these nations, these which remain among you, and intermarry with them, so that you associate with them and they with you, know with certainty that the LORD your God will not continue to drive these nations out from before you; but they will be a snare and a trap to you, and a whip on your sides and thorns in your eyes, until you perish from off this good land which the LORD your God has given you.

It is in this second usage that we get the full extent of this word's meaning, and Joshua's intent for using it, because its earliest connotations are of marriage, from Genesis 2:24: "For this reason a man shall leave his father and his mother, and *be joined to* his wife; and they shall become one flesh" [italics added]. Both Jesus and Paul quote this, that a husband and wife are to leave their family of origin and *cleave* [cling!] to one another to make something new (Matthew 19:5; Mark 10:7; 1 Corinthians 6:16; Ephesians 5:31).

God designed us to become permanently affixed to Him, and to our spouse – to be blessed by our life of faith and devotion! He wants us to understand we should expect to be destroyed by the breaking of our vows.

Seize the moment and cling to God with all your heart, soul, mind, and strength (Matthew 22:37). Maintain your vows with integrity!

JOSHUA 24
AS FOR ME AND MY HOUSE!

Every generation comes to an end, but how will they finish their race? What will their legacy be to the next generation?

Joshua's farewell address contains a very famous challenge, found in Joshua 24:14-15:

> Now, therefore, fear the LORD and serve Him in sincerity and truth; and put away the gods which your fathers served beyond the River and in Egypt, and serve the LORD. If it is disagreeable in your sight to serve the LORD, choose for yourselves today whom you will serve: whether the gods which your fathers served which were beyond the River, or the gods of the Amorites in whose land you are living; but as for me and my house, we will serve the LORD.

Joshua lived 110 years and served God faithfully throughout his life. He experienced God's rescue from Egypt, including the ten plagues, the miracles of the Exodus, and God's miraculous provision through the forty years of wilderness wanderings. Having personally witnessed the power of God, under the mentorship of Moses, he was charged with leading the conquest of the Promised Land.

Joshua 24:31 concludes of Joshua's life, "Israel served the LORD all the days of Joshua and all the days of the elders who survived Joshua, and had known all the deeds of the LORD which He had done for Israel." He accomplished the purpose of his life, and, before he died, Joshua challenged the next generation to be faithful to God, just as Moses had done in Deuteronomy, and just as every faithful leader of every generation must do. Joshua did all that was expected of him. The rest was now up to the next generation.

Have you fulfilled your purpose in your generation?

Seize the moment and choose this day whom you will serve! May our lives, today, inspire the next generation to live for God.

JUDGES

JUDGES 1
THE POWER OF STORY!

We are shaped by the stories we tell. Stories reveal our worldview — what we believe about God, the world we live in, people, and the purpose of our existence. What do the stories you tell reveal about your worldview?

Judges 1 is a historical recap with theological intention. It starts with these words in verse 1, "Now it came about after the death of Joshua that the sons of Israel inquired of the LORD, saying, 'Who shall go up first for us against the Canaanites, to fight against them?'"

The book of Judges explains what happened in the Promised Land, so that future generations would be warned and learn from their mistakes. God rescued Israel from Egypt, then, under Moses' leadership, they forged a new national identity through forty years in the wilderness, until Joshua assumed command and led them into their inheritance.

God commanded them to conquer all the nations of the Promised Land and to make no treaties with them, so that they could continue to build their own national and religious identity around God and His Law. God warned them of the consequences of not obeying His command.

Judges 1 makes it obvious that Israel had failed in fulfilling God's command. Moses and Joshua were dead, the people were living in the Promised Land, and everything should have been amazing, but it was not! Judges explains that it wasn't amazing because, without strong leadership, people do not obey God, but, rather, they do their own thing! Judges 21:25, the final verse of the entire book summarizes the theological intent behind the story told in the book of Judges, "In those days there was no king in Israel; everyone did what was right in his own eyes."

Seize the moment and obey God's commands — proclaim the better story of Jesus Christ, the King of Kings!

JUDGES 2
MAKING RIGHT CHOICES!

There are consequences to choices. God's Word is clear that obedience leads to blessings, and disobedience manifests curses. Before his death, Joshua had confronted the nation with a choice (Joshua 24:14-15). While they told Joshua they would remain faithful to the God who rescued them from Egypt, and brought them through the desert into the Promised Land, their actions proved otherwise. Judges 2:20-23 closes with a summary statement of Israel's condition after Joshua's death:

> So the anger of the LORD burned against Israel, and He said, "Because this nation has transgressed My covenant which I commanded their fathers and has not listened to My voice, I also will no longer drive out before them any of the nations which Joshua left when he died, in order to test Israel by them, whether they will keep the way of the LORD to walk in it as their fathers did, or not." So the LORD allowed those nations to remain, not driving them out quickly; and He did not give them into the hand of Joshua.

There are two reasons listed in this passage for why God was no longer going to drive out the nations before Israel as He had during the conquest of the Promised Land. First, it was an act of discipline for their transgressions of His covenant. Second, God desired to test their faithfulness, to see if "they will keep the way of the LORD." According to Deuteronomy 8:2, this was the same reason God led them in the wilderness for forty years, "You shall remember all the way which the LORD your God has led you in the wilderness these forty years, that He might humble you, testing you, to know what was in your heart, whether you would keep His commandments or not."

Seize the moment and obey God's commandments. He cares deeply about your choices, and He wants you to trust Him. God desires your heart, and your choices reflect who is on the throne of your heart.

JUDGES 3
A VICIOUS CYCLE!

Have you ever been caught in a vicious cycle that seemed to keep you stuck in a bad place, or prevented you from making forward progress in an area of your life? Unfortunately, a common cycle that 20% of spouses suffer is the vicious cycle of domestic violence; the cycle runs this way: tension builds in the relationship until there is an incident, which is followed by the honeymoon phase, which is followed by calm as the tension starts to build again.

Judges 3:9-14 describes the vicious cycle of violence in which Israel was caught:

> When the sons of Israel cried to the LORD, the LORD raised up a deliverer for the sons of Israel to deliver them, Othniel the son of Kenaz, Caleb's younger brother. The Spirit of the LORD came upon him, and he judged Israel. When he went out to war, the LORD gave Cushan-rishathaim king of Mesopotamia into his hand, so that he prevailed over Cushan-rishathaim. Then the land had rest forty years. And Othniel the son of Kenaz died. Now the sons of Israel again did evil in the sight of the LORD. So the LORD strengthened Eglon the king of Moab against Israel, because they had done evil in the sight of the LORD. And he gathered to himself the sons of Ammon and Amalek; and he went and defeated Israel, and they possessed the city of the palm trees. The sons of Israel served Eglon the king of Moab eighteen years.

Sin ensnared Israel in what we are going to see as a vicious cycle throughout the book of Judges. The people suffered in bondage and cried out to God for deliverance. God responded and raised up a powerful military leader who rescued them. They lived in peace for an extended period, until they did evil in the sight of God and another invader defeated them. This happened repeatedly, all because they wouldn't consistently remain obedient to God and His ways. They became complacent in times of peace and prosperity!

Seize the moment and break the vicious cycles in your life by returning to God today! Defeat complacency by committing yourself to growing stronger in your walk with Jesus.

JUDGES 4
PARTNERSHIPS FOR THE GLORY OF GOD!

Partnerships are necessary for life! There would not be a new generation of babies born if it were not for the partnerships of men and women coming together; healthy partnerships are required to bring thriving to our homes, churches, and lives.

Deborah the prophetess was judging Israel, as recorded in Judges 4:4-5:

> Now Deborah, a prophetess, the wife of Lappidoth, was judging Israel at that time. She used to sit under the palm tree of Deborah between Ramah and Bethel in the hill country of Ephraim; and the sons of Israel came up to her for judgment.

Deborah was unique during this period because she was judging in the ancient ways of Moses and his appointed judges. She is more akin to Samuel than the other judges of this time, who were all warriors raised up to defeat an oppressive regime. With this understanding in mind, she gave Barak God's command in an important exchange recorded in Judges 4:6-9:

> Then Barak said to her, "If you will go with me, then I will go; but if you will not go with me, I will not go." She said, "I will surely go with you; nevertheless, the honor shall not be yours on the journey that you are about to take, for the LORD will sell Sisera into the hands of a woman." Then Deborah arose and went with Barak to Kedesh.

Through their partnership, God won the victory, and the people experienced forty years of rest. But, as we saw in the continuation of this story, it was neither Barak, nor Deborah, who received the honor for this great victory, but, rather, the woman Jael (17-22; 5:24).

Seize the moment and work as a part of a God-designed team! It's amazing what God will do through us when we don't care who gets the honor, as long as God gets all the glory.

JUDGES 5
SING A DUET!

Do you have a favorite duet? Maybe when Barbra Streisand and Neil Diamond came together to sing, "You Don't Bring Me Flowers," or Faith Hill and Tony Bennett when they sang, "The Way You Look Tonight." There is something magical about a beautiful duet.

Did you know there is a duet in the Bible? The story of Deborah and Barak is an important story. We know this because it is told twice – Judges 4 tells the story in prose and Judges 5 shares it as poetry, in the form of a duet. Judges 5:1-3 introduces, then begins, their beautiful song, "Then Deborah and Barak the son of Abinoam sang on that day, saying, 'That the leaders led in Israel, that the people volunteered, bless the LORD! Hear, O kings; give ear, O rulers! I – to the LORD, I will sing, I will sing praise to the LORD, the God of Israel.'"

This is a rare discovery, because the next closest thing to a duet in the Bible was the Song of Miriam (Exodus 15:20-21), which immediately followed the Song of Moses (Exodus 15:1-19). They may have sounded like a duet, but their songs are not described as one.

Deborah and Barak sang, as one, of their victory, and they gave God all the glory! Just as foretold, the song gave honor to a woman for the victory, as Judges 5:24 declared of the heroine, "Most blessed of women is Jael, the wife of Heber the Kenite; most blessed is she of women in the tent." But, as you listen to their song, they are giving honor to many; they not only honor the champion, but the many from the tribes who fought, whether volunteer or commander.

Seize the moment and honor the people in your life who are fighting the good fight of faith as good soldiers of Jesus Christ for the glory of God! We are in this together (1 Corinthians 12:12-27)!

JUDGES 6
FOR THE FAME OF THE ONE NAME!

Have you ever done an important job, only to be overlooked? While the next three chapters, Judges 6-8, tell the story of the next great judge, Gideon, we first encounter an unnamed prophet in verses 7-10:

> Now it came about when the sons of Israel cried to the LORD on account of Midian, that the LORD sent a prophet to the sons of Israel, and he said to them, "Thus says the LORD, the God of Israel, 'It was I who brought you up from Egypt and brought you out from the house of slavery. I delivered you from the hands of the Egyptians and from the hands of all your oppressors, and dispossessed them before you and gave you their land, and I said to you, "I am the LORD your God; you shall not fear the gods of the Amorites in whose land you live. But you have not obeyed Me." ' "

That's it! No name mentioned, but a faithful word given. We may never know who this person was, unlike the prophetess Deborah, or the prophet Samuel, but God's will was done through his faithfulness just the same.

Does your faithfulness depend on recognition, fame, or notoriety?

In Philippians 2:3-4, Paul commands us to serve faithfully without need for personal gain, "Do nothing from selfishness or empty conceit, but with humility of mind regard one another as more important than yourselves; do not merely look out for your own personal interests, but also for the interests of others."

There is only one name that needs to be put up in lights and that is the name of Jesus Christ. So, don't be discouraged from doing good if you are overlooked; simply pray that your life will elevate the name of Jesus, the only name by which anyone can be saved (Acts 4:12; Romans 10:9).

Seize the moment and keep serving faithfully for the fame of the One name! Don't grow weary in doing good for God's glory (Galatians 6:7-10)!

JUDGES 7
WHEN GOD IS WITH YOU!

Have you felt like God could not use you because you weren't big enough, or smart enough, or significant enough? Well, do I have a story to tell you...

The story of Gideon is a powerful story of God working through a person, not because the person was big, strong, or important, but because God was with him. In Judges 7:2, God instructed Gideon to decrease the size of his army, commenting, "The people who are with you are too many for Me to give Midian into their hands, for Israel would become boastful, saying, 'My own power has delivered me.'" Even after cutting it in half, the army was still too impressive; so, in verse 4, God proclaimed to Gideon, "The people are still too many." God used only three hundred fighting men to achieve the victory (4-25).

From the beginning of Gideon's story, we saw that God was planning to do a great work amidst His people. Judges 6:15-16 captures an important point of the story:

> [Gideon] said to Him, "O Lord, how shall I deliver Israel? Behold, my family is the least in Manasseh, and I am the youngest in my father's house." But the LORD said to him, "Surely I will be with you, and you shall defeat Midian as one man."

The victory did not come through Gideon's power, or the size of his army, but through God. The same is true today! Paul made this clear in 1 Corinthians 1:27, "God has chosen the foolish things of the world to shame the wise, and God has chosen the weak things of the world to shame the things which are strong."

Seize the moment and trust that when God calls you to do something for Him, He will be with you. The victory comes *from* God *through* you, so be a living sacrifice for His glory today!

Dr. Jerry D. Ingalls

JUDGES 8
THE RULER OF YOUR LIFE!

Have you ever felt like someone said all the right things, but didn't follow through and live according to what they said?

After a great military victory that vanquished the enemy, the people of Israel wanted to make Gideon their king, but he said in Judges 8:23, "I will not rule over you, nor shall my son rule over you; the LORD shall rule over you."

If only his story ended with those words, but it doesn't! Gideon went on to essentially live like a king, functioning as the de facto king in the absence of one. He amassed wealth from the people and had seventy sons. Gideon said the right thing in that moment, but struggled to live it out with integrity, violating God's decrees for the king of Israel (Deuteronomy 17:17).

Most telling about Gideon's unofficial kingship, were the questions of hereditary rule that followed his death. In Judges 9:2, Abimelech poses the question, "Which is better for you, that seventy men, all the sons of Jerubbaal [Gideon], rule over you, or that one man rule over you?" If there is any further question to Gideon's unofficial kingship, Abimelech's name means, "my father is king."

Finally, we have the issue of the golden ephod, which was made from the willing tribute of the Ishmaelites in Judges 8:24-26, summarized by verse 27, "Gideon made it into an ephod, and placed it in his city, Ophrah, and all Israel played the harlot with it there, so that it became a snare to Gideon and his household."

Gideon will always be remembered as one of the heroes of faith for his military victories, as seen in Hebrews 11:32, but what should we emulate from his life?

Seize the moment and demonstrate your trust of Jesus as the ruler of your life through your actions; don't just declare Him to be the King of Kings.

JUDGES 9
STAND OUT BY TRUSTING GOD!

Judges 9 reads more like a Hollywood production than a Bible story, filled with political intrigue, family betrayal, and violence. It is a sad story about family politics, as an outcast child sows heartache and vengeance on his siblings and community. It is a disappointing story, as Gideon's progeny fall short of God's call. Ultimately, it is a true story about the human condition that teaches us to keep our eyes on God, and not put our trust in man, if we hope to walk true in our lives today.

Judges 9:22-24 provides a short summary of this story:

Now Abimelech ruled over Israel three years. Then God sent an evil spirit between Abimelech and the men of Shechem; and the men of Shechem dealt treacherously with Abimelech, so that the violence done to the seventy sons of Jerubbaal [Gideon] might come, and their blood might be laid on Abimelech their brother, who killed them, and on the men of Shechem, who strengthened his hands to kill his brothers.

Standing out like a beacon of light in this prevailing darkness, there is an intriguing character – Jotham, the youngest son of Gideon. He is the only son to escape Abimelech's murderous rage (5). After narrowly escaping death, and before his departure from the story, Jotham delivers a prophecy from God to Abimelech, and to the people of Shechem (7-21). The story ends with these words in verse 57, "the curse of Jotham the son of Jerubbaal came upon them."

Jotham was different! He, of all the characters in this story, was the only one who trusted God and did not take matters into his own hands. He trusted God in his dire circumstances, leaning not on his own understanding, but on God's promise, from Deuteronomy 32:35, "Vengeance is Mine."

Seize the moment and trust God for His promises (Proverbs 3:5-7)!

Dr. Jerry D. Ingalls

JUDGES 10
A DESPERATE PLEA!

Have you ever cried out to God in a desperate plea? We sometimes call these 9-1-1 prayers. Often, these are the prayers with which we cry out to God when we hit rock bottom. I often say to people that God does His best work when we are at our worst and weakest moments of life.

Judges 10:15 records the desperate plea the sons of Israel made to God, "We have sinned, do to us whatever seems good to You; only please deliver us this day." While I know we are still in the vicious cycle of sin and idolatry, I can't help but love this prayer. It's probably the reckless abandon of the words, "Do to me whatever seems good to You." There is a depth of trust in this prayer that only comes from knowing you can't trust yourself.

I have tried to make life work out for me, and it hasn't! How about you?

The definition of insanity is to do the same thing over and over again, expecting different results. The nation of Israel was "insane" during these dark and chaotic days of the Judges. They kept trying to make life work out for them, and would go to any source to do so. (Sounding familiar yet? We've all done some version of this!) When they finally found themselves at rock bottom, they heard God's just rejection of them in verse 14, "Go and cry out to the gods which you have chosen; let them deliver you in the time of your distress."

It was these words from God that broke them and brought them back to God. Just like the prodigal son went home to his father in Luke 15:21, "Father, I have sinned against heaven and in your sight; I am no longer worthy to be called your son."

Seize the moment and cry out to God! The Father is waiting to wrap His arms around you and welcome you home (Luke 15:22-24).

JUDGES 11
LEADERSHIP IN TIMES OF WAR!

Judges 11 is the story of Jephthah. He was a "valiant man," a warrior, who was hated and driven out of his community. Jephthah reminds me of Gunnery Sergeant Thomas Highway, Clint Eastwood's character from *Heartbreak Ridge*, a grizzled old medal of honor recipient who, when finishing his last years in the Marine Corps, had to go to war one last time. His commander critiqued that people like him should be behind glass displays that say, "Break glass only in the event of war!"

Judges 11:5-7 highlights that the people of Gilead had a similar opinion of Jephthah:

> When the sons of Ammon fought against Israel, the elders of Gilead went to get Jephthah from the land of Tob; and they said to Jephthah, "Come and be our chief that we may fight against the sons of Ammon." Then Jephthah said to the elders of Gilead, "Did you not hate me and drive me from my father's house? So why have you come to me now when you are in trouble?"

Leadership in times of war is different than in times of peace. It often requires a different skill set that is not usually acceptable at other times. With Jephthah, God used an unexpected person for His purposes. While we may not always understand why we are the way we are, we can still recognize that God has designed each of us for a purpose and desires us to impact our generation for His glory.

Seize the moment and ask God to use you today. You were created for such a time as this, so rise up and seize the moment!

JUDGES 12
THE CATASTROPHE OF CIVIL WAR!

Judges 12 appears to be a replay of the Gideon story (Judges 8:1), as the tribe of Ephraim confronts Jephthah about why he went to battle without them. But, unlike Gideon (Judges 8:3), Jephthah didn't have the diplomacy skills to satisfy their angry inquiry. The consequences are a senseless and bloody civil war, described in Judges 12:4-6:

> Then Jephthah gathered all the men of Gilead and fought Ephraim; and the men of Gilead defeated Ephraim, because they said, "You are fugitives of Ephraim, O Gileadites, in the midst of Ephraim and in the midst of Manasseh." The Gileadites captured the fords of the Jordan opposite Ephraim. And it happened when any of the fugitives of Ephraim said, "Let me cross over," the men of Gilead would say to him, "Are you an Ephraimite?" If he said, "No," then they would say to him, "Say now, 'Shibboleth.'" But he said, "Sibboleth," for he could not pronounce it correctly. Then they seized him and slew him at the fords of the Jordan. Thus there fell at that time 42,000 of Ephraim.

Can you imagine this catastrophic loss? That would be like us losing nearly every person in Henry County over an offense our mayor had with someone in Kentucky. They had become a divided people who would kill each other because of their regional accents. The loss of 42,000 people was not worth the offense that Ephraim took on themselves for Jephthah's victory apart from them. And 42,000 was too steep a price for Jephthah's hot-headed inability to come to the table and find a common ground that united them, rather than feed the fire of that which divided them.

Are we any better today?

Seize the moment and be a minister of reconciliation in the situations of your own life. Don't take on the offenses of others; rather seek that which unites us.

JUDGES 13
THE BIRTH OF A HERO!

It is an age-old question: Are heroes born, or are heroes made? The Samson story, which is told over the next four chapters of Judges, either confirms or denies your opinion based on whether you see this Judge of Israel as a hero. Judges 13:3-5 begins Samson's story with his birth narrative:

> Then the angel of the LORD appeared to the woman and said to her, "Behold now, you are barren and have borne no children, but you shall conceive and give birth to a son. Now therefore, be careful not to drink wine or strong drink, nor eat any unclean thing. For behold, you shall conceive and give birth to a son, and no razor shall come upon his head, for the boy shall be a Nazirite to God from the womb; and he shall begin to deliver Israel from the hands of the Philistines."

This is the only such birth narrative in the book of Judges. What made Samson different from the other biblical Judges was that he was mandated to live in a life-long Nazirite vow. God originally prescribes the Nazirite vow in Number 6:1-21 to be a voluntary and temporary vow to consecrate oneself from the world. The Nazarite vow was a choice to be made by a person who was responding to God's grace upon his life.

Without hesitation and with great fervor, Samson broke every regulation of the Nazirite vow. His life was a tragedy! He was born to be a hero, but he could have been so much more if he had committed his life to the pathway of becoming a hero – to being a living sacrifice for God's glory (Romans 12:1-2)!

Seize the moment and respond to the grace of Jesus Christ by willingly dedicating yourself to God as holy and pleasing sacrifice unto Him. Walk in the way of a hero of faith today!

Dr. Jerry D. Ingalls

JUDGES 14
THE POWER OF THE SPIRIT!

Samson's amazing feats of strength were possible only because of God's anointing. We see this twice in Judges 14. First, in verses 5-6, we see him defeat a lion:

> Then Samson went down to Timnah with his father and mother, and came as far as the vineyards of Timnah; and behold, a young lion came roaring toward him. The Spirit of the LORD came upon him mightily, so that he tore him as one tears a young goat though he had nothing in his hand; but he did not tell his father or mother what he had done.

The same phrase, "the Spirit of the LORD came upon him mightily," is used again in verse 19:

> Then the Spirit of the LORD came upon him mightily, and he went down to Ashkelon and killed thirty of them and took their spoil and gave the changes of clothes to those who told the riddle. And his anger burned, and he went up to his father's house.

Samson is not a likeable character, nor are his behaviors anything more than that of a man-child who wants what he wants and wants it now. He is certainly strong and courageous, but, beyond that, he is self-centered and disrespectful.

Judges 14:4 is the key to the Samson story, and this entire fiasco, "However, his father and mother did not know that it was of the LORD, for He was seeking an occasion against the Philistines. Now at that time the Philistines were ruling over Israel." God empowered Samson for *His* purposes to deliver and rescue Israel, not because of Samson's worthiness.

Seize the moment and walk in the power of the Holy Spirit, not by carrying out the desires of your flesh, but rather by doing the will of your heavenly Father (Galatians 5:16-26). God empowers you to live and work for His glory!

JUDGES 15
THE REVOLVING DOOR OF REVENGE!

The Hatfield-McCoy family feud is an infamous story. It started at the end of the American Civil War and escalated into a massacre, demonstrating the revolving door of revenge. This vicious cycle of violence will continue – either until the offenders are dead, or there is forgiveness.

We watch the revolving door of revenge in the Samson story in Judges 15. After being denied his wife, Samson stated in verse 3, "This time I shall be blameless in regard to the Philistines when I do them harm." Obviously looking for justification for his violence, Samson used the personal offense between him and his father-in-law as reason to burn the crops of the Philistines with torches bound to the tails of three hundred foxes (4-5). The revolving door of revenge commenced, and escalated to a great massacre in verses 6-8, just like with the Hatfield-McCoy family feud:

> Then the Philistines said, "Who did this?" And they said, "Samson, the son-in-law of the Timnite, because he took his wife and gave her to his companion." So the Philistines came up and burned her and her father with fire. Samson said to them, "Since you act like this, I will surely take revenge on you, but after that I will quit." He struck them ruthlessly with a great slaughter; and he went down and lived in the cleft of the rock of Etam.

The Philistines responded by marching to war against Judah until Samson was bound and brought to them, only to have Samson escape his bindings and kill one thousand Philistines using the jawbone of a donkey (9-16). While this was considered a great victory, it was not the end of the revolving door of revenge, which ended in Samson's death (Judges 16:28-31).

Seize the moment and put down your offense! A feud can only end in death, unless you choose to close the revolving door of revenge through forgiveness. Am I asking too much of you? Never forget that this is exactly what Jesus did for you with His substitutionary death on the Cross (Colossians 2:13-14; 1 Peter 2:24; 3:18; Isaiah 53:4-6). The feud is over!

JUDGES 16
BREAK UP WITH DELILAH!

What is your Delilah? Judges 16:4-6 introduces us to the woman that would be Samson's downfall, and, yes, her name was Delilah:

After this it came about that he loved a woman in the valley of Sorek, whose name was Delilah. The lords of the Philistines came up to her and said to her, "Entice him, and see where his great strength lies and how we may overpower him that we may bind him to afflict him. Then we will each give you eleven hundred pieces of silver." So Delilah said to Samson, "Please tell me where your great strength is and how you may be bound to afflict you."

Samson fell in love with a seedy woman; while the Bible gives us Delilah's motivation from the get-go, Samson seemed to be unaware of her intentions, or at least blinded to them by his infatuation with her. His romantic involvement prevented him from seeing straight. They do say love is blind, but, in this case, it wasn't love; instead, it was lust. Lust is a counterfeit, an enemy smoke screen to obscure the battlefield.

Delilah is not subtle about her efforts to sell Samson to his enemies, the Philistines, for riches beyond anything she would ever be able to earn through her normal nighttime activities. In fact, when you read Judges 16:6-20 you just want to pull Samson aside and talk some sense into him. Every time she asked him how to bind his strength, in the very next scene his enemies were doing it to him. Yet, Samson, in all his pride, kept returning to Delilah.

What is your Delilah? What do you keep returning to even though you know it is seeking to steel, kill, or destroy you (John 10:10a)?

Seize the moment and break up with your Delilah today – "Flee immorality" and "pursue righteousness" (1 Corinthians 6:18; 2 Timothy 2:22)!

JUDGES 17
OFFERING RIGHT WORSHIP!

As the book of Judges starts to come to an end with its final two stories, the situation has worsened for Israel. To explain the setting for the story of the Ephraimite Micah and his Levite priest, Judges 17:6 reminds the reader, "In those days there was no king in Israel; every man did what was right in his own eyes." The absence of a strong central leader in Israel was responsible not only for the anarchy of the tribes, culminating in civil war by the end of the book, but also for the widespread religious apostasy, which is the focus of this chapter.

Apostasy is not necessarily a walking away from being religious or spiritual; rather, it is the decision to step off the prescribed way of one's faith. Plainly speaking, it is a breaking of the covenant as established by God for our good. It's offering a form of worship that God does not accept. That is what is described in Judges 17:5, "And the man Micah had a shrine and he made an ephod and household idols and consecrated one of his sons, that he might become his priest."

Clearly Micah was a religious person, but the making of a house shrine, with the worship of household idols, and the consecration of his son as a priest, was not an acceptable form of worship to God. Micah was an ambiguous character. He does not seem to be filled with evil intent, but was simply doing what was right in his own eyes and wandered out of the way. It was this sort of misguided behavior that went unchecked by strong leadership, and ultimately led to the corruption of the priesthood, and the people, ending in the nation's destruction.

Seize the moment and walk in the prescribed and authorized way of God – follow Jesus and worship God in spirit and in truth (John 4:24).

JUDGES 18
NOT EVERY PROMOTION IS GOOD!

There are times in a person's career and working life where a decision must be made – to accept or decline a promotion, to stay or to go. For some, it is the right thing to do; it is the natural professional progression of experience and responsibility. For others it is not. Not every promotion is good!

The story of Israel's apostasy grows as six hundred men from the tribe of Dan seek to settle in the land near Micah's home, taking his household gods and the Levite priest while they are at it. Judges 18:18-20 captures the tragic scene of what happened in Micah's household as Dan's men are confronted by the priest during the burglary:

> When these went into Micah's house and took the graven image, the ephod and household idols and the molten image, the priest said to them, "What are you doing?" They said to him, "Be silent, put your hand over your mouth and come with us, and be to us a father and a priest. Is it better for you to be a priest to the house of one man, or to be priest to a tribe and a family in Israel?" The priest's heart was glad, and he took the ephod and household idols and the graven image and went among the people.

If you are invited to take a new opportunity outside of your current workplace, or receive a promotion within the organization, then I encourage you to be wise and discerning. Cry out to God, asking whether you should take it or leave it. Not every promotion should be accepted, and not every attractive job opportunity is the right thing to do.

Seize the moment and walk in the spirit of "power and love and discipline" (2 Timothy 1:7). Don't allow yourself to be intimidated into making a bad decision. Have the courage to serve God, and not your own advancement.

JUDGES 19
DO GOOD BY SHOWING HOSPITALITY!

Do you expect more from Christians than you do from the other people in your life?

Judges 19:11-13 sets up the final story of the book of Judges, with a Levite, his servant, and his concubine journeying from the concubine's father's house in Bethlehem back to their home in Ephraim:

> When they were near Jebus, the day was almost gone; and the servant said to his master, "Please come, and let us turn aside into this city of the Jebusites and spend the night in it." However, his master said to him, "We will not turn aside into the city of foreigners who are not of the sons of Israel; but we will go on as far as Gibeah." He said to his servant, "Come and let us approach one of these places; and we will spend the night in Gibeah or Ramah."

This is a story of great heart ache and pain. The Levite did not want to stay in or near Jebus, which was Jerusalem, because it was not yet under Israel control. The Levite did not like or trust the Jebusites, and did not want to have to depend upon them for hospitality. Instead, they pushed on to a town of Israel, believing God's people would care for them by showing them hospitality. But, as Judges 19:1 foreshadowed about this sad story, "Now it came about in those days, when there was no king in Israel."

When you read for yourself the horror of what happened in verses 14-30, your heart will break, remembering that the last time there was such brutality of a guest was in Sodom, which led to its destruction at God's hand (Genesis 19:1-28). This is not the way of God's people!

Hebrews 13:2 commands all believers, "Do not neglect to show hospitality to strangers, for by this some have entertained angels without knowing it."

Seize the moment and do good by showing hospitality (1 Peter 4:9; Romans 12:13).

Dr. Jerry D. Ingalls

JUDGES 20
THE NEAR DEATH OF BENJAMIN!

Have you ever had a near-death experience? The tribe of Benjamin did!

Judges 20 continues the story of how the nation of Israel responded to the appalling news of the Levite's concubine's rape and murder at the hands of the sons of Benjamin, in the city of Gibeah. They declared war on their cousins – eleven tribes against the one tribe of Benjamin. It was a massacre on both sides, as the Benjamites were fierce warriors (14-21). Judges 20:46-48 ends this heart-breaking chapter with the near-death experience of the tribe of Benjamin:

> So all of Benjamin who fell that day were 25,000 men who draw the sword; all these were valiant warriors. But 600 men turned and fled toward the wilderness to the rock of Rimmon, and they remained at the rock of Rimmon four months. The men of Israel then turned back against the sons of Benjamin and struck them with the edge of the sword, both the entire city with the cattle and all that they found; they also set on fire all the cities which they found.

Why did God preserve this rebellious tribe? Before his death, when Israel blessed his twelve sons, he spoke these words over Benjamin in Genesis 49:27, "Benjamin is a ravenous wolf; in the morning he devours the prey, and in the evening he divides the spoil." The Benjamites were on the verge of destruction because of the evil they did against the Levite's concubine. It was because of King Saul, the first king of Israel, who would come from the tribe of Benjamin that they were saved. Then, a thousand years later, came the Apostle Paul, God's appointed apostle to the Gentiles, who wrote thirteen letters of the New Testament. Beauty from ashes!

Seize the moment and be slow to judge a whole nation as deserving destruction. We never know what God may do in and through them for the good of all our futures.[11]

---

11 A scene that captures this action item comes from J.R.R. Tolkien's *The Fellowship of the Ring*, when Gandalf stated to Frodo, after Frodo had commented that Gollum deserved death for his many horrible deeds, "Many that live deserve death. And some that die deserve life. Can you give it to them? Then do not be too eager to deal out death in judgement. For even the very wise cannot see all ends."

JUDGES 21
SOMETHING MUST CHANGE OR ELSE!

Have you ever got to the end of your rope and realized that if something didn't change in your life, and quick, then there would be no future worth living? That is exactly where the people of God found themselves at the end of the book of Judges – something had to change or else!

The last five chapters of Judges turn my stomach, which is exactly the point. These final two stories are some of my least favorite stories in the Bible, and there are some horrifying stories in the Bible – like the judgment of all humanity through a world-wide flood. But there's no way to turn this level of debauchery into cute children's stories to domesticate the Bible and sanitize the absolute horror of its intended message.

Judges 17-21 intentionally closes out the history books of Joshua and Judges, transitioning between Moses and the monarchy. They have set the stage for Israel's need for a king. We know this because these last five chapters are bookended by its theme, "In those days there was no king in Israel; everyone did what was right in his own eyes" (Judges 17:6 & 21:25). With this thematic statement found at the beginning and end of these last five chapters, we know that everything between them is intended to illustrate this one point – Israel was a hot mess without a king!

Me too! I'm a hot mess without King Jesus ruling over my life. Furthermore, from my life, I have plenty of stories that should never be domesticated or sanitized to make my life look more presentable. In fact, some of my worst stories are what led me to bow my knee to King Jesus. Isn't that the point? I wasn't willing to surrender all until I realized that something must change – or else! How about you?

Seize the moment and submit your life to King Jesus! Apart from Him you are Hell-bent, but with Him you are Heaven-bound!

RUTH

RUTH 1
THE POWER OF CONVERSION!

The book of Ruth is a sad story with a happy ending. It is a short, four-chapter story, that takes place during the time of the Judges. It is the story of Elimelech and his wife, Naomi, who, with their two sons Mahlon and Chilion, traveled to the land of Moab to avoid a famine. They lived in the land for ten years, during which Naomi's husband died, the two sons took Moabite women as wives, then both sons died. This sad chain of events left Naomi alone, with two Moabite woman as her daughters-in-law. As Naomi prepared to return to Bethlehem, she released the two Moabite women from their commitments to her, but one of them would not depart. Ruth's response to Naomi's urging is found in Ruth 1:16-17:

> Do not urge me to leave you or turn back from following you; for where you go, I will go, and where you lodge, I will lodge. Your people shall be my people, and your God, my God. Where you die, I will die, and there I will be buried. Thus may the LORD do to me, and worse, if anything but death parts you and me.

Did you know that Ruth's proclamation of faith is the key to this entire story? As a Moabite woman, she would not be allowed to enter the assembly of God's people (Deuteronomy 23:3); however, her conversion brought great blessing to her and to Naomi. Without her declaration of loyal love, this story could be nothing more than another flagrant violation of the Law of God in the time of the Judges. With it, the Bible tells us a story of love and loyalty – a foreshadowing of God's redemptive love through Jesus Christ.

Seize the moment and declare your loyal love to God and His people. Your conversion transforms your story through the gospel of Jesus Christ.

RUTH 2
THE WILLINGNESS TO WORK HARD!

Are you willing to work hard? Naomi's daughter-in-law shows her true colors in Ruth 2:2-3:

> And Ruth the Moabitess said to Naomi, "Please let me go to the field and glean among the ears of grain after one in whose sight I may find favor." And she said to her, "Go, my daughter." So she departed and went and gleaned in the field after the reapers; and she happened to come to the portion of the field belonging to Boaz, who was of the family of Elimelech.

Ruth was an outsider, despised, because she was from Moab. She had only one chance at a new life in Bethlehem. There are many ways she could have responded to her circumstances, such as complain and grumble, but, instead, Ruth's character shined brightly. She labored willingly in the fields of Boaz, gleaning to survive while hoping for a miracle of provision that would care for Naomi. Her willingness to work hard paid off, as Ruth 2:11-12 captures Boaz's response to her selfless service to Naomi:

> All that you have done for your mother-in-law after the death of your husband has been fully reported to me, and how you left your father and your mother and the land of your birth, and came to a people that you did not previously know. May the LORD reward your work, and your wages be full from the LORD, the God of Israel, under whose wings you have come to seek refuge.

In Philippians 2:14-15, Paul commanded all believers to be like Ruth in their circumstances:

> Do all things without grumbling or disputing; so that you will prove yourselves to be blameless and innocent, children of God above reproach in the midst of a crooked and perverse generation, among whom you appear as lights in the world.

Seize the moment by letting your faith shine brightly through your willingness to work hard (Colossians 3:22-24)!

RUTH 3
BUILD A GOOD REPUTATION!

Do you have a good reputation? If you do, it is easier for people to trust you. People won't be quick to believe accusations against you, or listen to gossip about you. But, if your character has been compromised, people tend to think the worst of your actions, and mistrust your motives.

Ruth and Boaz have been presented as virtuous characters with righteous motives. Their good reputations are necessary for us not to read into their behavior on the threshing floor in Ruth 3, especially when reading Naomi's advice to Ruth in verses 3-4:

> Wash yourself therefore, and anoint yourself and put on your best clothes, and go down to the threshing floor; but do not make yourself known to the man until he has finished eating and drinking. It shall be when he lies down, that you shall notice the place where he lies, and you shall go and uncover his feet and lie down; then he will tell you what you shall do.

While we want to think the best of what Naomi is asking Ruth to do to secure Boaz, the biblical language is neither simple nor innocent. The Hebrew is suggestive, filled with idioms and sexual innuendo, which, honestly, would not be very surprising, considering this was happening in the time of the Judges, when people did what was right in their own eyes.

It is because of Ruth's and Boaz's good reputations that I interpret this story without it including a Hollywood scandal. It was Boaz himself who said of Ruth in verse 11, upon awakening to discover her at his feet, "Now, my daughter, do not fear. I will do for you whatever you ask, for all my people in the city know that you are a woman of excellence."

Seize the moment and build a good reputation (Proverbs 22:1; Ecclesiastes 7:1; 1 Timothy 3:7; 1 Peter 2:15).

RUTH 4
THE RESCUE OF RUTH!

Have you ever needed to be rescued? Maybe you have been lost, and needed to be found, or you got a cramp in the deep end of the pool, and needed someone to jump in to rescue you and set your feet on solid ground again.

That is exactly what Boaz was doing for Ruth and Naomi. He was rescuing them as their kinsmen-redeemer, the closest relative, with the responsibility to deliver them, and to set their feet on solid ground. Boaz testified of this in Ruth 4:9-10:

> You are witnesses today that I have bought from the hand of Naomi all that belonged to Elimelech and all that belonged to Chilion and Mahlon. Moreover, I have acquired Ruth the Moabitess, the widow of Mahlon, to be my wife in order to raise up the name of the deceased on his inheritance, so that the name of the deceased will not be cut off from his brothers or from the court of his birth place; you are witnesses today.

Interestingly, the same word used to describe Boaz as the kinsmen-redeemer in Ruth 4:14, was also used of God in Job 19:25a, when Job proclaimed, "As for me, I know that my Redeemer lives." This is also the same word God uses when promising Moses that He would rescue His people from slavery in Exodus 6:6. To redeem is to rescue and deliver!

Do you recognize your own need to be rescued and delivered? Ruth did! In Ruth 3:9, she asked Boaz to "spread your covering over your maid, for you are a close relative." This points to the living Redeemer, Jesus Christ, and why He came from Heaven to Earth – "to seek and to save that which was lost" (Luke 19:10).

Seize the moment and pray to God today that Jesus Christ would rescue you from sin and place your feet on the solid rock of His salvation!

1 SAMUEL

1 SAMUEL 1
THE POWER OF PETITION!

Have you ever petitioned God passionately for a miracle in your life?

Hannah did and, in doing so, she was misunderstood by Eli, the head priest. Hannah was a righteous woman and a good wife. But she was tormented by a rival concubine, and oppressed by an empty cradle. Weeping bitterly, she went to the temple of the Lord in Shiloh where she petitioned God passionately, making a vow that if God would grant her a son, then she would dedicate him as a Nazirite. Watch how Eli responds to what he saw, but couldn't hear, in 1 Samuel 1:14-18:

> Then Eli said to her, "How long will you make yourself drunk? Put away your wine from you." But Hannah replied, "No, my lord, I am a woman oppressed in spirit; I have drunk neither wine nor strong drink, but I have poured out my soul before the LORD. Do not consider your maidservant as a worthless woman, for I have spoken until now out of my great concern and provocation." Then Eli answered and said, "Go in peace; and may the God of Israel grant your petition that you have asked of Him." She said, "Let your maidservant find favor in your sight." So the woman went her way and ate, and her face was no longer sad.

The good news is that both Hannah's passionate petition and Eli's priestly blessing were heard by God, and God bestowed a son on Hannah (19-28). This is the birth narrative of Samuel, the last Judge of Israel, and the great prophet of God, who would ultimately anoint the first two kings of Israel – Saul and David. Samuel, the namesake of two books of the Bible, was Hannah's baby. All Samuel's works came about because of the effective prayer of a righteous woman (James 5:16).

Seize the moment and petition God passionately for the needs of your life.

1 SAMUEL 2
PREPARING FOR A LIFETIME OF SERVICE!

The summer of 2022 marks thirty years since I attended Cadet Basic Training at West Point. Duty, honor, and country were deeply instilled in us, as was our commitment to a lifetime of service to country.

Samuel's childhood was one of preparing him for a lifetime of service to God. First Samuel 2:18-19 & 21b gives us a glimpse of Samuel's life as a temple child:

> Now Samuel was ministering before the LORD, as a boy wearing a linen ephod. And his mother would make him a little robe and bring it to him from year to year when she would come up with her husband to offer the yearly sacrifice. ... And the boy Samuel grew before the LORD.

Furthermore, verse 26 elaborates, "Now the boy Samuel was growing in stature and in favor both with the LORD and with men."

There is an interesting connection between the boy Samuel and another boy that would come, over a thousand years later. The Gospel of Luke 2:52 describes, "And Jesus kept increasing in wisdom and stature, and in favor with God and men." The two verses read very similar. God used both boys' circumstances to prepare them for a lifetime of service!

God's high regard for Samuel was verified through prophecy, as declared to Eli in verse 35, "But I will raise up for Myself a faithful priest who will do according to what is in My heart and in My soul; and I will build him an enduring house, and he will walk before My anointed always." God was about to do something brand new in Israel, and he set apart Samuel for this very purpose.

Seize the moment and prepare the next generation for a lifetime of service to God. The next generation will serve someone or something, why not God?! Train them to seek first the Kingdom and His righteousness (Matthew 6:33).

1 SAMUEL 3
RESPOND TO GOD'S WORD!

In the days when the word of God was rare, Samuel's calling as a prophet was authenticated by his response to the word of God. It all started when Samuel was a young boy, lying down in the temple of the Lord, when he heard a voice call his name. He did not recognize the voice, but thought it was Eli, the high priest. First Samuel 3:7 explains this initial response, "Now Samuel did not yet know the LORD, nor had the word of the LORD yet been revealed to him."

It was Eli who taught him that it was God who was calling him by name, and to respond, "Speak, Lord, for Your servant is listening" (9). Samuel responded to the word of God, and his life was forever changed. Ironically, even though that first message was a word of judgment against Eli and his household for their unfaithfulness, Eli, who was far from a perfect mentor, gave him a faithful example that would set him up for success as a prophet of God's word, "It is the LORD; let Him do what seems good to Him" (18).

Samuel learned from Eli to listen for God and to trust that God is right and true in all that He says and does. He learned to respond to God's word in obedience and trust the outcome to God alone. First Samuel 3:19-21 describes how Samuel did just that:

> Thus Samuel grew and the LORD was with him and let none of his words fail. All Israel from Dan even to Beersheba knew that Samuel was confirmed as a prophet of the LORD. And the LORD appeared again at Shiloh, because the LORD revealed Himself to Samuel at Shiloh by the word of the LORD.

Seize the moment by trusting God. Take Him at His word, and He will prove you to be Jesus' disciple (John 8:31-32; 15:8).

1 SAMUEL 4
THE STORY OF ICHABOD!

Have you ever felt like God removed His presence from you?

In 1 Samuel 4, Israel experienced a day of great tragedy that culminated in such a feeling. In a series of battles against the Philistines, 34,000 men were killed (2, 10). Even with this tragic loss of life, the story emphasizes that the greatest loss was that of the ark of the covenant, which was where God would manifest His presence to the Israelites.

Upon hearing of this great defeat, which included the death of his two sons, Eli the high priest died (18). The story ends with the premature death of Phinehas' wife in childbirth, whose final words are recorded in 1 Samuel 4:21-22:

> And she called the boy Ichabod, saying, "The glory has departed from Israel," because the ark of God was taken and because of her father-in-law and her husband. She said, "The glory has departed from Israel, for the ark of God was taken."

Ichabod literally means, "inglorious," or "no glory." The glory of God describes God's favor and blessing upon His people; it is brought about by the giving of His presence. While we know that God is omnipresent, and it is impossible for God not to be where God always is, the removal of His manifest presence, His glory, is the removal of favor; it is judgment upon people for their sin. This woman felt the removal of God's presence in Israel, and named her son Ichabod – no glory!

There is only one answer when you feel that God has removed His favor from your life. James 4:8 invites you to "Draw near to God and He will draw near to you. Cleanse your hands, you sinners; and purify your hearts, you double-minded."

Seize the moment and seek God through confession and repentance. God is faithful and just to forgive you of your sin and to cleanse you from all unrighteousness (1 John 1:9).

1 SAMUEL 5
THE GRAVE DANGER OF A GRAVEN IMAGE!

Have you ever been tempted to put something or someone other than God on the throne of your heart? That is called idol worship. In 1 Samuel 5:2-4, God judged Dagon, the god of the Philistines, when the ark of the covenant was placed in the temple where the Philistines worshipped Dagon's idol:

> Then the Philistines took the ark of God and brought it to the house of Dagon and set it by Dagon. When the Ashdodites arose early the next morning, behold, Dagon had fallen on his face to the ground before the ark of the LORD. So they took Dagon and set him in his place again. But when they arose early the next morning, behold, Dagon had fallen on his face to the ground before the ark of the LORD. And the head of Dagon and both the palms of his hands were cut off on the threshold; only the trunk of Dagon was left to him.

God was communicating powerfully to the Philistines, not only that their god was beneath Him, and had been judged accordingly, but that they, as a people given over to idol worship, would end up just like Dagon – cut off from future life (headless) and powerless to do anything about it (handless).

Psalm 115:8 states of people who worship idols, "Those who make them will become like them, everyone who trusts in them" (cf. Psalm 135:18; Isaiah 44:9-11). First Samuel 5:6-12 demonstrates this truth; watch as God's judgement unfolds in verse 6, "Now the hand of the LORD was heavy on the Ashdodites, and He ravaged them and smote them with tumors, both Ashdod and its territories." Scholars believe that these tumors would have prevented their ability to have children, causing them to become like Dagon – cut off from future life, and powerless to change it.

Seize the moment and "guard yourselves from idols" (1 John 5:21). You are shaped by your life of devotion, so choose carefully what you allow on the throne of your heart.

Dr. Jerry D. Ingalls

1 SAMUEL 6
CURB YOUR CURIOSITY!

My daughter loves monkeys, so Curious George makes regular appearances in my life. He is such an adorable and funny character. His curiosity is constantly getting him into situations that could be avoided. That makes for great comedic relief, but in real life it can lead to serious situations. You have heard it said that curiosity killed the cat, but in 1 Samuel 6:19-21 curiosity killed a lot more than a cat:

> He struck down some of the men of Beth-shemesh because they had looked into the ark of the LORD. He struck down of all the people, 50,070 men, and the people mourned because the LORD had struck the people with a great slaughter. The men of Beth-shemesh said, "Who is able to stand before the LORD, this holy God? And to whom shall He go up from us?" So they sent messengers to the inhabitants of Kiriath-jearim, saying, "The Philistines have brought back the ark of the LORD; come down and take it up to you."

While there is some scholarly debate over the number of deaths, 70 or 50,070, due to some original language issues, the point of the story is unaffected – God can't let sin go unpunished! It is neither loving, nor holy, to do so – God is just in all that He does!

The ark of God had been returned after seven months of captivity. Upon it returning, the people of Beth-shemesh, most likely with the best of intent to ensure the contents were still in it, looked inside of it. Their curiosity manifested as a mistrust that God had protected the contents of the ark, and led them to take it upon themselves to look inside, violating the Law of God, and so He brought swift judgment upon them (Numbers 4:5, 15, 20; Romans 6:23).

Seize the moment and trust that God's ways are right and true for life and godliness (2 Peter 1:2-3). Don't let curiosity lead you astray from the way of God in your life.

1 SAMUEL 7
THE DAWNING OF A NEW DAY!

Today is a new day! Do you need a new beginning in an area of your life? The Israelites did, and Samuel gave it to them after a long season of mourning. First Samuel 7:2-4 marks the dawning of a new day for Israel under Samuel's faithful leadership:

> From the day that the ark remained at Kiriath-jearim, the time was long, for it was twenty years; and all the house of Israel lamented after the LORD. Then Samuel spoke to all the house of Israel, saying, "If you return to the LORD with all your heart, remove the foreign gods and the Ashtaroth from among you and direct your hearts to the LORD and serve Him alone; and He will deliver you from the hand of the Philistines." So the sons of Israel removed the Baals and the Ashtaroth and served the LORD alone.

As the Israelites were confronted by God's messenger, you have a choice to make if you want today to be the dawning of a new day in your life. I invite you to ask God to be your help in your pursuit to start afresh. Whether you desire a new vision, or the perseverance to see a previous vision fulfilled, you can't do it alone. Samuel demonstrated this in verse 12 with his fervent prayers for the Israelites, "Then Samuel took a stone and set it between Mizpah and Shen, and named it Ebenezer, saying, 'Thus far the LORD has helped us.'"

Ebenezer literally means, "stone of help." Samuel lifted an Ebenezer as a tangible reminder of the people's need for God. It was a proclamation of God's victory over their enemies, provision for His people's needs, and the power to fulfill His promises for His people.

Seize the moment and lift an Ebenezer by confessing your sins, repenting and offering yourself as a living sacrifice, and experiencing the dawning of a new day by walking in the way of Jesus Christ.

1 SAMUEL 8
DON'T TAKE REJECTION PERSONALLY!

Rejection hurts! When you let rejection in your heart, it can lead you down the road of discouragement. But we don't need to give ourselves over to those feelings of rejection because there is always more to the story than the painful words and hurtful actions of other people. Watch what happens between Samuel and the elders of Israel in 1 Samuel 8:4-7:

> Then all the elders of Israel gathered together and came to Samuel at Ramah; and they said to him, "Behold, you have grown old, and your sons do not walk in your ways. Now appoint a king for us to judge us like all the nations." But the thing was displeasing in the sight of Samuel when they said, "Give us a king to judge us." And Samuel prayed to the LORD. The LORD said to Samuel, "Listen to the voice of the people in regard to all that they say to you, for they have not rejected you, but they have rejected Me from being king over them."

The people referenced both Samuel's old age and his sons' inability to follow faithfully in his footsteps as reasons why they wanted him to appoint them a king. How could he not take that personally? But God made it clear to Samuel that he shouldn't. There was more to the story; it was because of Israel's recent history, the difficult days of the Judges, that the elders believed they needed a strong central leader, like the other nations. So, they asked for a king.

What caused them to reject the counsel of their trusted leader? Why would they reject their God and stubbornly insist that what they wanted is better than what He had for them? These were not Samuel's questions to answer. He sought God and learned there was more to the story that had nothing to do with him. Those are hard lessons to learn!

Seize the moment and don't take rejection personally. People will do what people do, and we shouldn't allow their choices to hijack our lives. There's always more to the story.

1 SAMUEL 9
THE LORD REIGNS OVER THE NATIONS!

The next three chapters cover the choosing and the anointing of the first king of Israel – King Saul. The account from 1 Samuel 9:15-17 ensures that all readers know that it was God who chose Saul, not Samuel, nor any person or committee of people:

> Now a day before Saul's coming, the LORD had revealed this to Samuel saying, "About this time tomorrow I will send you a man from the land of Benjamin, and you shall anoint him to be prince over My people Israel; and he will deliver My people from the hand of the Philistines. For I have regarded My people, because their cry has come to Me." When Samuel saw Saul, the LORD said to him, "Behold, the man of whom I spoke to you! This one shall rule over My people."

It can't get any clearer, but for those who know the rest of the story, it is important to remember that Saul was the Lord's chosen, and he was humbled by it. Saul's reluctant words to Samuel's favor are remembered in verse 21, "Am I not a Benjamite, of the smallest of the tribes of Israel, and my family the least of all the families of the tribe of Benjamin? Why then do you speak to me in this way?" God chose Saul to rule on purpose!

In today's world of self-promoting politicians, and endless committees of government bureaucracy, it is easy to forget the Bible's teaching from Romans 13:1b, "For there is no authority except from God, and those which exist are established by God." Paul was echoing Daniel 2:21b, "He removes kings and establishes kings." We must remember that, regardless of all that we can see, and no matter how hard it is to believe, the Lord reigns over all the nations.

Seize the moment and trust God. Don't allow current events to hijack your peace of mind (Philippians 4:6-7). Cast all your anxiety on God, because He cares for you (1 Peter 5:7).

1 SAMUEL 10
COME OUT OF HIDING!

Have you ever hidden from a responsibility? Maybe it was a social commitment you cancelled, a meeting you skipped, or a service opportunity you avoided. According to 1 Samuel 10:20-24, Saul did the same thing, but he couldn't hide for long:

> Thus Samuel brought all the tribes of Israel near, and the tribe of Benjamin was taken by lot. Then he brought the tribe of Benjamin near by its families, and the Matrite family was taken. And Saul the son of Kish was taken; but when they looked for him, he could not be found. Therefore they inquired further of the LORD, "Has the man come here yet?" So the LORD said, "Behold, he is hiding himself by the baggage." So they ran and took him from there, and when he stood among the people, he was taller than any of the people from his shoulders upward. Samuel said to all the people, "Do you see him whom the LORD has chosen? Surely there is no one like him among all the people." So all the people shouted and said, "Long live the king!"

There is a good chance that I would have wanted to hide from such a significant responsibility, too, and I hope that I would have people in my life, like Saul had, that didn't allow me to hide from God's calling. Importantly, while it was the community that went and got Saul, it was God who exposed his hiding spot.

You can run from your responsibilities, but you can't run from God; He can expose you at any time He chooses. Hebrews 4:13 explains, "there is no creature hidden from His sight, but all things are open and laid bare to the eyes of Him with whom we have to do."

Seize the moment and stop running from God's call. He is waiting for you, and has good plans for your life (Jeremiah 29:11).

1 SAMUEL 11
THE UNITY OF VICTORY!

Have you ever been a part of a great victory? Maybe you were a member of a winning sports team, or served on a sales team that made the big sale. Whatever role you played, when you experience a great victory, it feels like you can do anything together. Victory brings people together, and brings great momentum to do even greater things. In 1 Samuel 11:12-15, Saul seized the moment of a great military victory to solidify his kingship and unify the nation of Israel:

> Then the people said to Samuel, "Who is he that said, 'Shall Saul reign over us?' Bring the men, that we may put them to death." But Saul said, "Not a man shall be put to death this day, for today the LORD has accomplished deliverance in Israel." Then Samuel said to the people, "Come and let us go to Gilgal and renew the kingdom there." So all the people went to Gilgal, and there they made Saul king before the LORD in Gilgal. There they also offered sacrifices of peace offerings before the LORD; and there Saul and all the men of Israel rejoiced greatly.

Saul made a wise decision. Having just proved his kingship in battle, he essentially offered forgiveness to all who opposed him as king in a moment of great potential for national unity.

It is a rare leadership moment when you can bring people together and build momentum to do even greater things together than you could do apart. Jesus modeled this for us in Luke 9:50, when John tried to hinder someone from casting out demons in Jesus' name just because he wasn't part of Jesus' traveling squad; Jesus said to him, "Do not hinder him; for he who is not against you is for you."

Seize the moment and build unity around Jesus Christ and His victory on the Cross! We can do more together than we can apart (John 17:20-23).

1 SAMUEL 12
STAY IN THE WAY!

Have you ever had to follow through with a decision that couldn't be changed, even after you realized it wasn't a good decision in the first place? It's like, "Can I get a mulligan on this one?"

There are some choices that just can't be undone; you must see where the road leads you. In 1 Samuel 12:20-23 Samuel instructs Israel upon their realization that they sinned against God by asking for a king:

> Do not fear. You have committed all this evil, yet do not turn aside from following the LORD, but serve the LORD with all your heart. You must not turn aside, for then you would go after futile things which can not profit or deliver, because they are futile. For the LORD will not abandon His people on account of His great name, because the LORD has been pleased to make you a people for Himself. Moreover, as for me, far be it from me that I should sin against the LORD by ceasing to pray for you; but I will instruct you in the good and right way.

I love this passage and its relevance to all our lives. It is one thing to be able to confess your sin, stop doing it, and experience no further consequences, but it's entirely another situation when you confess, and repent, but the consequences of your past choices remain front and center. The answer is, as we used to say in the military, to drive on! C-M! Continue the Mission! These are all ways of expressing the same truth that Samuel was trying to get across to Israel. Yes, you made a mess of it, but keep following God, because that's still the way.

Seize the moment and stay in the way of Jesus! Regardless of the mess, or who made it, don't bail before the blessing! As Proverbs 3:6 promises, "In all your ways acknowledge Him, and He will make your paths straight."

1 SAMUEL 13
HOW TO MAKE GOOD DECISIONS!

Leaders must cultivate the capacity, and bear the responsibility, of being decisive in moments of great stress. Decision making requires a person to be able to effectively assess a situation, evaluate potential courses of action, weigh the pros and cons of each, make the best decision with the information available, and execute the decision with confidence. As a military officer, the Army trained this model into me until it was second nature, first in the classroom and then out in the field. When military leaders make bad decisions, there are grave consequences.

King Saul was in a difficult military situation. He was outnumbered by the Philistines, and his own soldiers were hiding in the mountains and trembling around him (5-7). He let the stress of the moment overwhelm him, and let the fear of his soldiers override his decision-making process. He made an impulsive decision that showed his heart and his lack of faith in God. In 1 Samuel 13:13-14, Saul hears the consequences for the decision he made:

> Samuel said to Saul, "You have acted foolishly; you have not kept the commandment of the LORD your God, which He commanded you, for now the LORD would have established your kingdom over Israel forever. But now your kingdom shall not endure. The LORD has sought out for Himself a man after His own heart, and the LORD has appointed him as ruler over His people, because you have not kept what the LORD commanded you."

In order to make good decisions, we must follow the wisdom of Joshua 1:8, God's counsel to a successful leader:

> This book of the law shall not depart from your mouth, but you shall meditate on it day and night, so that you may be careful to do according to all that is written in it; for then you will make your way prosperous, and then you will have success.

Seize the moment and train effective decision making by getting God's Word into your mind and heart!

Dr. Jerry D. Ingalls

1 SAMUEL 14
FROM HERO TO ZERO!

Have you ever experienced the pendulum swing of going from *hero* to *zero*? This happens a lot to leaders with the decisions they must make simply because, ultimately, someone must take responsibility and act decisively. Think of your favorite quarterback who, in one play, makes the decision that leads to a score, but, in the next quarter, throws the interception that costs the team the game. Still, the best athletes, just like the best leaders, want to have the ball in their hands when it matters most.

Jonathan, the son of King Saul, was an amazing man of God, and a decisive leader. He nearly went from war hero to living sacrifice in 1 Samuel 14:43-45:

> Then Saul said to Jonathan, "Tell me what you have done." So Jonathan told him and said, "I indeed tasted a little honey with the end of the staff that was in my hand. Here I am, I must die!" Saul said, "May God do this to me and more also, for you shall surely die, Jonathan." But the people said to Saul, "Must Jonathan die, who has brought about this great deliverance in Israel? Far from it! As the LORD lives, not one hair of his head shall fall to the ground, for he has worked with God this day." So the people rescued Jonathan and he did not die.

Jonathan had won a major battle, without Saul's knowledge, that highlighted how foolish Saul's oath was in verse 24, "Cursed be the man who eats food before evening, and until I have avenged myself on my enemies." If it wasn't for the intervention of the fighting men, who knew the full story of what Jonathan had done, then Saul would have murdered his own son. Unlike Jonathan, it was Saul who was going from being a hero to a zero!

Seize the moment and find out the full story before you say or do anything foolish.

1 SAMUEL 15
THE IMPORTANCE OF OBEDIENCE!

Have you ever delayed a job to such a point that, even if you did finally get around to it, it would no longer matter? It was too late; delayed obedience is no obedience at all, it is disobedience. The same is true with getting a job half done. When you send your kids to clean their room and, an hour later, there has been more playing than cleaning, and the room is only part-way clean, would you consider that obedience? Neither does God!

Samuel's final confrontation of Saul is precipitated by the king's disobedience to God's command. Saul was tasked with the utter destruction of the Amalekites, but 1 Samuel 15:9 tells the whole story:

> But Saul and the people spared Agag and the best of the sheep, the oxen, the fatlings, the lambs, and all that was good, and were not willing to destroy them utterly; but everything despised and worthless, that they utterly destroyed.

When confronted with his disobedience, Saul stated that he had been obedient, and then gave reasons why what he did was right – he justified his actions as right in his own eyes. To Samuel, that would have been very reminiscent of the time of the Judges, and he knew that this could not be tolerated; it would lead to the loss of everything. Samuel then spoke these dramatic and eternal words in verses 22-23:

> Has the LORD as much delight in burnt offerings and sacrifices as in obeying the voice of the LORD? Behold, to obey is better than sacrifice, and to heed than the fat of rams. For rebellion is as the sin of divination, and insubordination is as iniquity and idolatry. Because you have rejected the word of the LORD, He has also rejected you from being king.

Seize the moment and offer yourself to God as a living sacrifice by obeying His Word today! Trust and obey, for there's no other way to be happy in Jesus, but to trust and obey.

Dr. Jerry D. Ingalls

1 SAMUEL 16
LOOSENING THE GRIP OF GRIEF!

Have you ever felt paralyzed by the grip of grief? Do you know what it is like to be unable to move forward, even when you knew that God was calling you to take the next step? If you have experienced grief, then you know simplistic platitudes are not helpful, but a new purpose for your life is what's needed to loosen the grip of grief on you.

First Samuel 16:1 gives us a glimpse inside Samuel's broken heart over Saul:

> Now the LORD said to Samuel, "How long will you grieve over Saul, since I have rejected him from being king over Israel? Fill your horn with oil and go; I will send you to Jesse the Bethlehemite, for I have selected a king for Myself among his sons."

Suddenly, Samuel had a purpose to work toward, and a new vision to focus his faith and give him hope. We all need purpose in our lives, and we all need something to work toward. Apart from this, even the best of godly counsel may not loosen the grip of grief upon a person.

Samuel's new purpose, which God gave him at this moment of deep discouragement, set in motion a series of events that would change the world forever, through Samuel playing his part in the selection of, and anointing of, David as the next king of Israel (2-13). It is from the line of King David that Jesus Christ would come and be the Savior of the World (Romans 1:3-5; Revelation 22:16). He is our Living Hope (1 Peter 1:3)!

Seize the moment and break free from the grip of grief. Pray for God to give you a new purpose, as you take your focus off your grief and place it onto Jesus, who is "the resurrection and the life" (John 11:25). He promises to complete in you that which He has already begun (Philippians 1:6).

1 SAMUEL 17
THE POWER OF THE ANOINTING!

King Saul's reaction to Goliath, found in 1 Samuel 17:11, sets the stage for the contrast between himself and David, "When Saul and all Israel heard these words of the Philistine, they were dismayed and greatly afraid." Shockingly, there was not a person in Israel who was willing to face the giant.

Then the shepherd boy, David, walks on the scene. Without Saul's knowledge, he had been anointed by Samuel as the next king of Israel (1 Samuel 16:13). David's proclamation to Goliath about his impending defeat, found in 1 Samuel 17:45-47, demonstrated his faith in God's power:

> You come to me with a sword, a spear, and a javelin, but I come to you in the name of the LORD of hosts, the God of the armies of Israel, whom you have taunted. This day the LORD will deliver you up into my hands, and I will strike you down and remove your head from you. And I will give the dead bodies of the army of the Philistines this day to the birds of the sky and the wild beasts of the earth, that all the earth may know that there is a God in Israel, and that all this assembly may know that the LORD does not deliver by sword or by spear; for the battle is the LORD'S and He will give you into our hands.

Setting up this magnificent story of faith and victory, in 1 Samuel 16:14-15, God's Spirit fell mightily upon David at his anointing, and departed from Saul. This story is a graphic illustration of the importance of the anointing of God for His people to walk in His victory! Apart from Him, we can do nothing (John 15:5)!

Seize the moment and walk in the power of the Holy Spirit. It is by faith that mountains are moved, because it is God who defeats the giants!

1 SAMUEL 18
THE FORGING OF CHARACTER!

David's character was forged in the crucible of his relationship with Saul. As the anointed of Israel, next in line to be king, David easily could have become a peacock of a man, proud in his reputation as the man who killed Goliath, and arrogant in his boastings of being the rightful ruler of Israel. **But God...** David was a humble man, submissive to his king, competent in his work, and confident in his God. No matter what Saul threw at him, David remained faithful and true.

It was when Saul heard the song of the women in 1 Samuel 18:6-9 that David went from being a hero to a zero in Saul's eyes:

> It happened as they were coming, when David returned from killing the Philistine, that the women came out of all the cities of Israel, singing and dancing, to meet King Saul, with tambourines, with joy and with musical instruments. The women sang as they played, and said, "Saul has slain his thousands, and David his ten thousands." Then Saul became very angry, for this saying displeased him; and he said, "They have ascribed to David ten thousands, but to me they have ascribed thousands. Now what more can he have but the kingdom?" Saul looked at David with suspicion from that day on.

Saul was burning with jealousy. In verse 10, an evil spirit overcame him, and he became so enraged that he threw a spear at David. Saul tried to have him killed by sending him off to battle against the Philistines; when nothing could defeat him, Saul tried political intrigue and married him to his daughter. Everything Saul did to David, God used to forge David's character into being a man after His own heart.

Seize the moment and remain faithful and true. It is in moments of crisis that our character is forged the deepest.

1 SAMUEL 19
THE IMPORTANCE OF FRIENDSHIP!

Friendship is an important part of experiencing God's best for your life. As men and women made in the image of God, we are designed to exist in community. In fact, when I conducted my doctoral research on how to strengthen the spiritual vitality of pastors serving in local church ministry, I found that pastors who do have friendships experience a higher spiritual vitality than those who do not.

This was true for David in 1 Samuel 19, whose life was saved, three times, by other people he was in relationship with – his best friend Jonathan (1-7), his wife Michal (11-17), and the prophet Samuel (18-24). While all three of these relationships are crucial to understanding David's life, the story of Jonathan and David is a paradigm of biblical friendship. Jonathan was the son of King Saul, and had such a strong love for David that he was willing to jeopardize his own life to intercede with his father in verses 4-6:

"Do not let the king sin against his servant David, since he has not sinned against you, and since his deeds have been very beneficial to you. For he took his life in his hand and struck the Philistine, and the LORD brought about a great deliverance for all Israel; you saw it and rejoiced. Why then will you sin against innocent blood by putting David to death without a cause?" Saul listened to the voice of Jonathan, and Saul vowed, "As the LORD lives, he shall not be put to death."

David's friendship with Jonathan was a necessary, and important, relationship in David's journey to becoming the king of Israel. The Kingdom of God is a relational kingdom!

Seize the moment and invest time in building strong relationships. This is an important part of experiencing God's best for your life.

Dr. Jerry D. Ingalls

1 SAMUEL 20
KEEPING YOUR PROMISES CAN BE COSTLY!

Keeping your promises can be costly! Saul struck out at his own son, Jonathan, because he kept his covenant with David, as recorded in 1 Samuel 20:30-33:

> Then Saul's anger burned against Jonathan and he said to him, "You son of a perverse, rebellious woman! Do I not know that you are choosing the son of Jesse to your own shame and to the shame of your mother's nakedness? For as long as the son of Jesse lives on the earth, neither you nor your kingdom will be established. Therefore now, send and bring him to me, for he must surely die." But Jonathan answered Saul his father and said to him, "Why should he be put to death? What has he done?" Then Saul hurled his spear at him to strike him down; so Jonathan knew that his father had decided to put David to death.

Saul had lost his mind with jealousy for David. By this point, word must have gotten back to him that David had been anointed the next king; therefore, Saul was actively trying to kill him. This led to his verbal assault on Jonathan, and Jonathan's poor mother, and then, in a moment of absolute rage, Saul tried to kill his own son. At great cost to himself, Jonathan remained faithful to his covenant with David and protected him.

Seize the moment and keep your promises, even when they are costly! Thank you, Jesus, that you decided, in the Garden of Gethsemane, to keep Your word to the Father, "Abba! Father! All things are possible for You; remove this cup from Me; yet not what I will, but what You will" (Mark 14:36). You were willing to pay the price and I am eternally grateful.

1 SAMUEL 21
LIFTING THE BURDEN!

Much of what Jesus did in his earthly ministry was misunderstood, especially in His healing ministry on the Sabbath. Interestingly, Jesus used the rescue story from 1 Samuel 12:1-6 as His biblical defense of His actions. In this story, David and his companions were starving while fleeing from Saul's evil efforts to murder him, and a priest gave them the consecrated bread to eat. Jesus used this story to explain to the religious leaders that, not only were His works of deliverance lawful on the Sabbath, but they are God's intent in giving rest to His people, as commemorated on the Sabbath day. Jesus explained this in Mark 2:25-28:

> "Have you never read what David did when he was in need and he and his companions became hungry; how he entered the house of God in the time of Abiathar the high priest, and ate the consecrated bread, which is not lawful for anyone to eat except the priests, and he also gave it to those who were with him?" Jesus said to them, "The Sabbath was made for man, and not man for the Sabbath. So the Son of Man is Lord even of the Sabbath."

It's amazing how often people will miss the biblical principle in their great efforts to be right in the keeping of their own understanding of the Bible. Don't miss the heart of God in the gospel of Jesus Christ – the good news of rescue and deliverance by a holy and loving God. Jesus came to set His people free from sin to live for God through a relationship with Him, not to bury them under heavy burdens of religion.

Seize the moment and take on the easy yoke of Jesus and you will find rest for your soul (Matthew 11:28-30).

Dr. Jerry D. Ingalls

1 SAMUEL 22
BE WARNED OF DISPLACED LOYALTY!

In 1 Samuel 22:9-10, we see one of the mighty men of Israel start on an evil path in the name of loyalty to his king:

> Then Doeg the Edomite, who was standing by the servants of Saul, said, "I saw the son of Jesse coming to Nob, to Ahimelech the son of Ahitub. He inquired of the LORD for him, gave him provisions, and gave him the sword of Goliath the Philistine."

Then, when none of the king's guards would follow Saul's blasphemous command to murder the priest and his whole household for helping David, Doeg did, killing eighty-five priests and striking down Nob, the city of the priests, as recorded in verses 18-19.

This was an evil day for Israel, as King Saul demonstrated the evil that had now thoroughly consumed him in his jealousy for David. But it could not have happened if it weren't for Doeg and his misplaced loyalty to his own ambition, in the name of honoring his king.

In a place of great brokenness over this brutal slaughter, David showed humility by confessing to the priest's only living relative, Abiathar, that all of this was his fault because, when he saw Doeg at the priest's house, he knew that he would betray him to Saul, but did nothing to prevent it. In this place of deep sorrow, David penned Psalm 52 as a lament unto the Lord. David describes Doeg in verses 1-3:

> Why do you boast in evil, O mighty man? The lovingkindness of God endures all day long. Your tongue devises destruction, like a sharp razor, O worker of deceit. You love evil more than good, falsehood more than speaking what is right. Selah.

Seize the moment and be warned against displaced loyalty to your own ambition, even when you are doing something to provide for your family, or even in the name of God. Put your whole hope in Jesus Christ and walk in His ways.

1 SAMUEL 23
HONORING YOUR FRIENDSHIPS!

Do you remember the last time you saw a loved one or close friend before they went on to be with the Lord? Did you know that it would be the last time you saw one another? The last recorded meeting between David and Jonathan is found in 1 Samuel 23:15-18:

> Now David became aware that Saul had come out to seek his life while David was in the wilderness of Ziph at Horesh. And Jonathan, Saul's son, arose and went to David at Horesh, and encouraged him in God. Thus he said to him, "Do not be afraid, because the hand of Saul my father will not find you, and you will be king over Israel and I will be next to you; and Saul my father knows that also." So the two of them made a covenant before the LORD; and David stayed at Horesh while Jonathan went to his house.

This was the third time that they made a covenant together (1 Samuel 18:3; 20:16). Their commitment to one another was significant and would not be forgotten easily, or broken flippantly. In fact, David went to great lengths to keep his covenant with Jonathan, even after Jonathan died in battle. In 2 Samuel 9:1, after being established as king of Israel, David asked, "Is there yet anyone left of the house of Saul, that I may show him kindness for Jonathan's sake?" There was one son of Jonathan left, a man named Mephibosheth, and David showed him the kindness of God. David spoke to Mephibosheth in verse 7, "Do not fear, for I will surely show kindness to you for the sake of your father Jonathan, and will restore to you all the land of your grandfather Saul; and you shall eat at my table regularly."

Seize the moment and honor your friendships of old by loving, encouraging, and caring for the next generation. Go out of your way to honor their memory in a tangible way today.

1 SAMUEL 24
SET AN EXAMPLE WORTH FOLLOWING!

Do you set an example that is worth following? Paul said in 1 Corinthians 11:1, "Be imitators of me, just as I also am of Christ." People are watching – do they see Jesus in you? We are to set an example for others in our words and conduct, so that, in watching us, they may know the way of Jesus.

David set an example worth following when King Saul, who was trying to kill David, entered a cave and unknowingly put himself in the hands of David and his men. In 1 Samuel 24:6-7, listen to how David responded to his men who encouraged him to kill Saul with his own hands and take his rightful place as the next king:

So he said to his men, "Far be it from me because of the LORD that I should do this thing to my lord, the LORD'S anointed, to stretch out my hand against him, since he is the LORD'S anointed." David persuaded his men with these words and did not allow them to rise up against Saul. And Saul arose, left the cave, and went on his way.

What happened next would not have been possible without David's brave act of mercy. Saul finally came to terms with the judgment of God and recognized the righteousness of David, and God's anointing upon him as the next king (17-22). David's men watched all of this; because of David's unwillingness to set his hand against God's anointed, instead showing mercy and kindness, they experienced a powerful testimony of God's power working through a righteous man. Consequently, David, the anointed of God himself, protected his own future kingship, and that of his son Solomon's future reign, by not setting the precedent of "might makes right" as the way of succession in the kingdom.

Seize the moment and set an example worth following. Live by Jesus' Golden Rule, "Treat others the same way you want them to treat you" (Luke 6:31). You do this when you walk in a manner worthy of the gospel of Jesus Christ (Ephesians 4:1-3).

1 SAMUEL 25
LOVE WITH ABUNDANCE!

How do you handle disappointment when someone does not give you what you think you are owed? Whether through contract or custom, whether it was presumption on your part that you should receive something, or it was a breach of etiquette on their part for not doing what they should have done, how did you respond?

While David and his men were in exile, they faithfully cared for the local shepherds, who worked for a rich merchant named Nabal. In 1 Samuel 25:10-11, Nabal responded to David's humble request for provision with apathy for his neighbor, and negligence for his responsibilities as a patron:

> Who is David? And who is the son of Jesse? There are many servants today who are each breaking away from his master. Shall I then take my bread and my water and my meat that I have slaughtered for my shearers, and give it to men whose origin I do not know?

Thankfully for Nabal, his wife Abigail fulfilled his responsibilities to David and gave him and his men a feast out of their abundance. She said to David in verse 27, "Now let this gift which your maidservant has brought to my lord be given to the young men who accompany my lord." She loved them with abundance, and God honored her for her sacrifice. She also prevented bloodshed, as David was not responding to the offense so well, and was seeking vengeance with his own hand (32-33).

In Romans 13:8, Paul gives profound wisdom that can change your life and prevent a lot of disappointment and unnecessary conflict, "Owe nothing to anyone except to love one another; for he who loves his neighbor has fulfilled the law."

Seize the moment by loving with abundance and, like Abigail, God will honor you for your sacrifice. You never know what good will come from your act of love.

1 SAMUEL 26
KEEP ON THE ALERT!

I have an embarrassing military story to share from my time at the US Army Ranger School. I fell asleep on guard duty. I was laying in the prone position watching my sector of fire one moment, and the next I was being asked by a Ranger Instructor where my weapon was. I replied, oblivious to my own failure, that it was in my hands, and then he looked down. As my eyes followed his, there was my weapon disassembled in front of me. I failed to keep on the alert, and the consequences were grave.

King Saul's men failed to keep on the alert, allowing David to infiltrate their camp. As Abishai wanted him to, David could have killed the king, but would not raise his hand against God's anointed; instead, he took Saul's jug of water and his spear. In 1 Samuel 26:15-16, David confronted Abner, the commander of Saul's army, about his failure, "This thing that you have done is not good. As the LORD lives, all of you must surely die, because you did not guard your lord, the LORD'S anointed. And now, see where the king's spear is and the jug of water that was at his head."

In Matthew 26:40-41, like David to Abner, Jesus rebuked his closest friends for not being able to watch over Him while He prayed:

> And He came to the disciples and found them sleeping, and said to Peter, "So, you men could not keep watch with Me for one hour? Keep watching and praying that you may not enter into temptation; the spirit is willing, but the flesh is weak."

Seize the moment and keep on the alert in prayer by learning to trust in the strength of the Holy Spirit. As Jesus commanded in Mark 13:33, "Take heed, keep on the alert; for you do not know when the appointed time will come." Keep watch for Jesus (Matthew 25:1-13)!

1 SAMUEL 27
A TIME TO RETREAT!

A difficult lesson I learned in the military is that it is sometimes wiser, and more strategic, to retreat than to continue the advance. Even the best soldiers need to rest and regroup. David did this in 1 Samuel 27:1-2:

> Then David said to himself, "Now I will perish one day by the hand of Saul. There is nothing better for me than to escape into the land of the Philistines. Saul then will despair of searching for me anymore in all the territory of Israel, and I will escape from his hand." So David arose and crossed over, he and the six hundred men who were with him, to Achish the son of Maoch, king of Gath.

David took sixteen months away from Israel, and its internal politics dominated by Saul's jealousy of him. Saul was happy to see him go away. While David was retreating from Saul, he was also striking down the enemies of Israel from within their own borders. It turned out that David's time in retreat was more effective for the kingdom than if he had stayed.

This is not only true in military campaigns, but also in the spiritual life. Jesus modeled this in Luke 5:15-16, "But the news about Him was spreading even farther, and large crowds were gathering to hear Him and to be healed of their sicknesses. But Jesus Himself would often slip away to the wilderness and pray." Jesus set an example for His followers that it was best to strategically retreat for times of silence and solitude, in order to get the marching orders from His Father, not from the clamoring of the people, or the jealousy of the Pharisees.

Seize the moment and take time to retreat alone to the Word and in prayer with God. Rest and regroup with Jesus!

Dr. Jerry D. Ingalls

1 SAMUEL 28
SAMUEL'S LAST WORDS TO SAUL!

The prophet Samuel was dead. We first learned of this in 1 Samuel 25:1, and now again in 1 Samuel 28:3. The fate of Samuel was crystal clear – he was dead! I've now said it twice, just like God's Word, but there is more to this story; even though he was dead, we hadn't heard the last of him.

King Saul was desperate. He feared the Philistines, and God wasn't communicating with him (5-6). Since there was no David around to win the day for him, Saul took matters into his own hands and looked for a medium who could contact Samuel. *Did I mention that Samuel was dead?* Saul wanted to use a medium to get in touch with Samuel so that he would inquire of God for him. *Did I say Saul was desperate?*

Desperate people, more often than naught, find themselves in bad situations, and Saul was no exception. He received a message from God, through Samuel, through a medium, in verses 16-19:

> Why then do you ask me, since the LORD has departed from you and has become your adversary? The LORD has done accordingly as He spoke through me; for the LORD has torn the kingdom out of your hand and given it to your neighbor, to David. As you did not obey the LORD and did not execute His fierce wrath on Amalek, so the LORD has done this thing to you this day. Moreover the LORD will also give over Israel along with you into the hands of the Philistines, therefore tomorrow you and your sons will be with me. Indeed the LORD will give over the army of Israel into the hands of the Philistines!

Such contact with the dead was forbidden by God (Deuteronomy 18:9-14). Yet God authorized Samuel to communicate His judgment on Saul. This was an exceptional case, because God reserves the exclusive right to have the last word with the dead. Hebrews 9:27 states, "it is appointed for men to die once and after this comes judgment."

Seize the moment and put your trust in Jesus' last words, "It is finished" (John 19:30). Trust the One who already has the last word!

1 SAMUEL 29
THE POWER OF A REPUTATION!

What is your name worth to you? I have learned the power of a reputation. People anticipate what you *will* do based on what you *have* done. For example, growing up in a small town in Connecticut, I was a successful student-athlete, an Eagle scout, and a leader in the Civil Air Patrol. I was the only one surprised when I got accepted to West Point, because my reputation had gone before me, just like a resume goes before a job interview.

Even though David had a good reputation with Achish, the king of Gath, the lords of the Philistines were not willing to put their men at risk by having David fight with them. In 1 Samuel 29:4-5, we see why; David's reputation had gone before him:

> But the commanders of the Philistines were angry with him, and the commanders of the Philistines said to him, "Make the man go back, that he may return to his place where you have assigned him, and do not let him go down to battle with us, or in the battle he may become an adversary to us. For with what could this man make himself acceptable to his lord? Would it not be with the heads of these men? Is this not David, of whom they sing in the dances, saying, 'Saul has slain his thousands, And David his ten thousands'?"

The same is true today in our lives. For good or bad, our reputation goes before us. The power of your reputation is a compelling argument for why people will either give you the break you need, or you will hit the wall of their rejection. Proverbs 22:1 teaches, "A good name is to be more desired than great wealth, favor is better than silver and gold."

Seize the moment and build your life on the reputation of the powerful name of Jesus (1 Corinthians 3:11).

Dr. Jerry D. Ingalls

1 SAMUEL 30
TRUST GOD'S PROVIDENCE!

Have you ever been denied an opportunity, only to find out later that it was the best thing that could have happened to you?

David and his band of fighting men were sent away by the lords of the Philistines in 1 Samuel 29. David was upset! They were rejected and cast off, but it turned out to be the best thing that could have happened because, while they were gone, the Amalekites had raided their homes in Ziklag. It was a desperate situation for David, recorded in 1 Samuel 30:2-3:

> They took captive the women and all who were in it, both small and great, without killing anyone, and carried them off and went their way. When David and his men came to the city, behold, it was burned with fire, and their wives and their sons and their daughters had been taken captive.

Had David been allowed to fight for the Philistines, they would not have made it back to Ziklag in time to give chase to the Amalekites. By God's providence, they found a discarded sick Egyptian slave, who had been left in a field to die, and he showed them the location of the Amalekites (11-16). This led to a great victory for David, described in 1 Samuel 30:18-19:

> So David recovered all that the Amalekites had taken, and rescued his two wives. But nothing of theirs was missing, whether small or great, sons or daughters, spoil or anything that they had taken for themselves; David brought it all back.

If David had not been rejected by the Philistines, they would have missed the opportunity to rescue their families, restore their animals and possessions, and capture a great spoil that David used to secure alliances with key leaders in Israel (20-31).

Seize the moment and trust God's providence. What may feel like rejection, or denial, in the moment may be God's greatest opportunity for your life.

1 SAMUEL 31
RESPOND TO DEFEAT WITH RESILIENCE!

How do you respond to defeat?

The King was dead! As foretold in 1 Samuel 28:19, Israel's army was defeated by the Philistines, with Saul and his three sons killed in action. In the face of defeat, three communities of Israel, who lived close to the enemy, abandoned their cities to the Philistines. The Philistines, in an act of defiance, desecrated Saul's body, and declared their gods as victorious over Israel's.

Israel responded to defeat by giving themselves over to their fear, which made their circumstances worse. By all appearances, the book of 1 Samuel was ending in utter ruin, as defeat led to despair, except for a small group of valiant men who responded to the Philistines' disgraceful abuse of their king's body in 1 Samuel 31:11-13:

> Now when the inhabitants of Jabesh-gilead heard what the Philistines had done to Saul, all the valiant men rose and walked all night, and took the body of Saul and the bodies of his sons from the wall of Beth-shan, and they came to Jabesh and burned them there. They took their bones and buried them under the tamarisk tree at Jabesh, and fasted seven days.

Recently, one of my track athletes was tested mentally in a big competition; her first two efforts in the discus throw did not go well. She was on the verge of giving herself over to defeat, and despair was knocking on the door of her heart. But, through some positive coaching (and, unbeknownst to her, a lot of praying) she won the mental battle and came back to throw a seasonal best to earn an unexpected third place. She fought off despair and responded to defeat with resilience! I am so proud of her for learning this life skill at a young age!

Seize the moment and respond to defeat with resilience! Don't let defeat lead to despair; allow it to bring out your very best!

2 SAMUEL

2 SAMUEL 1
BLESS YOUR ENEMY!

Have you ever rejoiced at the death of an enemy?

Welcome to the tenth book of the Old Testament, and it begins with David doing a surprising thing in 2 Samuel 1:17-18, "Then David chanted with this lament over Saul and Jonathan his son, and he told them to teach the sons of Judah the song of the bow; behold, it is written in the book of Jashar." We understand David's grief over Jonathan, but why Saul? While Saul was the anointed of Israel, and David's king, Saul was also the mad man who had made the last eight years of David's life miserable. Burning with jealousy, and fueled with anger, Saul had relentlessly sought David's life.

But David, a man after God's own heart, not only refused to raise a hand against his king, the anointed of God, he lamented his death through this psalm, as recorded in 2 Samuel 1:19-27. David set an example for us to follow. Don't dance on the graves of your enemies; grieve for them and pray for their salvations.

Jesus commanded us to love our enemies, and to pray for those who persecute us, in Matthew 5:44-45. The Apostles taught the way of Jesus to the early church. Paul emphasized this teaching in Romans 12:17 and 1 Thessalonians 5:15. Peter captured it in 1 Peter 3:8-9:

> To sum up, all of you be harmonious, sympathetic, brotherly, kindhearted, and humble in spirit; not returning evil for evil or insult for insult, but giving a blessing instead; for you were called for the very purpose that you might inherit a blessing.

Seize the moment and seek first the Kingdom of God and His righteousness by being a blessing to all – this is the way of Jesus! Do not return evil for evil; instead, seek to be a blessing. You never know how God is preparing you for even greater things.

2 SAMUEL 2
EMBRACING THE TWISTS AND TURNS OF LIFE!

Do you ever wish that your story had fewer twists and turns? While we may wish that for our lives, the reality is that none of us would enjoy a movie or book that had no plot twists. A story without drama doesn't have opportunity for human intrigue, adventure, crisis, and redemption – the ingredients of all great epic stories.

The story of Israel becoming a united kingdom under King David's reign is a twisted story, just like all great stories. King Saul was dead, and while we were led to believe that his sons were dead alongside him in battle, a twist appeared in 2 Samuel 2:8-11:

> But Abner the son of Ner, commander of Saul's army, had taken Ish-bosheth the son of Saul and brought him over to Mahanaim. He made him king over Gilead, over the Ashurites, over Jezreel, over Ephraim, and over Benjamin, even over all Israel. Ish-bosheth, Saul's son, was forty years old when he became king over Israel, and he was king for two years. The house of Judah, however, followed David. The time that David was king in Hebron over the house of Judah was seven years and six months.

The great general of Saul's armies, Abner, propped up Saul's living son, Ish-bosheth, as the rightful heir to the throne. Was Abner using him to keep himself in power, and to continue the fight against David and his men? Time would tell, but, for the meantime, David continued to be forged in the twists and turns of Israel's toxic political environment. This drama served to prepare him for his kingship, one that would unite the twelve tribes.

Seize the moment and embrace the twists and turns of your life. Trust that God is sovereign and "causes all things to work together for good to those who love God, to those who are called according to His purpose" (Romans 8:28).

2 SAMUEL 3
LIVE ABOVE REPROACH!

Have you ever been accused of something that you didn't do? How did you prove your innocence? In 2 Samuel 3:6-8 there is an exchange between Ish-bosheth, the king of Israel, and Abner, the general of Israel's armies:

> It came about while there was war between the house of Saul and the house of David that Abner was making himself strong in the house of Saul. Now Saul had a concubine whose name was Rizpah, the daughter of Aiah; and Ish-bosheth said to Abner, "Why have you gone in to my father's concubine?" Then Abner was very angry over the words of Ish-bosheth and said, "Am I a dog's head that belongs to Judah? Today I show kindness to the house of Saul your father, to his brothers and to his friends, and have not delivered you into the hands of David; and yet today you charge me with a guilt concerning the woman."

Notice the context that Abner was, "making himself strong in the house of Saul." The king did more than accuse him of sleeping with one of Saul's concubines. He was accusing him of a military coup, because that activity was considered a public signal of an attempt to overthrow the king (e.g., 2 Samuel 16:21-22).

Abner was furious, and he moved against the king to put David on the throne of Israel. Abner soon died at the hands of Joab and Abishai, who sought revenge for the death of their brother Asahel in the battle of Gibeon (2 Samuel 2:23; 3:26-30). David grieved Abner's death and was frustrated with his men for killing him (31-39). It was a mess of personal agendas and political intrigue!

Seize the moment and live above reproach. Don't get caught up in personal agendas and political intrigue; rather, "Keep a good conscience so that in the thing in which you are slandered, those who revile your good behavior in Christ will be put to shame" (1 Peter 3:16).

Dr. Jerry D. Ingalls

2 SAMUEL 4
HAVE COURAGE AND ENCOURAGE OTHERS!

Courage is an important quality to be found in a person, especially a leader. When people speak and act with conviction in the face of fear, they put courage in others, which encourages them to speak and act likewise.

The political intrigue continued as the king responded to the death of his general in 2 Samuel 4:1, "Now when Ish-bosheth, Saul's son, heard that Abner had died in Hebron, he lost courage, and all Israel was disturbed." Furthermore, Ish-bosheth was assassinated and the nation of Israel found itself leaderless and grieving with the only living heir to the throne described in verse 4:

> Now Jonathan, Saul's son, had a son crippled in his feet. He was five years old when the report of Saul and Jonathan came from Jezreel, and his nurse took him up and fled. And it happened that in her hurry to flee, he fell and became lame. And his name was Mephibosheth.

Saul and his lineage were now effectively cut off from the kingship.

Ish-bosheth's lack of courage in the face of Abner's death sent a ripple effect throughout the nation, which ultimately led to his own assassination, and the discouragement of his people. Contrast that with David's behavior.

The two assassins brought news of their treachery to David, hoping for a reward and a place of honor in his entourage. David, now the king of Judah, remembering his vow to Saul to not cut off his line entirely, executed them instead for their cold-blooded actions against the king (9-12).

David showed courage in the face of political intrigue. He remained steadfast to his convictions, and faithful to his vows. Therefore, as we will see in the next chapter, David was installed as king over all of Israel. His courage encouraged the nation!

Seize the moment and "be strong and courageous! Do not tremble or be dismayed, for the LORD your God is with you wherever you go" (Joshua 1:9). Have courage and you will encourage others!

2 SAMUEL 5
DAVID'S FIRST ORDER OF BUSINESS!

Politicians seek votes by making campaign promises. They do so to gain popularity, but it is not until they are in office that we see their true priorities. David's first order of business as the newly installed king of the united kingdom of Israel is found in 2 Samuel 5:6-10:

> Now the king and his men went to Jerusalem against the Jebusites, the inhabitants of the land, and they said to David, "You shall not come in here, but the blind and lame will turn you away"; thinking, "David cannot enter here." Nevertheless, David captured the stronghold of Zion, that is the city of David. ... So David lived in the stronghold and called it the city of David. And David built all around from the Millo and inward. David became greater and greater, for the LORD God of hosts was with him.

It was Jerusalem! This was not the first time the Israelites had tried to seize the high ground of the Promised Land from the Jebusites. We find them mentioned as far back as the spies' fearful report to Moses in Numbers 13:29, and again in two failed attempts in Joshua 15:63 and Judges 1:21. David had his eyes on establishing a unified kingdom, with Jerusalem as the capital, and because of God's favor he was able to fulfill his first order of business as the king of Israel.

God continued to bless David's priorities because David gave all glory to God, as evidenced by verse 12, "And David realized that the LORD had established him as king over Israel, and that He had exalted his kingdom for the sake of His people Israel."

Seize the moment by putting God's glory as the first order of business in all that you do. Just as Jesus taught us in Matthew 6:33, "But seek first His kingdom and His righteousness, and all these things will be added to you."

2 SAMUEL 6
WALK IN THE AUTHORIZED WAY OF GOD!

We are becoming progressively more utilitarian and results-oriented in our society, and we are often so focused on the end-product that we forget the importance of the process. There is a right way to do things, and there are consequences when you take short cuts. As you have heard it said, if a job is worth doing, it is worth doing right.

The importance of doing something the right way is emphasized in the story of King David, when he is leading the effort to move the ark of God to Jerusalem. For whatever reason, David and his men were not following the authorized way to move the ark. First, they put the ark on a cart so that the oxen could pull it, instead of using poles so that people could walk with it (Exodus 25:13-14). Then, this led to an accident when one of David's men reached out and touched that which was forbidden, bringing God's wrath upon himself in 2 Samuel 6:6-7:

But when they came to the threshing floor of Nacon, Uzzah reached out toward the ark of God and took hold of it, for the oxen nearly upset it. And the anger of the Lord burned against Uzzah, and God struck him down there for his irreverence; and he died there by the ark of God.

Uzzah appears to have had the best of intentions in securing the ark, but he was still struck down for touching it. It is not that God doesn't want people to approach Him (the ark manifested God's presence during this time in Israel's history), it is that God establishes an authorized way to come to Him; we must submit to His ways, regardless of our good ideas or best of intentions for how we want to experience God.

Seize the moment and approach God through His Son Jesus Christ – the only authorized way to come to Him (John 14:6).

2 SAMUEL 7
TRUST GOD FOR HIS BETTER YES!

Have you ever had a knee-jerk response to a person's request, then later realized it was the wrong response? Were you able to go back to the person and rectify the situation?

In 2 Samuel 7:3, Nathan the prophet gives a knee-jerk response to David's request to build God a temple, "Go, do all that is in your mind, for the LORD is with you." And why not?!? David was now the king of a unified Israel, anointed by the great prophet Samuel, victorious over his enemies, and the one who brought the ark of God to the newly conquered city of Jerusalem. Why would God *not* want David to do this for Him?

But Nathan was wrong! God's plans were bigger than anything Nathan the prophet could imagine, and more than anything King David was prepared to ask for. God's "no" to David was because He had a bigger yes in mind. Thankfully, Nathan's integrity went beyond the stubborn pride of keeping his own word and demonstrated the humble faithfulness to keep every Word of God. After faithfully going to prayer with David's request, he gave this word to David in 2 Samuel 7:12-13:

> When your days are complete and you lie down with your fathers, I will raise up your descendant after you, who will come forth from you, and I will establish his kingdom. He shall build a house for My name, and I will establish the throne of his kingdom forever.

Thank God Nathan the prophet did not let his pride prevent him from rectifying the situation, so that God could use him to give David a better yes.

Seize the moment and be willing to put your trust more in God's Word than in your own ideas and plans. Open your hands, mind, and heart to God's better yes!

2 SAMUEL 8
BE FAITHFUL TO YOUR WORK!

King David was a military man with much blood on his hands from years of campaigning. This was the reason God did not allow him to build His temple (1 Kings 5:3; 1 Chronicles 22:8). Immediately after God established a covenant with him and his household in 2 Samuel 7, David went back out on military campaign and brutally conquered the Philistines, Moabites, Zobahites, Arameans, and Edomites. Essentially, David ran a textbook military conquest, which built a name for him, and established Israel's dominance over the Promised Land, as summarized in 2 Samuel 8:13-15:

> So David made a name for himself when he returned from killing 18,000 Arameans in the Valley of Salt. He put garrisons in Edom. In all Edom he put garrisons, and all the Edomites became servants to David. And the LORD helped David wherever he went. So David reigned over all Israel; and David administered justice and righteousness for all his people.

While there was still work to be done, as we will see in future chapters, the reality is that David did not sit back and sulk after God told him he couldn't lead the building campaign of the temple; instead, David got back to the work he was called to do, building the kingdom of Israel through military conquest and right administration. He was preparing the way for his son, Solomon, who would build the temple because he would not have to dirty his hands with military conquest, as David had to do.

Each of us has been chosen by God to do specific good works for God's glory. Paul taught us this in Ephesians 2:10, "For we are His workmanship, created in Christ Jesus for good works, which God prepared beforehand so that we would walk in them."

Seize the moment and be faithful to the work God has chosen for you to do in this season of your life.

2 SAMUEL 9
ACT WITH A CLEAR CONSCIENCE!

Have you ever been exceedingly generous to a person, church, or charity, only to wonder later if what they did with your generosity was the right thing, or a good stewardship of your trust?

Sandwiched between chapters of war and conquest, today's chapter stands out as a breath of fresh air as David, moved by covenant faithfulness to Jonathan, blessed Mephibosheth, Saul's grandson, the son of Jonathan who was "crippled in his feet" (2 Samuel 4:4). In 2 Samuel 9:9-11, David entrusted the care of Saul's estate to Ziba:

> Then the king called Saul's servant Ziba and said to him, "All that belonged to Saul and to all his house I have given to your master's grandson. You and your sons and your servants shall cultivate the land for him, and you shall bring in the produce so that your master's grandson may have food; nevertheless Mephibosheth your master's grandson shall eat at my table regularly." Now Ziba had fifteen sons and twenty servants. Then Ziba said to the king, "According to all that my lord the king commands his servant so your servant will do." So Mephibosheth ate at David's table as one of the king's sons.

Did David go too far in bestowing royal favor upon Mephibosheth? Was Ziba trustworthy of such a large stewardship responsibility? The answers to these questions are not clear, as 2 Samuel 16:1-4 portrays Mephibosheth as being disloyal, while Ziba comes across as a faithful servant. Later, 2 Samuel 19:24-30 conveys the opposite, portraying Mephibosheth as the faithful one, a victim of Ziba's duplicity. Regardless of what they did with David's favor and generosity, what is clear is that David acted with a clear conscience as he honored his word to Saul and kept his covenant to Jonathan.

Seize the moment and give generously with a clear conscience. You are only responsible to do what God has put on your heart to do. Surrender the results to Him!

2 SAMUEL 10
FOCUS!

Do you like to think of yourself as an effective multitasker? I used to! I learned that, while it is possible to do two things at once, it's difficult to give either of them my attention effectively. For example, I can't listen to a person sitting in front of me effectively while checking my text messages. In that same way, I can't attend to a phone call while reading emails. I need to pick one or the other to focus my concentration on one person, or one task, at a time.

Israel found themselves in a battle on two fronts and Joab, the general of their army, made the decision to give his full attention to one front and entrust the other to his brother, Abishai. He galvanized his brother into action with these words from 2 Samuel 10:11-12:

> If the Arameans are too strong for me, then you shall help me, but if the sons of Ammon are too strong for you, then I will come to help you. Be strong, and let us show ourselves courageous for the sake of our people and for the cities of our God; and may the LORD do what is good in His sight.

Joab knew that he couldn't personally lead the battle on both fronts, so he delegated authority so that his attention was not split; both fronts had a leader with their full focus on the task. To win the battle, regardless of whether it is physical, mental, emotional, relational, or spiritual, you must give your full attention to the situation at hand and trust God with the results on every front in your life. Trust God with everything so you can focus on one thing.

Seize the moment and work with a whole heart, and an undivided mind (Colossians 3:23)! Rather than multitasking, focus on the person, task, or situation at hand and watch God win the battle.

2 SAMUEL 11
BE WHERE YOU ARE SUPPOSED TO BE!

The greatest scandal of King David's life happened in 2 Samuel 11 – his affair with Bathsheba, her pregnancy, and the murder of Uriah, her husband. It all happened because David was not where he was supposed to be, as highlighted in verse 1, "Then it happened in the spring, at the time when kings go out to battle, that David sent Joab and his servants with him and all Israel, and they destroyed the sons of Ammon and besieged Rabbah. But David stayed at Jerusalem."

The situation got worse, and everyone knew about it, including Uriah, whom David had brought back from the front line in a failed attempt to cover his shame for his abuse of power. Uriah's response to David in verse 11, when David asked him why he had not gone home to be with his wife, made the situation abundantly clear:

> The ark and Israel and Judah are staying in temporary shelters, and my lord Joab and the servants of my lord are camping in the open field. Shall I then go to my house to eat and to drink and to lie with my wife? By your life and the life of your soul, I will not do this thing.

Uriah was not letting David off the hook. He emphasized that everyone was where they were supposed to be, except David! Uriah refused to cover David's shame, but instead multiplied it. The situation escalated out of control, and David ordered his death. The chapter ends with David's honor in doubt, as verse 27 declares, "the thing that David had done was evil in the sight of the LORD." Sin is progressive by nature; while it may start small, it seeks to devour you in the end.

Seize the moment and be where you are supposed to be, and do what you are supposed to do; don't give evil a foothold in your life.

Dr. Jerry D. Ingalls

2 SAMUEL 12
WE ALL NEED A NATHAN!

When was the last time God confronted you through a person who loved you enough to tell you the truth? When has He used a person you trust, who has permission to hold you directly accountable for your walk with Jesus? Do you have a Nathan in your life?

In 2 Samuel 12:1-15, Nathan the prophet used a story of injustice to confront King David for his sin against Uriah and Bathsheba. David was pierced to the heart through this direct confrontation, and, by God's grace, confessed his brokenness before God in 2 Samuel 12:13, "Then David said to Nathan, 'I have sinned against the LORD.' And Nathan said to David, 'The LORD also has taken away your sin; you shall not die.'" Even though David experienced mercy for his sin, it was not without grave consequences.

For thousands of years, David's deep contrition for his sin, as recorded in Psalm 51, has resonated with countless people who have found themselves in a place of brokenness over their own sin. I, too, have prayed these words of repentance, as first heard in verses 1-4:

Be gracious to me, O God, according to Your lovingkindness; according to the greatness of Your compassion blot out my transgressions. Wash me thoroughly from my iniquity and cleanse me from my sin. For I know my transgressions, and my sin is ever before me. Against You, You only, I have sinned and done what is evil in Your sight, so that You are justified when You speak and blameless when You judge.

We all need to experience brokenness over our sin; therefore, we all need a Nathan in our lives who has permission to speak truth to us with a genuine love and a gentle spirit (Galatians 6:1). Who is your Nathan?

Seize the moment and ask God to give you a clean heart, to renew a steadfast spirit in you, and to restore the joy of your salvation (Psalm 51:10, 12).

2 SAMUEL 13
DISCIPLINE IS DESIGNED FOR GOOD!

Have you ever experienced discipline that seemed hard, but later, you realized, was an important and essential part of your development? The Bible speaks of the importance of parental authority, and the urgency of discipline, for the character development of children.

Second Samuel 13 is a heartbreaking chapter, as David's children sin against one another, not because David was absent from their lives, but because he wouldn't discipline them for their wrongdoing. David's firstborn son, Amnon, lusted after his half-sister, Tamar, and devised a plan to take her as his own; upon taking her, he hated her with a greater intensity than that of his former obsession, and abandoned her (1-19). This is an ugly tale that fueled a deep hatred within Absalom's heart. Absalom was the full brother of Tamar, and, upon seeing David do nothing in response to this situation (21), he devised a plan to punish Amnon (20-39). He murdered him, and later sought the death of his father when he led a military coup against him (2 Samuel 15-18). Absalom's hatred burned hot!

Could Absalom's spiral into murder and betrayal have been avoided if David disciplined Amnon for his gross sin against Tamar? Hebrews 12:9-11 states the importance of a father's discipline:

> Furthermore, we had earthly fathers to discipline us, and we respected them; shall we not much rather be subject to the Father of spirits, and live? For they disciplined us for a short time as seemed best to them, but He disciplines us for our good, so that we may share His holiness. All discipline for the moment seems not to be joyful, but sorrowful; yet to those who have been trained by it, afterwards it yields the peaceful fruit of righteousness.

Seize the moment and submit yourself to the loving discipline of the Lord and His authorized agents in your life; God has good plans for you (Jeremiah 29:11).

2 SAMUEL 14
SEIZE THE MOMENT FOR RECONCILIATION!

Have you experienced a moment of reconciliation with a person you thought you would never see again, or whom you assumed would remain estranged to you forever? Did someone help facilitate that moment? David and Absalom experienced a moment of reconciliation in 2 Samuel 14:33, "So when Joab came to the king and told him, he called for Absalom. Thus he came to the king and prostrated himself on his face to the ground before the king, and the king kissed Absalom."

After killing his brother Amnon, David's firstborn son, Absalom fled to Geshur for three years (2 Samuel 13:37-39). David mourned for his sons, the one who was dead and the one who fled, but, even upon his return to Jerusalem, David did not see Absalom for two more years (2 Samuel 14:28). That's five years of estrangement and heartache compounded over time, until Joab, the mighty general of David's armies, intervened. It may be that Joab understood, in a unique way, the plight of Absalom, because Joab had incurred the wrath of David for avenging his own brother's murder years earlier (2 Samuel 3:26-30). Joab, more than anyone else, knew that reconciliation was possible, and necessary, so he facilitated the process.

Are you a minister of reconciliation? Are you open and available to get right with the people in your own life, and are you willing to facilitate the process of reconciliation for others? Like with David and Absalom, it may not last, as we will see in the next chapters, but that doesn't mean that the moment wasn't both important and meaningful. Paul commands us in 2 Corinthians 5:18, "Now all these things are from God, who reconciled us to Himself through Christ and gave us the ministry of reconciliation."

Seize the moment and look for moments of reconciliation in your own life; be a peacemaker to those you encounter (Matthew 5:9).

2 SAMUEL 15
THE CONTAGION OF DISCONTENTMENT!

Did you know that discontentment can be contagious?

Absalom was a discontented man bent on the downfall of his father, David. Fueled by ambition and anger, the man who murdered his own brother was now conspiring for the throne of Israel, as evidenced by 2 Samuel 15:3-6:

> Then Absalom would say to him, "See, your claims are good and right, but no man listens to you on the part of the king." Moreover, Absalom would say, "Oh that one would appoint me judge in the land, then every man who has any suit or cause could come to me and I would give him justice." And when a man came near to prostrate himself before him, he would put out his hand and take hold of him and kiss him. In this manner Absalom dealt with all Israel who came to the king for judgment; so Absalom stole away the hearts of the men of Israel.

Absalom systematically worked a contagion into the hearts and minds of God's people – discontentment! He conspired against his father by causing the people to believe that they couldn't trust King David to meet their needs, but they could trust him. In 1 Timothy 6:6-9, Paul provides the antidote to Absalom's rebellion against God's rightful authority, which continues to be a tool of the enemy against God's people to this day:

> But godliness actually is a means of great gain when accompanied by contentment. For we have brought nothing into the world, so we cannot take anything out of it either. If we have food and covering, with these we shall be content. But those who want to get rich fall into temptation and a snare and many foolish and harmful desires which plunge men into ruin and destruction.

Seize the moment and be content in your circumstances so that you can be motivated to work with your whole heart, for the glory of God, in all that you do (Philippians 4:11-13; Colossians 3:23).

2 SAMUEL 16
GET BOTH SIDES OF THE STORY!

Have you ever been offended on behalf of another person, only to find out later that the person's version of the story was not the whole story? It is a terrible feeling to have taken someone's side only to discover that you should have listened to both sides of the story before making the decision to defend one person, or go on the attack against the other person. King David fell into this trap when Ziba accused Mephibosheth of rebellion in 2 Samuel 16:3-4:

> Then the king said, "And where is your master's son?" And Ziba said to the king, "Behold, he is staying in Jerusalem, for he said, 'Today the house of Israel will restore the kingdom of my father to me.'" So the king said to Ziba, "Behold, all that belongs to Mephibosheth is yours." And Ziba said, "I prostrate myself; let me find favor in your sight, O my lord, the king!"

Absalom was overthrowing his father's throne in a military coup, and David was fleeing Jerusalem. Ziba arrived with significant supplies to assist him with the escape, and told David that Mephibosheth was not with him. We find out later, in 2 Samuel 19:24-30, that there was another side of the story. David's son, Solomon, reflected in Proverbs 18:17, "The first to plead his case seems right, until another comes and examines him."

Due process is a necessary part of the law, as commanded in Deuteronomy 19:15, "on the evidence of two or three witnesses a matter shall be confirmed." Jesus commanded the need for involving others as witnesses to the process of reconciliation in Matthew 18:16. Getting the whole story is a necessary part of making good decisions.

Seize the moment and get both sides of the story; be slow to make judgments. James teaches us in James 1:19-20, "This you know, my beloved brethren. But everyone must be quick to hear, slow to speak and slow to anger; for the anger of man does not achieve the righteousness of God."

2 SAMUEL 17
PURSUE THE COUNSEL OF GOD'S WILL!

Have you ever felt your advice was disregarded? If so, don't fret; God may be doing something bigger than you can imagine. Pray for God's will to be done.

Absalom seized Jerusalem and sought separate counsel for his next steps from two men, Ahithophel and Hushai. The former was personally willing to lead a strike force of 12,000 men to strike down David, who was weary and his army was in disarray. The latter, who was still loyal to David, advised against such a quick attack. Hushai seized the moment, and wisely played against Absalom's fears and pride.

While Absalom was manipulated by a master politician, the reality of the situation is revealed in 2 Samuel 17:14:

> Then Absalom and all the men of Israel said, "The counsel of Hushai the Archite is better than the counsel of Ahithophel." For the LORD had ordained to thwart the good counsel of Ahithophel, so that the LORD might bring calamity on Absalom.

This was God's response to David's prayer in 2 Samuel 15:31, "O LORD, I pray, make the counsel of Ahithophel foolishness." He used Hushai to thwart Absalom's rebellion. In fact, David had sent Hushai into Absalom's ranks for this very reason (34).

Tragically, Ahithophel committed suicide soon after Absalom's rejection of his counsel. He felt the shame would have been too great, and certain judgment would befall him upon David's victorious return to Jerusalem.

Don't follow his example! Remember, when situations don't work out the way you think they should, that is a reason to trust God and surrender to His will. Your choice is either to submit to God's will or to seek after your own will – one leads to life and freedom, the other to death and slavery (2 Corinthians 7:9-10).

Seize the moment and pursue the counsel of God to walk in His will for your life.

2 SAMUEL 18
BE A FAITHFUL MESSENGER!

I had the privilege of coaching at the Regional Championships for girls high school track and field this season. In addition to watching some great throwing, highlighted by my discus thrower competing like a champion to earn third place and secure her spot at the Indiana State Championships, I watched a lot of amazing running on the track.

In 2 Samuel 18:19-22, Joab's favorite runner wanted to be the messenger of the good news that Absalom had been defeated and the battle was won – the kingdom was secure! Joab knew that David tended to shoot the messenger when there was bad news, and Absalom's death would not be well received by his father, so he refused Ahimaaz this privilege and sent another, the Cushite. But Ahimaaz would not be denied his opportunity to be the messenger of the good news.

With Joab finally relenting, Ahimaaz beat the Cushite to the king to deliver the good news, but when David asked about the well-being of his son, the swift-footed herald of the good news equivocated (29). It was the Cushite who gave David the whole story – the good and the bad news of the victory.

Who was the more faithful messenger – the eager, persistent one who concealed the bad news of the battle, or the faithful one who told the whole story? As messengers of the gospel of Jesus Christ, we are commanded to tell the whole story of Christ's victory. Paul summarized the good with the bad in Romans 6:23, "For the wages of sin is death, but the free gift of God is eternal life in Christ Jesus our Lord." People will not understand the victory of Jesus Christ for the forgiveness of their sin, the free gift of God, if they don't first hear the truth about God's punishment for their sin.

Seize the moment and be a faithful messenger of the gospel; tell the whole story!

2 SAMUEL 19
MEPHIBOSHETH AND THE REST OF THE STORY!

Have you ever been in a situation where you are invited to help two people, but their perspectives are not the same? I'm often in this position, especially in marital counseling. I prayerfully listen to both people, and seek a compromise that will bring them together, for their good and God's glory.

Absalom's rebellion had been defeated, and David was returning to his throne in Jerusalem. While David was trying to restore unity throughout the twelve tribes of Israel, he was also trying to pass right judgments upon those people who had been disloyal. One critical relationship to David was with Jonathan's son, Mephibosheth. Ziba, his servant, had approached David when he was fleeing from Jerusalem to inform him of Mephibosheth's disloyalty, but he was now hearing the rest of the story from the man himself in 2 Samuel 19:25-27:

> It was when he came from Jerusalem to meet the king, that the king said to him, "Why did you not go with me, Mephibosheth?" So he answered, "O my lord, the king, my servant deceived me; for your servant said, 'I will saddle a donkey for myself that I may ride on it and go with the king,' because your servant is lame. Moreover, he has slandered your servant to my lord the king; but my lord the king is like the angel of God, therefore do what is good in your sight."

What was David to do? David had previously judged Mephibosheth at the word of Ziba; now, as he learned the other side of the story, Ziba was accused of opportunistically betraying his master and lying to the king. David decided in verse 29, "You and Ziba shall divide the land." It was a compromise to bring both sides together – for their good, and for the unity of the kingdom.

Seize the moment, by "being diligent to preserve the unity of the Spirit in the bond of peace" (Ephesians 4:3).

2 SAMUEL 20
USE YOUR BRAIN BEFORE YOUR BRAWN!

Have you ever been in a situation where you used your brawn instead of your brain?

Immediately after Absalom's rebellion was put down, another one, led by Sheba, the son of Bichri, a Benjamite, revolted against David. Sheba blew a trumpet and declared in 2 Samuel 20:1, "We have no portion in David, nor do we have inheritance in the son of Jesse; every man to his tents, O Israel!"

Trouble was following David, and the kingdom of Israel, at every turn! Not only was there a political division in the twelve tribes, but there was also a power struggle in the military. David promoted Amasa to lead the army, but Joab, the former general who had killed Absalom, could not accept his demotion, so he murdered Amasa. Joab was starting to flex his military might, again, when a wise woman called out to him in 2 Samuel 20:15-16:

> They came and besieged him in Abel Beth-maacah, and they cast up a siege ramp against the city, and it stood by the rampart; and all the people who were with Joab were wreaking destruction in order to topple the wall. Then a wise woman called from the city, "Hear, hear! Please tell Joab, 'Come here that I may speak with you.'"

She knew there was a better way to put down this rebellion than to see her entire city destroyed, so she called for a negotiation. Essentially, she asked Joab what he wanted, and she gave it to him – the death of Sheba. Using her brains instead of her brawn, this unnamed woman won the victory, the army went home, and her city was left in peace (17-22).

Paul teaches us in Romans 12:18, "If possible, so far as it depends on you, be at peace with all men." Think about how you bring the peace of God to the situations around you.

Seize the moment and use your brain to be at peace with all people before you use your brawn to create the appearance of peace.

2 SAMUEL 21
TRAIN THE NEXT GENERATION!

One of my hobbies is training for, and competing in, USA Track & Field Masters competitions. Even with a few national championships under my belt, I will be the first to tell you that, as I get older, I am not able to throw the 16-pound Olympic hammer as far as I did when I was younger. (Evidence of this happened, recently, with my second-place finish at the 2022 USATF Masters Championships.) This is one of the reasons why being a coach makes sense at this point in my life. It's time to pass on the knowledge gained from my former successes to aid the next generation to be even more successful.

There is a reality to getting older that requires one generation to entrust to the next generation their skills and responsibilities. We must pass it on (2 Timothy 2:2)! As David matured in his kingship, we witness a critical turn of events happen in 2 Samuel 21:15-17:

> Now when the Philistines were at war again with Israel, David went down and his servants with him; and as they fought against the Philistines, David became weary. Then Ishbi-benob, who was among the descendants of the giant, the weight of whose spear was three hundred shekels of bronze in weight, was girded with a new sword, and he intended to kill David. But Abishai the son of Zeruiah helped him, and struck the Philistine and killed him. Then the men of David swore to him, saying, "You shall not go out again with us to battle, so that you do not extinguish the lamp of Israel."

At one time David was the only one in Israel who had the courage to face the giant Goliath (1 Samuel 17). That was no longer true, and praise God it wasn't, because if David hadn't trained the next generation to defeat the giants, he may not have survived that day of battle.

Every generation will face their giants! Who are you training to win the victory?

Seize the moment and train the next generation to face their giants (Psalm 22:30-31; 78:6).

2 SAMUEL 22
WALK IN COVENANT FAITHFULNESS!

David pens a psalm of praise for God's deliverance in his life, expressing his complete dependence and absolute loyalty to the God of Israel, starting with these words in 2 Samuel 22:2-4:

> The LORD is my rock and my fortress and my deliverer; my God, my rock, in whom I take refuge, my shield and the horn of my salvation, my stronghold and my refuge; my savior, You save me from violence. I call upon the LORD, who is worthy to be praised, and I am saved from my enemies.

This song of David is virtually identical to Psalm 18, so why do we find it near the end of this book? The author of Samuel was bookending his work, which began with Hannah's song of praise for God's provision, starting with these words in 1 Samuel 2:1-2:

> My heart exults in the LORD; my horn is exalted in the LORD, my mouth speaks boldly against my enemies, because I rejoice in Your salvation. There is no one holy like the LORD, indeed, there is no one besides You, nor is there any rock like our God.

In the Hebrew Bible, Samuel was originally in the format of one book, not two. The author's intent was to encourage the people of the divided kingdom to walk with the Lord in covenant faithfulness – with complete dependence and absolute loyalty to Him in all circumstances.

David and Hannah's songs, the bookends of Samuel, emphasize the sovereignty of God. He is powerful to act, bringing about His purposes from their dire circumstances, for the good of His people and His glory. God, Israel's rock, was the only hope in their time of dire need!

Seize the moment and praise God for His power and provision to bring about His purposes in all circumstances (Genesis 50:20; Romans 8:28). Put your hope in God alone (Psalm 62:5-8)!

2 SAMUEL 23
THE HOPE OF A SUNRISE!

When was the last time you set apart time to enjoy the sunrise? As part of my rhythm of writing these daily devotions, I intentionally stop to watch the first light of the morning as the sun crests the horizon in the East. For me, it is a time of hope and awe – a daily promise of God's faithfulness! As you may know about me, by now, I believe that every promise of God comes with a praxis for my daily life – the sunrise is a time of covenant renewal to live faithfully, with faith, hope, and love, once again, today.

The "last words of David" are recorded in Samuel as a song of praise to God for establishing a covenant with His house. In typical Davidic style, as evidenced by his writing of over half the psalms, David poetically expresses the validity of his own kingship, and the security of God's covenant, in 2 Samuel 23:3-5:

> The God of Israel said, the Rock of Israel spoke to me, "He who rules over men righteously, who rules in the fear of God, is as the light of the morning when the sun rises, a morning without clouds, when the tender grass springs out of the earth, through sunshine after rain." Truly is not my house so with God? For He has made an everlasting covenant with me, ordered in all things, and secured; for all my salvation and all my desire, will He not indeed make it grow?

Every day that the sun rises, you also can experience the reminder of God's covenant faithfulness, and rejoice in His promises (Lamentations 3:22-24). Additionally, like David, your life can shine every day like the rising sun, bringing life and flourishing to all that you touch. Just as the sun rises every day, you are called to be a hope-bearer every day.

Seize the moment and embrace the covenant renewal opportunity that comes with each sunrise – live faithfully by shining God's light (Matthew 5:14-16)!

2 SAMUEL 24
COSTLY MISTAKES REQUIRE COSTLY SACRIFICE!

Have you ever made a costly mistake?

King David did! He ordered a census, which took over nine months to complete (2 Samuel 24:1-9). His costly mistake brought judgment upon the nation of Israel. God confronted David and offered him three options on how that judgment would unfold; David chose pestilence, because he trusted that God's mercy would prevail in the end (2 Samuel 24:10-14). As the king, he knew that the only way to reconcile the situation, and see God relent from judgment, was to bear the cost himself, as seen in 2 Samuel 24:24-25, the last verses of Samuel:

However, the king said to Araunah, "No, but I will surely buy it from you for a price, for I will not offer burnt offerings to the LORD my God which cost me nothing." So David bought the threshing floor and the oxen for fifty shekels of silver. David built there an altar to the LORD and offered burnt offerings and peace offerings. Thus the LORD was moved by prayer for the land, and the plague was held back from Israel.

This foreshadows the ministry of Jesus, and what He did for all people; Jesus bore the cost of God's judgment for humanity's sin upon Himself, as expressed in 1 Peter 2:24, "He Himself bore our sins in His body on the cross, so that we might die to sin and live to righteousness; for by His wounds you were healed." Jesus, who knew no sin, took on our sin, so that we might become the righteousness of God in Him (2 Corinthians 5:21).

In response to Jesus' great act of mercy for your healing and reconciliation, are you willing to make a costly sacrifice to God?

Seize the moment and "present your bodies a living and holy sacrifice, acceptable to God, which is your spiritual service of worship" (Romans 12:1). Paul expounds on how to do this in Romans 6:12-13, "Therefore do not let sin reign in your mortal body so that you obey its lusts, and do not go on presenting the members of your body to sin as instruments of unrighteousness; but present yourselves to God as those alive from the dead, and your members as instruments of righteousness to God."

1 KINGS

1 KINGS 1
MEN PLOT AND GOD WILLS!

As we begin a new book of the Bible, we start with the same old story of people acting out of their fears, manipulating current events, and plotting to gain power. Not much has changed over the last three thousand years. As David laid on his death bed, Adonijah, like Absalom before him, took the initiative to make himself the next king of Israel. The heart of the drama is found in 1 Kings 1:13-14, where Nathan organized a plan with Bathsheba, the mother of Solomon, to counter Adonijah's conspiracy:

> So now come, please let me give you counsel and save your life and the life of your son Solomon. Go at once to King David and say to him, "Have you not, my lord, O king, sworn to your maidservant, saying, 'Surely Solomon your son shall be king after me, and he shall sit on my throne'? Why then has Adonijah become king?" Behold, while you are still there speaking with the king, I will come in after you and confirm your words.

Nathan the prophet had access to David, and used it to bring about God's will for the building of His temple through Solomon, as foretold to David (1 Chronicles 22:9-10). This was of paramount importance to David, as it was on his heart to do this for God. In the 2 Samuel 7 account, Nathan had mistakenly given David permission to build the temple, before being given a word from God that forbade David from building the temple, but secured a dynastic succession. Adonijah, as the eldest living son of David, thought that he could put himself on the throne of Israel, but that was the way of men. God is the one who establishes authority (Romans 13:1). Men plot and God wills!

Seize the moment and stop your plotting; trust God's sovereign rule over the nations (Psalm 22:28; 47:8; 1 Chronicles 16:31).

1 KINGS 2
DEAL WITH THE ENEMY WITHIN!

Have you ever felt like the greatest threat to your own happiness and well-being was not from the outside, but from the enemy within?

In his final charge to Solomon, King David commanded the new king to deal with the enemies within his own gates; he started with these instructions recorded in 1 Kings 2:2-4:

> I am going the way of all the earth. Be strong, therefore, and show yourself a man. Keep the charge of the LORD your God, to walk in His ways, to keep His statutes, His commandments, His ordinances, and His testimonies, according to what is written in the Law of Moses, that you may succeed in all that you do and wherever you turn, so that the LORD may carry out His promise which He spoke concerning me, saying, "If your sons are careful of their way, to walk before Me in truth with all their heart and with all their soul, you shall not lack a man on the throne of Israel."

Wisely, David gave Solomon God's instructions for a king from Deuteronomy 17:18-20 and passed on to his son God's covenantal promise from 2 Samuel 7:12-16. David believed the greatest threat to Solomon would be the enemies within the gate, including Joab and Shimei (1 Kings 2:5-9).

By the end of this chapter, it looked as if the enemies within the gate had been dealt with successfully, except for one! Solomon seemingly didn't deal with the worst of the enemies within the gate that David warned him of – himself! As we will see in the very next chapter, Solomon sowed the seeds of his own failure, not from a lack of wisdom, but from a lack of submission to God's ways in the most intimate places of his life (Deuteronomy 17:17; 1 Kings 11:1-6).

Seize the moment and "watch over your heart with all diligence, for from it flow the springs of life" (Proverbs 4:23; Mark 7:15; Galatians 5:16-21; Romans 7:21-23).

1 KINGS 3
THE OPPORTUNITY OF A LIFETIME!

If God gave you the opportunity to ask for anything you want, what would you ask for? Before you give a flippant response to this question, take time to think deeply upon this opportunity of a lifetime. Your answer reveals your heart, and determines the way in which you will walk.

Solomon is the new king of Israel, and, in his great wealth, he offered a large sacrifice to God, after which the Lord appeared to him in a dream and said, "Ask what you wish me to give you" (1 Kings 3:5). Solomon's response, in 1 Kings 3:9, pleased God, "Give Your servant an understanding heart to judge Your people to discern between good and evil. For who is able to judge this great people of Yours?"

A thousand years later, in Mark 10:51-52, a blind beggar was crying out to Jesus from the side of the road, when Jesus responded:

"What do you want Me to do for you?" And the blind man said to Him, "Rabboni, I want to regain my sight!" And Jesus said to him, "Go; your faith has made you well." Immediately he regained his sight and began following Him on the road.

Two men, one a rich ruler and the other a poor beggar, are given the opportunity of a lifetime. The first received the ability to hear with his heart, and the second the ability to see with his eyes. Both, in response, are invited to follow in the way to demonstrate that they have received the true gift – a relationship with the Gift-Giver. Today, God is offering you the same opportunity of a lifetime.

Seize the moment and "delight yourself in the LORD; and He will give you the desires of your heart. Commit your way to the LORD, trust also in Him, and He will do it" (Psalm 37:4-5).

1 KINGS 4
GOD KEEPS HIS PROMISES!

Are you waiting on God to fulfill a promise?

King Solomon's reign was unique in the history of Israel. It was a time of rest for the nation as they experienced the fulfillment of God's promise to Abraham, according to 1 Kings 4:20-21 & 25:

> Judah and Israel were as numerous as the sand that is on the seashore in abundance; they were eating and drinking and rejoicing. Now Solomon ruled over all the kingdoms from the River to the land of the Philistines and to the border of Egypt; they brought tribute and served Solomon all the days of his life. ... So Judah and Israel lived in safety, every man under his vine and his fig tree, from Dan even to Beersheba, all the days of Solomon.

You may recognize the phrase "as numerous as the sand that is on the seashore," because it was a promise of God, given to Abraham in Genesis 22:17, "indeed I will greatly bless you, and I will greatly multiply your seed as the stars of the heavens and as the sand which is on the seashore; and your seed shall possess the gate of their enemies." God later reiterated this promise to Israel (Jacob) in Genesis 32:12.

God yoked the promise of abundance and the promise of rest with the giving of the Promised Land, which He covenanted to give to Abraham in Genesis 15:18. That was later affirmed by Moses to the twelve tribes of Israel in Deuteronomy 12:10, "He gives you rest from all your enemies around you so that you live in security."

Just as God's promises of abundance and rest were fulfilled in the days of Solomon, so they are today in Jesus Christ (John 10:10; Matthew 11:28-30; Hebrews 4:9-11; 2 Corinthians 1:20).

Seize the moment and wait upon the Lord with faith, hope, and love; God never fails to keep His promises!

1 KINGS 5
THE HEAVY BURDEN OF FORCED LABOR!

Have you ever been forced to do a job you didn't like, or didn't want to do? Imagine being conscripted by the President to be a forced laborer for a grand national project in Washington, D.C.

First Kings 5:13-16 explained how Solomon conscripted 183,300 workers to do the hard labor of building the temple:

Now King Solomon levied forced laborers from all Israel; and the forced laborers numbered 30,000 men. He sent them to Lebanon, 10,000 a month in relays; they were in Lebanon a month and two months at home. And Adoniram was over the forced laborers. Now Solomon had 70,000 transporters, and 80,000 hewers of stone in the mountains, besides Solomon's 3,300 chief deputies who were over the project and who ruled over the people who were doing the work.

These men quarried and cut the stones for the foundation of the temple, as well as transported and prepared the necessary timber for this grand national project in Jerusalem. Unstated in this account are the countless farmers, laborers, and servants who would support this undertaking, providing for the terms of the purchase agreement with Hiram, the king of Tyre (1-12).

We read through all this way too quickly! We remain deaf and blind to the suffering of the people living under the heavy burden of Solomon's aggressive agenda. In 1 Kings 12:4, after forty years of Solomon's rule, the people petition Solomon's son, Rehoboam, "Your father made our yoke hard; now therefore lighten the hard service of your father and his heavy yoke which he put on us, and we will serve you." When he refused, the people rebelled (1 Kings 12:13-19). People can only take the heavy burden of forced labor for so long!

Seize the moment and find rest for your soul from the oppressive regime of sin by breaking the world's heavy yoke and getting in the easy yoke of Jesus; His burden is light (Matthew 11:28-30).

1 KINGS 6
THE HEART OF WORSHIP!

Why do we gather as the church? What is the heart of worship? Is it about a building, or a service with songs and a sermon, or is worship something more than all of these?

The detailed description of Solomon's temple has two distinct parts in 1 Kings 6. Verses 2-10 describe the exterior, and verses 14-38 describe the interior. While most of this chapter is focused on the details of the construction of the temple, the heart of the temple project is found in 1 Kings 6:11-13:

> Now the word of the LORD came to Solomon saying, "Concerning this house which you are building, if you will walk in My statutes and execute My ordinances and keep all My commandments by walking in them, then I will carry out My word with you which I spoke to David your father. I will dwell among the sons of Israel, and will not forsake My people Israel."

Obviously, the temple was an important place, but it should not be surprising that God would remind His people that, at the heart of its construction, and its future usage, was the life of obedience to His commandments. God taught the heart of worship previously in 1 Samuel 15:22-23a:

> Has the LORD as much delight in burnt offerings and sacrifices as in obeying the voice of the LORD? Behold, to obey is better than sacrifice, and to heed than the fat of rams. For rebellion is as the sin of divination, and insubordination is as iniquity and idolatry.

While building projects, event planning, song selections, and sermon writing are important parts of how we practice our faith in contemporary Christianity, let us never forget that the heart of worship has always been, and will always be, obedience to God and His ways. We are the temple of His presence on the Earth (1 Corinthians 6:19-20).

Seize the moment and worship God by obeying His Word. Behold, to obey is better than sacrifice!

1 KINGS 7
ACQUIRE WISDOM AND GET UNDERSTANDING!

While it is important to be a competent and capable person, your character is of the greatest importance.

The construction of the temple was complete, and it was time for the intricate details to be crafted. Accordingly, in 1 Kings 7:13-14, King Solomon called upon the best artisan, a skilled worker who was filled with wisdom and understanding:

> Now King Solomon sent and brought Hiram from Tyre. He was a widow's son from the tribe of Naphtali, and his father was a man of Tyre, a worker in bronze; and he was filled with wisdom and understanding and skill for doing any work in bronze.

This passage is reminiscent of God's words to Moses, during the building of the tabernacle, in Exodus 31:1-3, "See, I have called by name Bezalel, the son of Uri, the son of Hur, of the tribe of Judah. I have filled him with the Spirit of God in wisdom, in understanding, in knowledge, and in all kinds of craftsmanship."

When God chooses a person for an important job, it is not only for their competency, but also for their character. The skilled artisans Solomon and Moses selected were people of wisdom and understanding. This pairing of "wisdom and understanding" in the Bible is used to describe the quality of a person's spiritual maturity – they feared God and listened for His instructions. Isaiah 11:2a details this truth in a messianic prophecy, "The Spirit of the LORD will rest on Him, the spirit of wisdom and understanding."

God desires for His people to be empowered by His Spirit in all their work, not to lean upon their own understanding, no matter how educated or trained. It is good to further your education, and pursue your training, but don't neglect the fear of the Lord!

Seize the moment and "acquire wisdom; and with all your acquiring, get understanding" (Proverbs 9:10).

Dr. Jerry D. Ingalls

1 KINGS 8
BLESSED TO BE A BLESSING!

The word "blessed" has become commonplace in our culture recently. There is nothing wrong with using it, if you know that God's blessings always come with a stewardship responsibility – a charge from God to be a blessing!

There was a big celebration in Jerusalem, and throughout Israel, as the ark of God was relocated to the temple. As it was placed inside the most holy place, the cloud, the glory of God, filled the house of the Lord (1 Kings 8:1-11). God was with them! King Solomon spoke (12-21), gave a prayer of dedication (22-54), and then in verses 56-61, he blessed the people:

Blessed be the LORD, who has given rest to His people Israel, according to all that He promised; not one word has failed of all His good promise, which He promised through Moses His servant. May the LORD our God be with us, as He was with our fathers; may He not leave us or forsake us, that He may incline our hearts to Himself, to walk in all His ways and to keep His commandments and His statutes and His ordinances, which He commanded our fathers. And may these words of mine, with which I have made supplication before the LORD, be near to the LORD our God day and night, that He may maintain the cause of His servant and the cause of His people Israel, as each day requires, so that all the peoples of the earth may know that the LORD is God; there is no one else. Let your heart therefore be wholly devoted to the LORD our God, to walk in His statutes and to keep His commandments, as at this day.

Solomon's blessing was filled with gratitude and faith, yet it also charged the people to live for God wholeheartedly, according to His commandments, and to bless the nations for His glory. God's blessings always come with a stewardship responsibility – give to others what God so freely gave to you!

Seize the moment and walk in God's blessing by living out God's charge upon your life – you have been blessed to a blessing!

1 KINGS 9
THE SCORE AT HALF-TIME!

What is the least important statistic in sports? The score at half-time!

Fast forward twenty years; King Solomon's building projects were finished (1 Kings 9:10). As we get this glimpse of Solomon's kingship, at the halfway point of his forty-year reign, we see that he has been blessed by God and is prospering in every way. Unfortunately, there were also strong indicators of his eventual defeat, if he doesn't shore up his weak areas. God, like a good coach who challenges his players to play like champions in the second half of the game during the half-time locker room talk, confronted Solomon in 1 Kings 9:6-9:

> But if you or your sons indeed turn away from following Me, and do not keep My commandments and My statutes which I have set before you, and go and serve other gods and worship them, then I will cut off Israel from the land which I have given them, and the house which I have consecrated for My name, I will cast out of My sight. So Israel will become a proverb and a byword among all peoples. And this house will become a heap of ruins; everyone who passes by will be astonished and hiss and say, "Why has the LORD done thus to this land and to this house?" And they will say, "Because they forsook the LORD their God, who brought their fathers out of the land of Egypt, and adopted other gods and worshiped them and served them, therefore the LORD has brought all this adversity on them."

Solomon did not heed the Coach's wisdom, and all of God's warnings were fulfilled in the destruction of Jerusalem in Jeremiah 52. Regardless of the score at half-time in your life, or ministry, live like a champion today, all the way to finish line (1 Corinthians 9:24-27).

Seize the moment and finish strong; persevere until the end (Matthew 24:13).

Dr. Jerry D. Ingalls

1 KINGS 10
SOMETHING GREATER THAN SOLOMON!

Have you ever had a chance to meet a powerful or famous person? Did that person live up to your expectations?

King Solomon received many important visitors, and one of the most famous was the Queen of Sheba. After spending time with Solomon, and inspecting every aspect of his kingship, she concluded in 1 Kings 10:6-7:

It was a true report which I heard in my own land about your words and your wisdom. Nevertheless I did not believe the reports, until I came and my eyes had seen it. And behold, the half was not told me. You exceed in wisdom and prosperity the report which I heard.

As a point of comparison, Jesus referenced this story in Matthew 12:42:

The Queen of the South will rise up with this generation at the judgment and will condemn it, because she came from the ends of the earth to hear the wisdom of Solomon; and behold, something greater than Solomon is here.

To further illustrate this contrast, 1 Kings 10:23-24 says this about Solomon's power and fame, "So King Solomon became greater than all the kings of the earth in riches and in wisdom. All the earth was seeking the presence of Solomon, to hear his wisdom which God had put in his heart."

What can possibly be greater than the greatest king on Earth? It is the Kingdom of God, the sovereign rule of God over all creation, Heaven and Earth, through the rightful kingship of the King of Kings, God's only begotten Son, Jesus Christ. Jesus declared that He was ushering in "something greater," and that was His wisdom, His riches, and His rule, which far exceed all who had ever come before Him, including King Solomon. Jesus has put all things in subjection under His feet (1 Corinthians 15:23-28).

Seize the moment and put your faith in King Jesus; He will never fall short of the power and fame ascribed to Him.

1 KINGS 11
KEEP YOUR FOCUS ON JESUS!

As I read about the sad ending to Solomon's life in 1 Kings 11, I couldn't help but reflect on how I want to finish my race – with my eyes on Jesus. Solomon experienced a long season of peace and prosperity during the first half of his kingship, but his final years were marked by anxiety and turmoil. Solomon lost focus on God! In 1 Kings 11:11-13, God declared His verdict on Solomon for his idolatry:

> Because you have done this, and you have not kept My covenant and My statutes, which I have commanded you, I will surely tear the kingdom from you, and will give it to your servant. Nevertheless I will not do it in your days for the sake of your father David, but I will tear it out of the hand of your son. However, I will not tear away all the kingdom, but I will give one tribe to your son for the sake of My servant David and for the sake of Jerusalem which I have chosen.

God raised up adversaries against Solomon, including Jeroboam, the man who would be the one to fulfill this prophetic judgment. Ahijah the prophet declared Jeroboam to be the future king over ten of the tribes of Israel, dividing the kingdom after Solomon's death (29-39).

God had given Solomon's kingdom great peace, and abundant prosperity, for many years, but instead of using that time and wealth to lead his nation to love and worship God more deeply, Solomon sought pleasure from many women, and privilege from his position. His loss of focus destroyed his life, and divided Israel. It's amazing how one person's focus can bring life or death, blessings or curses, upon himself and others.

Seize the moment and keep your eyes on Jesus, all the way to the finish line of your life (Hebrews 12:1-3).

1 KINGS 12
THE IMPORTANCE OF WISE COUNSELORS!

How do you approach making big decisions? Do you make your big decisions all by yourself, or do you seek the counsel of others?

Proverbs 15:22 teaches, "Without consultation, plans are frustrated, but with many counselors they succeed." The Bible emphasizes the importance of having a trusted community of wise counselors in your life. These people don't have to be professional therapists, but they do need to be trusted friends and family members who will give you biblical and timely wisdom. They should neither make your decisions for you, nor serve as your rubber-stamp committee; rather, they should be brothers and sisters who love you enough to ask the hard questions, to ensure you are living for Jesus in every area of your life.

A great example of the need for such a community comes from 1 Kings 12:1-15. Rehoboam, the son of Solomon, and successor to the throne of Israel, was ambivalent on how to respond to the plea of his people in verse 4, "Your father made our yoke hard; now therefore lighten the hard service of your father and his heavy yoke which he put on us, and we will serve you." The elders counseled him to lessen the people's burden, whereas his contemporaries counseled him to increase their burden (6-11). In fulfillment of God's judgment, Rehoboam forsook the wise counsel of the elders to follow the foolish counsel of the young men he grew up with. Henceforth, the people rebelled, forsook him as king, and the kingdom was divided from that day forward (13-33).

From this story, we learn that we must choose our counselors wisely. It takes time and effort to find them, but surround yourself with people who will walk in the way of Jesus with you, to the glory of God.

Seize the moment and build a community of wise counselors for your life (Proverbs 11:14; 24:6).

1 KINGS 13
THE CALL TO RADICAL OBEDIENCE!

Has God ever asked you to fast from food for a prolonged time? There was a time when I was in the US Army, faced with a difficult challenge, when the Lord asked me to fast from food for three days in preparation for a significant meeting. I didn't understand why at the time, but in retrospect, I see that God has always had a better plan than any of my plans.

In 1 Kings 13, an unnamed man of God from Judah traveled to Bethel to confront Jeroboam, the king of Israel, and to prophesy God's judgment against the altar he had built at Bethel (1-10). The prophet spoke with authority, and gave a sign, but Jeroboam didn't repent, and Israel remained in its apostasy (33-34).

Strange, but true, God authenticated this man as His prophet through a call to radical obedience – a complete fast from food and water. He told Jeroboam in 1 Kings 13:9, "For so it was commanded me by the word of the LORD, saying, 'You shall eat no bread, nor drink water, nor return by the way which you came.'"

The prophet walked in submission to God, until, on his way home to Judah, he ate in the home of a deceptive old man. It was his last meal. Shortly after, God struck him down by a lion, proving that he was a prophet, his calling authenticated by God's immediate judgment of his disobedience (11-32). One hundred years later, the prophet's words were proven true by King Josiah, as recorded in 2 Kings 23:15-20, as this prophet was remembered as the harbinger of God's judgment of the altar at Bethel.

Seize the moment and obey God's call, because you never know the impact of one act of radical obedience. You may not know why God asks you to do certain things, but trust that God's Word never returns void (Isaiah 55:11).

Dr. Jerry D. Ingalls

1 KINGS 14
REMAIN FAITHFUL TO GOD!

In our secular-humanist culture, with the wall between religion and state, it is hard for us to imagine how religion and politics were yoked in Israel. God's prophets would foretell the rise and fall of kings and kingdoms. We see this in the prophetic ministry of Ahijah the Shilonite and the rise and fall of King Jeroboam.

Ahijah was introduced during the reign of Solomon, immediately after Jeroboam was first introduced in 1 Kings 11:28 as a "valiant warrior" and "industrious." In verses 30-40, Ahijah, reminiscent of the prophet Samuel's anointing of David during Saul's reign, endorsed Jeroboam as the next king, and spoke of him tearing away ten of the tribes from David's household. Just like when Saul ripped Samuel's cloak, Ahijah ripped his own cloak into twelve pieces to symbolize the tearing of the kingdom (30-31). Additionally, he used dynastic language, similar to Nathan's prophecy to David (38).

In 1 Kings 14, fast forward to the end of Jeroboam's twenty-two-year kingship, and his son Abijah was sick. Jeroboam turned to Ahijah, now an old man who had gone blind, and God gave him a final prophetic word for Jeroboam and Israel, a heart-breaking reversal of his first word. In 1 Kings 14:16, he proclaimed, "He will give up Israel on account of the sins of Jeroboam, which he committed and with which he made Israel to sin."

Ahijah remained faithful in his role as God's prophet, but can you imagine how he must have felt, since his ministry was intimately yoked with the rise and fall of Jeroboam? His ministry was filled with moments of hope and exaltation when Jeroboam was coronated, then with grave disappointments as he watched God's man rebel against the very one who put him into office. Yet, Ahijah himself remained faithful to God, regardless of these circumstances and Jeroboam's bad choices.

Seize the moment and be faithful to God, regardless of your circumstances and the bad choices of others. It's your choice!

1 KINGS 15
THE WAY OF KINGS!

What is the way of kings? According to 1 Kings 15, it is war. Listen to three passages that demonstrate how three different sets of kings spent their kingships waging a civil war between the northern ten tribes of Israel and the southern two tribes of Judah:

1. "There was war between Rehoboam and Jeroboam all the days of his life" (1 Kings 15:6; cf. 1 Kings 14:30).
2. "And there was war between Abijam and Jeroboam" (1 Kings 15:7).
3. "Now there was war between Asa and Baasha king of Israel all their days" (1 Kings 15:16, cf. 1 Kings 15:32).

God's people were divided after the death of Solomon, and, from that time forward, the way of kings was the sword. Jesus warned Peter in Matthew 26:52, "Put your sword back into its place; for all those who take up the sword shall perish by the sword." So, while the way of worldly kings is war, the way of the King of Kings is peace.

Jesus not only commanded Peter to put away the sword, but He commanded all His followers to work as peacemakers in a world caught in a perpetual cycle of violence (Matthew 5:9). In Luke 6:27-28, Jesus gave us one of the hardest commands we are to follow, "But I say to you who hear, love your enemies, do good to those who hate you, bless those who curse you, pray for those who mistreat you."

Just as violence breeds violence, so love begets love! Jesus gave Himself over to violent men as the eternal solution to the way of kings. He invites us to follow Him (Mark 1:17). You must choose for yourself: the way of kings, or the way of the King of Kings.

Seize the moment and walk in the way of Jesus – the Prince of Peace (Isaiah 9:6-7)!

Dr. Jerry D. Ingalls

1 KINGS 16
COUNT THE COST OF YOUR AMBITION!

What is the price tag on your ambition?

At the end of 1 Kings 16, an overview of six successive evil kings of Israel, there is a one-verse description of the cost of rebuilding Jericho, in verse 34:

> In his days Hiel the Bethelite built Jericho; he laid its foundations with the loss of Abiram his firstborn, and set up its gates with the loss of his youngest son Segub, according to the word of the LORD, which He spoke by Joshua the son of Nun.

Whereas the material and labor costs would have been substantial to Hiel, those would have paled in comparison to the value of his two sons, who died in fulfillment of the ancient curse against the rebuilding of this city, recorded in Joshua 6:26:

> Then Joshua made them take an oath at that time, saying, "Cursed before the LORD is the man who rises up and builds this city Jericho; with the loss of his firstborn he shall lay its foundation, and with the loss of his youngest son he shall set up its gates."

While most industrious people, today, would laugh off the concept of ancient curses, there are blessings and curses built into the Law of God, which, like gravity, are at work, regardless of whether you believe in the Creator of those laws. Like gravity, there is a consequence upon those who teeter on the cliff of their own ambition. In Mark 8:36, Jesus gave us a principle to sober us in our ambitions, "For what does it profit a man to gain the whole world, and forfeit his soul?"

What is the price tag on your ambition: your marriage, your children, your health, or your soul? Be warned of what you are sacrificing on the altar of your success, those may end up being your greatest regrets! We each have such a short life to live, please, invest your life wisely.

Seize the moment and count the cost of your ambition today. Step back from the cliff and discover contentment in Jesus (Philippians 4:12)

1 KINGS 17
THE MIRACLE OF MULTIPLICATION!

Dire circumstances can turn the smallest request into a great act of faith. During a time of drought, a judgment of God against Israel, Elijah the prophet asked a widow for some water and a piece of bread. Normally, that request would have been nothing memorable, but, as seen in 1 Kings 17:12-16, the widow's dire circumstances turned a simple act of hospitality into a great act of faith:

> But she said, "As the LORD your God lives, I have no bread, only a handful of flour in the bowl and a little oil in the jar; and behold, I am gathering a few sticks that I may go in and prepare for me and my son, that we may eat it and die." Then Elijah said to her, "Do not fear; go, do as you have said, but make me a little bread cake from it first and bring it out to me, and afterward you may make one for yourself and for your son. For thus says the LORD God of Israel, 'The bowl of flour shall not be exhausted, nor shall the jar of oil be empty, until the day that the LORD sends rain on the face of the earth.'" So she went and did according to the word of Elijah, and she and he and her household ate for many days. The bowl of flour was not exhausted nor did the jar of oil become empty, according to the word of the LORD which He spoke through Elijah.

The widow's obedience led to her experiencing God's revelation of power and provision. Her willingness to give the last of what she had, in faith, led to a miracle of multiplication that transformed her scarcity into an abundance. This was a foretaste of the gospel of Jesus Christ, who took five loaves, and two fish, and fed a multitude (Matthew 14:15-21). Jesus took one child's sacrifice of his meager peasant's meal, and transformed it into a grand feast for a multitude of thousands (John 6:9).

Seize the moment and trust God to multiply whatever He asks of you in faith, whether it is the giving of your time, talents, or treasures. God can transform any sacrifice, made in faith, "to do far more abundantly beyond all that we ask or think" (Ephesians 3:20).

Dr. Jerry D. Ingalls

1 KINGS 18
MOUNTAINTOP EXPERIENCES!

Have you ever had a mountaintop experience? This is an experience where you encounter the power of God; it is a moment of clarity and exultation. Elijah experienced the mountaintop, literally and spiritually, on Mount Carmel, where he defeated 850 pagan prophets for the glory of God, and the devotion of His people.

The story began with God taking on Baal, the pagan storm god, with a three-year drought, which Elijah announced in 1 Kings 17:1. Then, in 1 Kings 18, God called for an end of that drought, and for a showdown to occur between His prophet, Elijah, and the pagan prophets, who were serving under the evil king, Ahab, and his blasphemous wife, Jezebel. Forty-six verses later, Elijah is on the run, down from the mountaintop, having just personally experienced God's justice against a grave evil. The purpose of this showdown was to win back the hearts of God's people to a singular devotion to the one true God. As Elijah confronted the people in 1 Kings 18:21, "How long will you hesitate between two opinions? If the LORD is God, follow Him; but if Baal, follow him."

The purpose of mountaintop experiences is to return us to a life of wholehearted devotion to the one true God. God grants them for His glory, and our good, but we can't be dependent on them for our daily walk with Jesus. None of us are intended to live on the mountaintop itself, but the mountaintop experience is intended to embolden how we live. This was true of Jesus, who, even after His Transfiguration, which happened on a high mountain, had to come down and face the reality of everyday life (Matthew 17). Jesus brought the experience and knowledge of His mountaintop experience into His everyday life and ministry.

Seize the moment and live with a wholehearted devotion to Jesus today by remembering the clarity and exultation of your mountaintop experiences.

1 KINGS 19
THE VALLEY OF THE SHADOW!

Did you know that the "valley of the shadow of death," a famous phrase coined by King David in Psalm 23:4, is not exclusively referencing death, but includes any experience of peril? Have you ever experienced the valley of the shadow? How did you handle it?

From the highest of highs to the lowest of lows, Elijah went from the mountaintop experience, with the defeat of the 850 pagan prophets on top of Mount Carmel, to the valley of the shadow with the unveiled threat to his life by the wicked queen Jezebel. Elijah was now in the wilderness, literally and spiritually, as told in 1 Kings 19:4:

> But he himself went a day's journey into the wilderness, and came and sat down under a juniper tree; and he requested for himself that he might die, and said, "It is enough; now, O LORD, take my life, for I am not better than my fathers."

Elijah was experiencing the valley of the shadow, which led him to suicidal ideation. This is one of the primary Bible stories that Christian counselors use when researching a biblical understanding of depression, and like issues. Elijah, in this low moment, did the most important thing that any of us can do when we are low; he did a 9-1-1 call to God. In his dark shadow, he didn't turn inwards to find help, he cried out to God with an honest prayer. Like King David before him, he learned that God's presence with him overcomes the worst things he can face in his life – "Even though I walk through the valley of the shadow of death, I fear no evil, for You are with me; Your rod and Your staff, they comfort me" (Psalm 23:4).

God responded to Elijah's prayer by giving him sleep and nourishment, two essential ingredients to survive any valley experience. God then gave him a journey to travel, to Mount Horeb, where he would learn that there was still a purpose for his life (9-21).

Seize the moment by calling out to God with an honest prayer; no matter how deep the shadow, God's light will pierce the darkness.

1 KINGS 20
THE LORD OF MOUNTAINTOPS AND VALLEYS!

Genesis 1:1 proclaims, "In the beginning God created the heavens and the earth." This truth is the key to Ahab's victory over the king of Aram. In fact, it was for the honor of the one true God's sovereignty over all that He granted Ahab a dramatic victory over the Arameans, as articulated in 1 Kings 20:28:

> Then a man of God came near and spoke to the king of Israel and said, "Thus says the LORD, 'Because the Arameans have said, "The LORD is a god of the mountains, but He is not a god of the valleys," therefore I will give all this great multitude into your hand, and you shall know that I am the LORD.'"

As clearly portrayed in this passage, and again in verse 23, the king of Aram made his battle plans based on the ancient supernatural assumption that gods were either functional, such as a harvest or fertility god, or geographical, gods of different cultures and their corresponding regions. The fact that there was one God, who was the Lord over the battle fields of both mountains and valleys, was radically new, and unimaginable. This revelation of the limitlessness of God's dominion was to King Aram and his officials like that of the Copernican Revolution to sixteenth century astronomers – it was an entire paradigm shift! Every time Israel put their faith in the Creator God, who is sovereign over all, He gave them unparalleled victories as a testimony to His power.

Yahweh is not simply one of the *elohim*, in competition with many for supremacy, He is God over all His creation. As the prophet declared in Jeremiah 32:17, "Ah Lord GOD! Behold, You have made the heavens and the earth by Your great power and by Your outstretched arm! Nothing is too difficult for You."

Seize the moment and put your full confidence in the Lord God of all, who is victorious, regardless of whether you are on the mountaintop, or in the valley.

1 KINGS 21
OBEY GOD'S BETTER WAY!

Have you ever been restless, irritable, and discontent? It's a dangerous cocktail of emotions that often leads to poor decision making. In the recovery movement, these three words are often used together to remind us that we must care for our emotional well-being by doing the right thing. A similar word combination is used in the story of Ahab, the king of Israel.

Twice, in short order, we find Ahab "sullen and vexed." The first time was in 1 Kings 20:43, after the prophet rebuked him for disobeying God by making a covenant with Ben-hadad of Syria. The second occurrence was in 2 Kings 21:4:

> So Ahab came into his house sullen and vexed because of the word which Naboth the Jezreelite had spoken to him; for he said, "I will not give you the inheritance of my fathers." And he lay down on his bed and turned away his face and ate no food.

In both cases, the most powerful man of Israel was experiencing this dangerous cocktail of emotions because his appetites and ambitions were being limited by God's Word. It was his own disregard for doing what was right that caused him to become distraught. The antidote was obvious – to obey God and experience serenity – but, Ahab, like a child, wanted what he wanted, and he wanted it now. He didn't like getting his hand slapped at the cookie jar!

God is a loving parent! The purpose of God's Word in establishing clear boundaries on right and wrong is to prosper and protect you. Insatiable appetites, and unrestricted ambitions, seek to consume you, as you progressively need more to bring you a sense of ease from being sullen and vexed. The love of God, through the Holy Spirit, restrains our flesh so that we may live in freedom from sin and its ensnaring grip upon our lives.

Seize the moment and find peace from the storm of your inner turmoil, by learning from Jesus how to deny yourself and obey God's better way of the Cross (Luke 9:23-24). As Paul testified in Galatians 2:20, "I have been crucified with Christ; and it is no longer I who live, but Christ lives in me; and the life which I now live in the flesh I live by faith in the Son of God, who loved me and gave Himself up for me." This is our victory!

1 KINGS 22
SEEK TRUTH FROM GOD'S WORD!

Ahab, king of Israel, was surrounded by false prophets, who tickled his ears by affirming his desires and approving his decisions. In 1 Kings 22:7-8, after Ahab had received the rubber-stamp affirmation from his four hundred prophets to go to battle, Jehoshaphat, the king of Judah, challenged Ahab to truly inquire of the Lord:

> But Jehoshaphat said, "Is there not yet a prophet of the LORD here that we may inquire of him?" The king of Israel said to Jehoshaphat, "There is yet one man by whom we may inquire of the LORD, but I hate him, because he does not prophesy good concerning me, but evil. He is Micaiah son of Imlah." But Jehoshaphat said, "Let not the king say so."

Clearly Ahab and Micaiah had some history. Jewish historian, Josephus, believed Micaiah was the prophet who had prophesied against Ahab in 1 Kings 20:39-43, after he had disobediently made a covenant with Ben-hadad of Syria.[12] Ahab hated Micaiah because he was no respecter of men, but of God and His Word. Micaiah was faithful and courageous! He ended up in prison after giving an honest report to the king and his false prophets (13-28).

Like many today, Ahab was easily deceived, because he surrounded himself with people who told him what he wanted to hear; they affirmed his desires and approved his decisions. In 2 Timothy 4:2-3, Paul warned his protégé that many would become like Ahab:

> For the time will come when they will not endure sound doctrine; but wanting to have their ears tickled, they will accumulate for themselves teachers in accordance to their own desires, and will turn away their ears from the truth and will turn aside to myths.

Seize the moment and seek truth from God's Word for every area of your life, so that God, and His will, is your desire, and His Word directs your decisions (Psalm 19:7-14; 119; 2 Timothy 3:16-17).

---

[12] Jason Darrell Coplen, "Micaiah the Prophet," ed. John D. Barry et al., *The Lexham Bible Dictionary* (Bellingham, WA: Lexham Press, 2016).

ACKNOWLEDGMENTS

A teenage girl once said, "For nothing will be impossible with God" (Luke 1:37). Because of her faith, God chose Mary to bring His indescribable gift of Jesus Christ into the world. With that same belief, I acknowledge that it is only in abiding in Jesus Christ that anything good can come from my pastoral or writing ministry. May the Holy Spirit transform our souls to the glory of God, through the reading of His Word.

I continue to acknowledge the loving people who support my pastoral ministry at First Baptist Church of New Castle, Indiana. It is to them that I have dedicated this book. Please see the acknowledgments from the first book in the series, *Seize the Moment: New Testament Devotions for Today*, to learn more about the many who make this possible. It is not only impossible apart from God, but it would also be impossible for me to write without His people working together as the one body of Christ. It amazes me that 440 people, from our congregation and beyond, continue to receive our church's daily phone call, which inspired the original material for these daily devotions. While I take responsibility for this book, and any errors that may be found in it, I am filled with gratitude for each person who supports me in this long, slow obedience of writing a daily devotional on each of the 1,189 chapters of the Bible.

This book is the product of a small team of dedicated people from our congregation. It is unique, that within our faith family, we have a gifted professional editor in Emily Hurst, who has edited my writing ministry from the beginning, including my doctoral work. Additionally, we have a professional publisher in Sean Slagle, who has worked closely with me to publish this devotional series through AGF Publishing. Sean's example as an author, and his encouragement of my writing, has inspired me to publish my work for the larger Christian community. Furthermore, I want to thank Pastor Ken Durham for assisting me by doing the Saturday morning phone calls so that I can faithfully take a Sabbath day of rest. He writes special materials not only for the Saturday calls, but also for when I am on vacation, so that I can spend time with my wife and three children. Finally, a word of appreciation to Michael Dabrowski and Richard Kinnaird, who have faithfully produced videos on each of my daily devotions. You can find a link to those videos, my sermons, blogs, and other materials at www.newcastlefbc.com.

A special word of thanks to Kimberly, my beloved wife, and our three precious children – Beorn, Alana, and Willow. Each of you is a gift from God – I love you! Thank for your patience and perseverance. Though we are at the half-way point of this significant writing project, you keep encouraging me with your love, support, and prayers. We are running this race together.

> Praise God, from whom all blessings flow.
> Praise Him, all creatures here below.
> Praise Him above, ye heavenly host.
> Praise Father, Son, and Holy Ghost.
> Amen.

ABOUT THE AUTHOR

Jerry D. Ingalls serves as the Lead Pastor of First Baptist Church of New Castle, Indiana. He is an ordained minister and has been serving ABC-USA churches in pastoral ministry since 2003. Prior to serving in pastoral ministry, Jerry honorably served in the US Army as an Infantry Officer with assignments in the 82nd Airborne Division and the US Army's World Class Athlete Program, earning awards such as the US Army Ranger Tab, Airborne Wings, Air Assault Wings, and the Expert Infantryman Badge. Additionally, Jerry served as a Chaplain Candidate and graduated from the US Army Chaplain School (2007). He has earned a Doctor of Ministry (DMin) in Pastoral Studies from Grace Theological Seminary (2020), a Master of Divinity (MDiv) from Fuller Theological Seminary (2008), an MS in Counseling and Student Development from the C.W. Post Campus of Long Island University (2000), and a BS in Psychological Engineering from the United States Military Academy at West Point (1996). Jerry was a 1996 Academic All-American athlete at West Point and still holds the Academy and Patriot League records in the hammer throw. He married Kimberly in 1999 and by God's grace they have been blessed with three wonderful children – Beorn, Alana, and Willow. Jerry enjoys reading with his children, camping with his family, backcountry hiking, trail running, coaching high school track and field, and competing in masters track and field.

SEIZE THE MOMENT: NEW TESTAMENT DEVOTIONS FOR TODAY BY DR. JERRY D. INGALLS

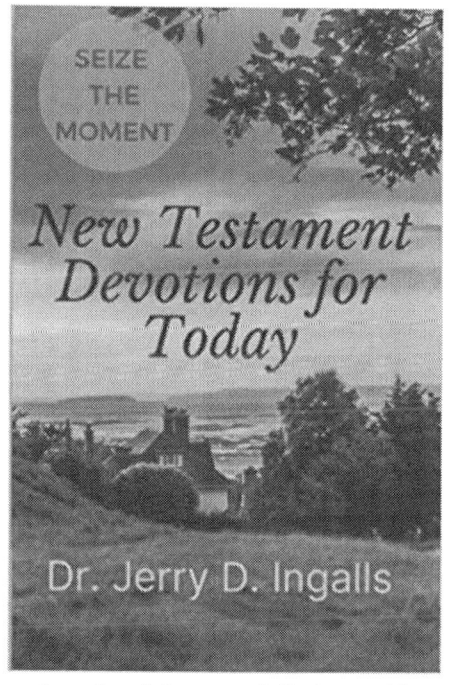

The devotional book that kicked off the Seize the Moment Series!

Walk through each of the 260 chapters of the New Testament.

Be daily blessed as you learn to find rest for your soul in the easy yoke of Jesus Christ.

"This book is written in a reader friendly manner, and is easy to follow examples of how to communicate with God through using His Word to assist us in knowing how to pray. Interesting life experiences of this author are invaluable in relating situations to Biblical truths. It is very hard for me to use it as a daily devotional, because I find myself wanting to read numerous passages in one setting…which I think speaks volumes for the content!" – 5-Star Amazon Review

"The daily devotions in this book take only about 5 minutes of your time, but often leave you thinking about the content for the rest of the day. The tone of this book is one that is so fitting to the world we are living in today. Written during the earliest days of the COVID-19 pandemic, this book gives practical, Biblically sound counsel on how to live a life connected to the Father, and to the church, in practical ways, even when meeting in person is not possible. This book would be a great resource for personal use or for use by a church, Sunday School class, or small group that is looking for something to work through that unifies them in mind and spirit." – 5-Star Amazon Review

LIVE LIKE A CHAMPION TODAY!
THE 40 PROMISES IN 40 DAYS CHALLENGE
BY DR. JERRY D. INGALLS

40 days can change a habit or create a new one.

Embark upon the journey of learning how to live like a champion.

Live a victorious life by trusting God.

Walk in His promises in your everyday life.

Be a valuable member of God's championship team.

"This book was a very practical approach to understanding how scripture is God's game plan for each and every one of us and how we can put that plan into action. Easy to understand, yet very thought provoking. It helped me go from a vague idea of following scripture to a re-energized plan for living God's Word." – 5-Star Amazon Review

"Live Like a Champion Today provides an accessible look at the many promises of God. Athletes will no doubt enjoy the metaphorical language with God as the coach, scripture as the playbook, and team members as fellow believers. But if you are more of a 'cheer from the stands' type, don't let the sports vernacular make you think this isn't for you. Whether you have been a believer for your whole life, or you are a new Christ follower, or you are still seeking, you will definitely find something new to love about Jesus as you read through this book. My personal favorite section of the book is section 3, which dives into the scriptural foundation of being 'partakers of the divine nature.' If you are looking for a fresh perspective on oft-quoted scriptures, pick this book up and give it a try!" – 5-Star Amazon Review

CHECKOUT THESE NEW RELEASES FROM AGF PUBLISHING AND NORTHSIDE BOOKS & MEDIA

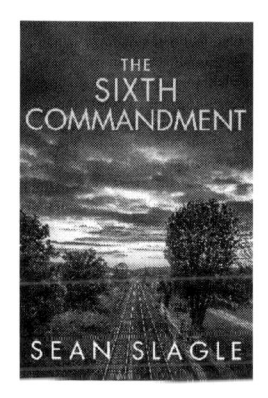

THE SIXTH COMMANDMENT
BY SEAN SLAGLE

Michael James is the pastor of a small church in Short Ridge, Kentucky, a community in the foothills of Appalachia. Life seems normal until Judd Simmons, a local drug lord, tries to kill his own family and Michael is called on to help, which has consequences beyond that one evening. Alycen Loveless is a new journalist at The Outlook. She rushes onto the scene to report on the terrors the family faced. Later, as she delves into the town's dark side and fears, she finds an unlikely romance with the pastor from that fateful night. But love has a hard time blossoming when the couple is stalked, threatened, and harassed to the point that Michael questions if he can take another man's life.

SEEK FIRST
BY ANDREA ATWOOD

Using first person accounts and observations, Andrea Atwood shares about the importance of seeing God's truth, listening to His small, still voice, and walking in His power and grace.

Atwood leads you into a deeper understanding of life's circumstances and the importance of seeking God first in all things.

AGF PUBLISHING LLC

We publish books and media in an array of genres, always aiming to entertain, educate, inform, and inspire people of all ages and reading levels. We encourage and train writers from all backgrounds to work with us in bringing their stories and knowledge to a worldwide audience. Learn more about the company and all its offerings at www.agfpublishingcompany.com

NORTHSIDE
AN AGF IMPRINT

NORTHSIDE BOOKS & MEDIA
AN AGF PUBLISHING IMPRINT

Northside Books & Media encourages and equips Christians worldwide through fiction and nonfiction. Look for more titles, author information and call for manuscripts at http://agfpublishingcompany.com

Made in the USA
Columbia, SC
29 October 2024